The Anthropology of Religious Conversion

The Anthropology of Religious Conversion

Edited by Andrew Buckser and Stephen D. Glazier

ROWMAN & LITTLEFIELD PUBLISHERS, INC.
Lanham • Boulder • New York • Toronto • Oxford

ROWMAN & LITTLEFIELD PUBLISHERS, INC.

Published in the United States of America
by Rowman & Littlefield Publishers, Inc.
A wholly owned subsidiary of The Rowman & Littlefield Publishing Group, Inc.
4501 Forbes Boulevard, Suite 200, Lanham, Maryland 20706
www.rowmanlittlefield.com

PO Box 317, Oxford, OX2 9RU, UK

British Library Cataloguing in Publication Information Available

Library of Congress Cataloging-in-Publication Data
The anthropology of religious conversion / edited by Andrew Buckser and
Stephen D. Glazier.
    p. cm.
Includes bibliographical references and index.
  ISBN 0-7425-1777-2 (cloth : alk. paper) — ISBN 0-7425-1778-0 (pbk. :
alk. paper)
  1. Conversion. I. Buckser, Andrew, 1964– II. Glazier, Stephen D.
  BL639.A58 2003
  306.6'91—dc21
                                    2003007435

Printed in the United States of America

∞™ The paper used in this publication meets the minimum requirements of American
National Standard for Information Sciences—Permanence of Paper for Printed Library
Materials, ANSI/NISO Z39.48-1992.

In Memoriam: Morton Klass

In November 2000, Professor Morton Klass organized a symposium on the anthropology of conversion at the American Anthropological Association annual meeting in San Francisco, California. Mort had recently retired from a distinguished teaching and research career at Barnard College, during which he had become one of the leading figures in the anthropological study of religion. He had conducted extensive fieldwork in South Asia and Trinidad, leading to such books as *East Indians in Trinidad*, *From Field to Factory*, and *Singing with Sai Baba*. In books like *Ordered Universes* and *Across the Boundaries of Belief*, he had also contributed greatly to developing a theoretical understanding of the meaning of religion across cultures. Mort had served as the first president of the Society for the Anthropology of Religion, and he continued to be active in the field after his retirement. The conversion symposium represented a new field of endeavor for Mort, one that he felt could contribute greatly to our understanding of religious experience. After it received an enthusiastic response from the assembled scholars, he began considering publishing a volume on the subject in collaboration with the undersigned.

Mort's sudden death on April 28, 2001, came as a shock to those of us who had known him. He was an extraordinarily vital man, a witty raconteur who could hold a lecture hall or a dinner table spellbound with equal ease. He was also a man of uncommon warmth, extended as much to students and young scholars as to his many longtime friends. Perhaps most of all, he was a man of energetic ideas, whose passion for anthropology was unmistakable and infectious. This passion never diminished; he continued debating, researching, and writing about anthropology through his very last day. Several projects remained unfinished at his death, including the collection on conversion, then in its preliminary stages.

Mort's theoretical vision and editorial grace are irreplaceable, and this volume would surely have been much richer had Mort been able to edit it, as he had planned. We hope, however, that we have preserved some of his vision for the collection, especially his interest in opening new directions for ethnographic and theoretical work on conversion. If the essays here prompt readers to think anew about the meaning of religious experience, if they spur any of us to wonder again about the connections between the cultures we live in and the heavens we live under, they will constitute the best memorial we could raise to Mort's memory.

It is in this spirit that we dedicate this book to the late and much missed Professor Morton Klass, our dear friend and teacher.

Andrew Buckser
Stephen D. Glazier
September 2002

Contents

Afterword

Preface

Religious conversion poses a powerful challenge to anthropological theories concerning the connection between culture and the self. Anthropologists have long argued that religion involves more than just ideas about the supernatural; it constitutes a theory of the world, a way of constructing reality that seems uniquely real to those who experience it. If this is true, how can it be that individuals suddenly choose new religions? To change one's religion is to change one's world, to voluntarily shift the basic presuppositions upon which both self and others are understood. The fact that this is possible—that it is, indeed, almost routine in certain religious traditions—raises difficult questions about the relationship of individuals to their cultural surroundings. What can prompt such an abrupt and total transformation? How is it achieved, and what are its effects? What does conversion mean for anthropological theories of agency and the cultural construction of reality?

Conversion also raises important questions about the social processes within which religion is embedded. Conversion is usually an individual process, involving a change of worldview and affiliation by a single person, but it occurs within a context of institutional procedures and social relationships. Religious groups structure the ways in which adherents may move in and out, and in many cases they place converts in a unique social position. These processes articulate with other dynamics within groups—their internal divisions, their authority structures, their political rivalries, and more. In many cases, religious groups are also held accountable to the restrictions and requirements of state authorities. How do these social structures incorporate the intense and often unpredictable experience of the individual convert? How does temporal power constrain the sense of divine power so integral to many conversions? What effects does conversion produce in the group that gains a convert, and what does it do to the group that loses one? Conversion highlights the interaction, and in many cases the tension, between individual consciousness and the structural requirements of community life.

In this book, we approach these questions through ethnography. The first step in understanding what conversion is and how it works is to explore the different ways that other cultures have understood it. To that end, this volume brings together fourteen case studies of conversion, written by anthropologists working in a variety of settings and religious traditions. Each case study presents a different set of theoretical questions addressed in different ways by each contributor. The goal of the book is not to integrate these case studies into a single theoretical statement. To the contrary, authors have been encouraged to pursue the questions raised by their particular subjects of study. Our aim is not to advance a single analytical approach, nor to resolve any specific theoretical question. It is, rather, to suggest the variety of avenues for investigation that an anthropology of religious conversion can offer. We hope to open a conversation about conversion in which anthropology has in many ways yet to engage.

This is not a conversation limited to anthropology. If conversion has serious implications for anthropologists, it has profound ones for theologians and religious believers. In many religious traditions, conversion marks the time when the hand of the divine is most plainly visible; conversion narratives overflow with expressions of supernatural agency, in which the individual feels guided, or coerced, or enraptured by a divine presence. For many, conversion marks a moment of epiphany, when a traumatic or seemingly chaotic past is revealed as the subtle handiwork of a benevolent God. To suggest— as anthropologists do—that even this moment owes something of its shape to cultural systems is to intrude culture into the very core of the religious experience. Doing so poses a challenge for the many believers, lay and academic, who have looked to anthropology for a perspective on their faith in recent decades. If believers really wish to engage with anthropological insights, to fully face the cultural dimensions of the religious experience, they must be critically interested in what anthropology has to say about this, the time in which the cultural dimension seems most irrelevant, when the hand of God seems most palpable.

Religious conversion has interested social scientists for over a century. Early research was dominated by psychologists who—like G. Stanley Hall and his students at Clark University—focused on sudden, emotional conversion occurring during adolescence (see Hall 1902). Sociologists and social psychologists came to dominate the field in the middle of the twentieth century, particularly after 1960, as interest in new religious movements became a central focus of sociology. Sociological studies examined processes of individual conversion from a "gradualist" perspective, based mainly on participant observation and on interviews with believers. These studies also examined issues of apostasy and deconversion, which, as Hall might have predicted, were found to be linked to problems of late adolescence and early adulthood. In general, social scientists have moved from a tight focus on evangelical Protestantism to a growing interest in non-Western religions, and they have increasingly emphasized gradual rather than sudden conversion (Hood et al. 1996).

Early anthropology seldom directly addressed the topic of religious conversion, although individual anthropologists — like Franz Boas — were present at the inception of conversion studies in the United States. (It was Hall's two-volume study *Adolescence* that Boas sought to debunk when he sent Margaret Mead into the field to find a society without adolescent stress.) Serious anthropological attention to the subject has developed only over the past few decades. This attention has included a few extended case studies, such as Harriet Whitehead's analysis of conversion to Scientology (1987), as well as several more general analyses of international trends in conversion. Most of the latter work has dealt with issues of modernity and colonialism. Hefner (1993), Van der Veer (1996), and Viswanathan (1998), for example, all explore conversion's role in advancing (and at times contesting) the expansion of Western colonial power. Although such studies have brought conversion into anthropological discourse, they have done so in the context of strong theoretical statements; they have often lacked the ethnographic detail that allows an exploration of the differences, as well as the common features, of conversion in different cultures.

This volume seeks to provide that detail, the attention to the intimate, small-scale dynamics of conversion for which the ethnographic perspective is uniquely suited. This approach allows the book to take a broad approach to religious conversion, exploring a wide variety of ethnographic and theoretical questions. Its essays span a range of geographical areas, from Melanesia to South America to the Middle East, as well as Western Europe, the Caribbean, and the United States. Contributors discuss not only conversion to mainstream Christianity — the subject of most conversion research — but also conversion to Judaism, Hinduism, Rastafarianism, Spiritualism, and a variety of alternative Christian movements. Its theoretical orientation is equally diverse. Authors discuss the definition of conversion, the politics of conversion, the place of conversion in bodily experience, the social implications of conversion, and much more. Two essays by distinguished scholars of conversion bracket the case studies. The first discusses the place of conversion studies in anthropology, and the second relates the anthropology of conversion to the larger field of religious studies.

BOOK STRUCTURE

The volume begins with a general introduction to the anthropological study of conversion by Diane Austin-Broos. Austin-Broos argues that conversion research raises issues of central importance to contemporary anthropological theory, especially its interaction with nationalism, state formation, and the construction of authority. Her discussion deftly positions the chapters in this volume and the field of conversion studies as a whole within a larger disciplinary context. The book then turns to fourteen detailed case studies, each of which considers conversion in a distinct ethnographic setting. These studies have been divided into three sections according to their primary ethnographic emphases. These sections represent a rather artificial division, however, since common questions run through them all, and readers will find elements in many chapters that bridge all three sections.

The first section considers conversion and its relationship to social processes. Much of the literature on conversion has focused on its psychological dimensions, the transformation in individual consciousness that a religious change implies. That transformation takes place, however, within a social matrix, as converts detach themselves from one group of believers and affiliate with another. In many cases, that matrix has considerably more impact in motivating the conversion than any individual religious experience. In all cases, the social group structures the intellectual and experiential process through which conversion occurs. The papers in this section explore some of the questions that this social dimension of conversion implies. In what ways, for example, does conversion influence group identity and solidarity? How do the social and political divisions within groups affect the ways that particular individuals convert? How does the individual agency so central to most conversions articulate with the authority of religious leaders and bureaucracies? And how do relationships of power more generally influence the understanding and practice of conversion?

The papers in this section approach these issues from several different directions. Simon Coleman begins with a penetrating analysis of a charismatic Protestant church in Uppsala, Sweden. Known as the Word of Life, this congregation builds much of its rhetoric and outreach activity around the activity of conversion, despite the fact that its efforts generate relatively few actual converts. Coleman suggests that the significance of conversion for the group lays largely in its metaphorical qualities, in the paradigm it offers its members for understanding personal identities and social experience. Such continuous aspects of conversion, he argues, may mean as much as the radical disjunctures upon which conversion studies have usually focused. Don Seeman's paper also explores the ongoing effects of conversion, this time among people for whom it has become enmeshed with bureaucracy and political oppositions. The subjects of the study, known as Felashmura, have sought Israeli citizenship on the basis of their descent from Ethiopian Jews; since their ancestors converted to Christianity, however, the Felashmura must convert "back" to Judaism in order to qualify for admittance. As he follows converts through the disheartening and often humiliating bureaucratic maze involved, Seeman points out the multiple and often changing meanings of conversion for individual Felashmura. He urges anthropologists not to try to rationalize away such indeterminacy in their analyses of conversion, but rather to embrace it as a central feature of the phenomenon.

Seeman's case study underscores the political implications of conversion, a theme that also animates the chapters by Kalyani Menon and Charles Farhadian. Menon analyzes understandings of conversion among Hindu nationalists in contemporary India. Hindutva activists have accused Christian missionaries of using deception and bribery to attract converts, charges that have led to incendiary rhetoric and anti-Christian violence. As Menon demonstrates, however, Hindus employ nearly identical tactics when converting Christians "back" to Hinduism. She argues that the different valuations on these practices derive from Hindutva understandings of the relationship between religious affiliation and individual nature; the actions of Christian missionaries are threatening not because they involve any trickery, but because they contradict the assumptions about Hinduism and Indian identity central to the Hindutva movement. Farhadian examines two waves of conversion among the Dani of Irian Jaya. In the first, widespread conversion to Methodism creates a new sense of intertribal identity among previously separated groups in Irian Jaya. This sense of identity then makes possible a second conversion, decades later, when new Christian movements became the basis of Papuan opposition to Indonesia's New Order government. Farhadian's case illustrates the potential volatility of conversion as a political force; although the initial conversions in many ways served colonial purposes, they generated social solidarities and symbolic resources that made new forms of indigenous resistance possible.

The final two papers in this section explore the role of conversion in defining boundaries, both within and among religious groups. For the Copenhagen Jews of Andrew Buckser's study, group boundaries are the subject of ongoing dispute among community factions. On a daily basis, the proprieties of community life paper over such differences; the process of conversion, however, brings them vividly to the surface. Buckser discusses two typical cases of conversion to Judaism and the debates over the nature of Jewishness and rabbinical authority that accompany them. Although these debates can and do produce hard feelings—at times even schism—they also create opportunities for expressing family solidarity and consolidating political power. Marie Pia Di Bella's study focuses on the marginality involved in the boundary-crossing of conversion, suggesting that the marginal position of the convert can be crucial to understanding the linguistic and symbolic patterns associated with the process. In one of her two case studies, marginality is essential to the conversion—the converts are convicts, living in jail cells for the short interval between their condemnations and their executions. In the other, marginality derives from the requirements of group membership, as Pentecostal converts who have not experienced glossolalia find themselves excluded from the center of their new group. Di Bella explores the ritual and symbolism of conversion in both settings, highlighting the ways that marginality both informs and reflects the social experience of the converts.

Cross-cultural analyses of conversion inevitably encounter difficulties when they try to define their subject. Academic models of conversion tend to draw heavily on Christian imagery, particularly on such dramatic scenes as Paul's vision on the road to Damascus. These images construct conversion as a radical, sudden change of belief, one in which old ways and associations are left behind as a result of a new theological outlook. How can such models encompass non-Christian religions, which often regard belief as less important than religious practice? How can they accommodate the slow and partial stages through which conversion often takes place? Even more difficult, how can they accurately describe cultures for which belief, practice, and membership have profoundly different meanings than they do in Western society? The papers in the second section explore this question directly, using four different case studies. For each, they suggest an alternative way of conceptualizing conversion, one based on the indigenous conceptions of religious transformation among the people under study.

Robert Priest, for example, looks at the transformation of the notion of sin among Aguaruna converts to Christianity in Brazil. Scholarly analysis has often seen sin as a fundamentally Western concept that non-Westerners assimilate and accept as part of the conversion process. The Aguaruna, however, have a complex traditional vocabulary for sin and wrongdoing, one that they retain even when they have "discovered their sin" as part of Christian conversion. What changes upon becoming Christian is not the notion of sin, but the direction of blame: converts see themselves as culpable for actions they would previously have attributed to witchcraft or spirits. This change produces personal transformations of a rather different sort than those of Augustine and Paul. Roger Lohmann offers yet another variant in his analysis of the Asabano of Papua New Guinea. The Asabano conceive volition very differently than does the Western tradition: thoughts and desires come not from the head, but from the belly, and they are generated by two types of resident spirits.

Conversion, therefore, is not a matter of rethinking the nature of reality, but of "turning the belly," changing the individual's relationship with the spiritual beings who direct his or her volition. Lohmann presents a model of conversion based on relationships with spiritual beings, one that he finds truer not only to Asabano experience but to many facets of Western experience as well.

Robert Anderson and Thomas Brown focus on contexts much more familiar to American readers; Anderson discusses the history of Christian conversion in Iceland, and Brown explores Spiritualist congregations in California. Even here, however, local understandings of conversion suggest a rethinking of academic models. Anderson challenges the notion that conversion must involve a total movement from one pattern of religious practice to another. Such movements occur, he argues, only where church and state authorities have the power to demand exclusive religious affiliations. Where authorities lack such power—as in Iceland at the turn of the first millennium, and again at the turn of the second—conversion has involved the selective adoption of particular practices, rather than complete religious transformation. Anderson calls on anthropologists to recognize the structures of constraint that underlie their definitions of conversion. Brown, in his study, questions the notion of conversion as a discrete and clearly identifiable event. The Spiritualists he studies do think of it that way, and many of them describe specific paranormal experiences as the occasions of their conversions. His interviews suggest, however, that for many the process actually takes much longer and, indeed, that transitions to Spiritualism are often conditional and incomplete. He concludes that the essence of conversion lies less in particular changes of belief than in more general changes in individual understandings of group membership and personal identity.

The third section of the book addresses the subject that has dominated most of the academic research on conversion: the place of conversion in personal experience. How does conversion make sense and feel to those who go through it? What motivates them to convert, and what sorts of emotional and cognitive changes does conversion involve? The chapters here take an anthropological approach to these questions, asking how different cultural and historical settings shape the conversion experience. The answers are seldom simple. Steven Glazier, for example, finds conversion taking a variety of forms for Rastafarians and Spiritual Baptists on the island of Trinidad. These two movements share a number of features, including extensive African imagery and an individualist orientation; their philosophies and ritual practice differ considerably, though, as do their norms of bodily comportment. Glazier follows a number of individuals who move back and forth between the groups, exploring both the motivations for their conversions and the social concomitants of their memberships. Rebecca Norris looks at converts to a variety of faiths in New England, focusing on the continuities between their old faiths and their new ones. She argues that conversion must always involve such continuities. Not only must a new faith make sense in terms defined by a lifetime in the old one, but it must also work with the bodily attitudes and accustomed gestures with which the convert has grown up. Her case studies depict conversion as a gradual process for individuals, a matter not of sudden insight but of extended and often unconscious learning.

Mary Ann and Van Reidhead illustrate this process with an extended case study from the American Midwest. They follow a woman from her initial conversion to Catholicism to her subsequent decision to join a Benedictine monastic order. In both cases, her conversions (the first from Jehovah's Witness to Roman Catholicism, and the second to Benedictine monasticism) involve the kinds of overpowering religious experiences that conversion studies have generally explored and that might seem to suggest a total transformation of worldview before and after. Yet even as a Benedictine postulant, the subject of the study acknowledges the profound ongoing impact of her Jehovah's Witness upbringing on her understanding of religion. Despite changes in affiliation and practice, her activist approach to religion and her personal relationship with the Holy Spirit—the cornerstones of her childhood religion—have remained central to her experience. Marcela Mendoza describes a similar pattern on a broader scale in the final case study of the volume. Among the Western Toba of Argentina, converts to Christianity draw similarities between the Christian conception of Heaven and the indigenous image of the House of God in the sky. These similarities produce an interesting effect. On the one hand, they make conversion easier by making Christian imagery more plausible to potential converts. On the other, they seem to confirm the image of the spiritual world advanced by traditional shamans. As a result, conversion can produce a kind of validation of the very religious tradition it rejects.

The book ends with an afterword by the eminent psychologist of religion Lewis Rambo, the only one of our contributors from outside anthropology. Rambo puts conversion studies in a broader context, suggesting ways in which anthropology can inform and learn from the other disciplines that have analyzed the subject. He calls strongly for more interdisciplinary work on conversion; the virtual blindness of academics to developments outside their fields, he suggests, has deprived anthropologists, sociologists, historians, and others of excellent methodological and theoretical resources. A concerted effort to build bridges among these isolated disciplines could produce major advances in conversion studies and a corresponding enrichment of each.

Acknowledgments

This volume originated in two symposia on the anthropology of religious conversion at the 2000 American Anthropological Association annual meeting. We would like to thank the Society for the Anthropology of Religion and the Society for the Anthropology of Consciousness for their joint sponsorship of those sessions. We would also like to express our appreciation to some of the people who helped bring this volume to fruition. Our editor, Dean Birkenkamp, has been an expert and uncommonly patient guide throughout the development of the text. We are also grateful to Manfred Kremser, Barry Chevannes, Mort Klass, and Janet Jacobs, who commented on earlier drafts of some of these papers. The staff of the Purdue Department of Sociology and Anthropology offered a great deal of help with the production of the volume; special thanks are due to Marcy Jasmund, Evelyn Douthit, Dianne Livingston, and Dawn Stahura. Finally, many thanks are due to our families, especially Susan Buckser and Rosemary C. Glazier, for their patience and support through the twists and turns of the project. To these people, and to the contributors, goes much of the credit for what is of value in this collection. As editors, we jealously guard our credit for the mistakes.

The Anthropology of Conversion: An Introduction

Diane Austin-Broos

Recent years have seen a resurgence in the study of conversion as anthropologists have focused increasingly on the interplay between religion and identity.[1] This topic commands particular attention now, when the very idea of the secular state is being contested in many parts of the world. Conversion has implications for many of the dynamics involved in this struggle—the shifting relations between nation-states and a global economy, the new forms of identity politics within and between nations, and the increasing importance of religion in the lives of individuals. In a world of instant information and seeming heterogeneity, moreover, controversies over conversion also reflect a new variability in the status of authoritative texts, both scientific and religious. Testing authorities and turning to others are integral parts of religious practice in many localities. Conversion thereby shapes aspirations and reorients social life. In the case of whole communities, it can involve a "paradigm shift" compelled by circumstance and sometimes by conquest.[2] Most of all, renewed interest in conversion reflects the revision of a century of verities concerning secularism and modernity. The view that the rise of the modern state with its bureaucratic modes would supersede religion has proven mistaken. New departures and confrontations involving the world's religions mean that the dynamics that draw people to one religion or away from another intrigue us as never before.

CONVERSION AS PASSAGE

Conversion is a form of passage, a "turning from and to" that is neither syncretism nor absolute breach.[3] Previous attempts to grasp conversion have often relied on one of these ideas. Some have seen conversion as diffuse, yet others have sought to contain it in a particular event. With its roots in trait analysis, syncretism fits well with ideas of cultural flow, with the cosmopolitan and the hybrid. These are notions that evoke the image of *bricoleurs*, experimenters and iconoclasts involved in cultural pastiche. Conversion is a cultural passage more robust than this. Possibly experimental at first, it becomes a deliberate change with definite direction and shape. It shows itself responsive to particular knowledge and practices. To be converted is to reidentify, to learn, reorder, and reorient. It involves interrelated modes of transformation that generally continue over time and define a consistent course. Not mere syncretism, neither can conversion involve a simple and absolute break with a previous social life. Learning anew proceeds over time and requires a process of integrating knowledge and experience. Even in the context of conquest, the aspiration of another power to "know," "domesticate," "name," and "claim" is difficult to accomplish (see Dirks 1996). Comprehensive reform of another is in fact an elusive goal, because a cultural being can never entirely even know herself. In the shadowy terrain between explicit and implicit culture, the person hides from herself and among her practiced dispositions. She therefore can only cooperate somewhat in any project to negate the past. Thinking about conversion as passage, and about passage as more than syncretism or breach, suggests a further dimension to conversion, a quest for human belonging.

Rather than simple cultural breach, the voiding of a past social self, the language of converts expresses new forms of relatedness. The public aspect of this belonging is perhaps a new identity, a newly inscribed communal self defined through the gaze of others. But for the person who has converted or allowed herself to be converted, the issue is a larger one and also more intimate. Conversion is a type of passage that negotiates a place in the world. Conversion as passage is also quest, a quest to be at home in a world experienced as turbulent or constraining or, in some particular way, as wanting in value.[4] The passage of conversion is a passage to some place rather than no place. It is not a quest for utopia but rather for habitus.[5] It involves a process of continual embedding in forms of social practice and belief, in ritual dispositions and somatic experience. Cultural passage generally, and the passage of conversion in particular, are then more than "travel" in the sense that Clifford proposed, and they are more than migration.[6] Conversion involves an encultured being arriving at a particular place.

The passages in conversion can be remarkably diverse. Some involve immediate and intense somatic experience. Others are more akin to the "long conversation" that the Comaroffs described for Africa, the development of new hegemonies partly apprehended and partly not (Comaroff and Comaroff

1991: 198–251). Some conversions interweave these phenomena; still others involve more immediate reorientations of practice within the same religion or national culture. The forms of passage are numerous, and most are extended through time. As this collection shows, they can at times seem to have little in common. Yet all these passages from and to are directed to a home in the world, structured through particular knowledge and modes of ritual practice. Heterogeneous they certainly are, and yet they comprise a discernible phenomenon—for all their increasing engagement with the political, conversions are religious practice in the world rather than politics.

If conversion simply involved individuals and their passages, this heterogeneity might be noted but merely attributed to culture's creativity. The widespread prevalence of conversion events that prompts a collection such as this, however, speaks to something more, some broader historical dynamics spanning a number of cultures and times. The chapters in this collection cover a range of geographical settings: Europe (Buckser, Coleman, Di Bella, and Anderson), Papua New Guinea (Lohmann and Priest), Irian Jaya (Farhadian), the United States (Norris, Brown, and Reidhead and Reidhead), Trinidad (Glazier), Peru (Priest), Argentina (Mendoza), India (Menon), and Israel (Seeman). The chapters provide accounts of passages between various modes of Christian practice and between statuses within Christianity; passages between different world religions (Christianity and Judaism, Hinduism and Christianity, and Christianity and Sufi Islam); various Christian engagements with Spiritualism; and passages from one regional religion to another. What are the historical dynamics involved in these various movements, and are there connections between them that prompt such a plethora of passages in the world today?

CONVERSION AND HISTORICAL DYNAMICS

Some of the conversions discussed in this collection involve the familiar transition between local and indigenous religions and Christianity. Reflecting on Weber, Hefner has argued that world religions, and especially Christianity, should not be seen simply as the artifact of one or another colonizing process.[7] World religions have been able to create some of the largest transnational milieus in the world today by virtue of their highly systematized forms of transcendentalism, their organized ritual forms, and their effective socialization of converts. Sahlins has remarked that the dominant metaphors of modern society come from the market, as it elaborates its links around the world (1976: 166–67). Geertz's way of underlining the power of Islam in 1950s Java was to connect religion and the market. Marveling at Islam's dynamic progress in the region, he termed it "as simple and easily marketable a religious package as has ever been prepared for export" (1960: 123). Not mere shadows of the market, however, these world religions have their own dynamics that engage with other ontologies and cosmologies in quite particular ways.

In this collection, Priest's account of Aguaruna conversions in villages of northern Peru offers an especially interesting example of this form of passage. He describes narratives concerning "sin," noting that the Aguaruna have had their own extensive vocabulary of badness and wrongdoing, with a variety of moral categories including turpitude, damage, maliciousness, and malevolent deception. Contrary to the view of some anthropologists that "sin" is perhaps an exclusively Indo-European concept, Priest proposes that Aguaruna use these indigenous categories to elaborate reflections on sin. Transgressive wrongdoing, in other words, is not strange to Aguaruna. What was strange and has changed among them is the attribution of sin to the self rather than to others. The latter, once usual practice was often embedded in witchcraft beliefs and tied to social dramas of revenge. From Priest's account, one might surmise that the "guilty self" could only emerge with a degree of individuation that supersedes the "dividual" actors of immediate, local, and intensely transactional cultures. The link in this transition is between forms of individualism of a type that absorbed Dumont, and the engagement with a specific Christian rendering of sin.[8]

Mendoza offers an equally interesting perspective on world religion and changing local cosmology. The Western Toba of Argentine Chaco have reordered their world to engage Christianity, but only by inserting its transcendentalism into their previous cosmology as elaborated by shamans. Christianity's heaven is the house in the sky that their shamans knew of, but could not enter; the Toba can enter now because they are Christians. Curiously, in this passage, Christianity's transcendentalism, although more rigorous, has nonetheless been subsumed within Toba ideas of the world. A complex interaction between the universal and the particular also characterizes Lohmann's account of the Asabano in Papua New Guinea. The conversion process there presents features that both Weber and Horton would readily recognize (see Weber 1991 [1948] and Horton 1975). And yet it is particular—Asabano conversion involves new relations with a new spirit, a spirit able to engage with any and all human beings. For them, cognition takes place "in the belly," and the conversion process involves "turning the belly" to house and be animated by a universal Holy Spirit.

Weber's view of modernity had definite direction, and his world religions were a part of it. They were systems that subsumed others and, with their systematicity, acted relentlessly to homogenize the world. The passage involved in much conversion has often followed this historical direction. Yet these examples, along with others provided by Norris, Farhadian, Menon, and Seeman, show that the world religions also open up new possibilities that cannot always be contained within a greatly extended system. The world religions do assimilate, but they also create a new diversity, in which numerous passages are possible.

The dynamic of world religions also intersects with that of nation-states. This is a second historical process that complicates Weber's vision in a way that he half saw but never integrated with his writing on religion. Nation-states are another form of modern imagined community, one in which the struggle to establish shared symbols and institutions can become intense and threaten to split the state apart. As Tambiah has argued, the progress of nationalism and nation-states in the twentieth century is multistranded. It involves the spread of the Western European form of secular nation, a system that fostered privatization of religion during the eighteenth and nineteenth centuries. At the same time, though, it also involves other "ethnonationalisms," European and non-European, often mainly based on language, public religion, or both. These different nationalisms may also appeal to "mytho-historical charters" and claims of common "blood descent or race" in order to build solidarity (Tambiah 1996).[9] When these two forms of nationalism meet, the demands of the homogenizing nation-state either for secularism or for religious conformity can precipitate conflict. Farhadian's account of Dani Christianity in Irian Jaya is such a case. Christianity there has moved from the status of private religion to a Melanesian rallying call against Indonesia with its Muslim face and assimilating thrust. Hindu nationalism presents the other, majority side of this confrontation between national projects. Contesting a secular politics, Hindus struggle aggressively to make their mark on the nation-state. Menon describes the ways in which nationalists identify and castigate the tricks involved in Christian conversion. Nationalist efforts to draw minorities into Hinduism, on the other hand, are not identified as conversion but rather as a returning of citizens to their essential Hindu being. Menon's account reveals the manner in which religion intertwines with primordialism in Indian nationalism.

There are also other ways in which the circumstance of nation-states mediates conversion. Conversion can become the medium of passage between nation-states. In the case of the Ethiopian "Felashmura" or Beta Israel Christians, their passage to Judaism as immigrants to Israel was encouraged because they were thought to be the descendants of Jews who in Ethiopia had been involved in an "ethnic defection" to Christianity. Like the Hindu nationalists, Seeman suggests, the Jewish state did not regard this passage as conversion, but more as a return precipitated by turmoil in Ethiopia. Just as interesting are Spiritual Baptists in Trinidad who experiment with Rastafarianism. This Caribbean black nationalism, beginning in Jamaica, proposed the

Ethiopian Haile Selassie as the returned Christian savior. A variety of New World Ethiopianism, Rastafarianism seeks to provide through religion a sense of nation in island societies that struggle to articulate autonomous cultures in the shadow of the United States. That some early Jamaican Rastafarians "returned" to Ethiopia and still reside there shows how the passages involved in conversion can make new links between worlds.

In a fascinating discussion of very different kinds of conversion in Italy, Di Bella shows that religious passage can be between nations and also between states of being. Contemporary returned emigrants to the United States use their newly acquired Pentecostalism to mark off themselves and their relatives from their Italian neighbors. The *Bianchi* of the sixteenth and seventeenth century, by contrast, converted the bodies of the condemned. By proposing that ritual submission on the gallows would return them to the Kingdom of God, this Sicilian company kept the convicted quiet and possibly provided comfort. They also offered to the watching crowd a mystification that masked the cruelty involved and made an uncanny reference to Christ's own crucifixion.

Although the nation may inform and sometimes encourage conversion, its power to do so is never unlimited. Anderson presents an account of Icelandic engagements with Christianity in which the religion on more than one occasion has singularly failed to socialize believers into its view of the world. He describes the situation of Icelanders around the year 1000 C.E. when, although people took up a public Christian commitment, there was no way that "pagan" practice could possibly be expunged from remote and scattered farms. Similarly, the spiritism that pervaded Iceland in the early twentieth century has been excluded again from Christian orthodoxy, but not from the orientations and everyday interests of many Icelanders. These brakes on the assimilating power of Christianity show other forms of rite and belief as "idioms of intimacy," regional identifications that resist Christianity.[10] Herzfeld's felicitous phrase can describe not simply the spoken word but also the practice of rite and song, not to mention humor, that pervade both private and public life.

Buckser's account of Copenhagen Jews also points to major blocks in religious passage. Judaism as a national religion has not been inclined to proselytize. Aspiring converts who are not believed to have appropriate Jewish descent may not be rejected but often are not encouraged either. And Islam, although it has spread around the world, has failed to engage a Christendom that identifies itself with European descent. Similarly, for many in the Middle East today, the nationalization of religion makes passage between Judaism and Islam almost unimaginable as would be passage between Hinduism and Islam for many in the Indian subcontinent. Again, even prior to the rise of modern nationalisms, Christianity had only modest impact in much of Asia.

The study of conversion must address these ideas about race, religion, and politics that preclude or discourage religious passage. They suggest that conversion on a large and patterned scale is not common between literate and stable civilizations. Though not simply a colonization, conversion does require significant flux and also, perhaps, a real perception of unequal degrees of power attached to different forms of knowledge.

CONVERSION, MEANING, AND PRACTICE

In addition to world religions and the rise of modern nationalisms, a third historical trend bears on conversion: changes in the rendering of knowledge about the world, especially in the secular West. As Klass has observed, the relevant issues were prefigured in the emergence of the tension between religion on the one hand and humanism and science on the other. These have been pitted against each other in the course of the rise of the secular state, so much so that de Certeau described a repositioned Christianity as the mere "sacred theater" of the system that would take its place. Like Klass, de Certeau envisioned a complementary relationship between science and religion, the former describing the natural world and the latter providing a social-moral orientation.[11] Nonetheless, the unresolved tensions between Christianity and science have retained an ability to relativize both. This circumstance was intensified by the rise of nation-states. The cultural identities of these states have presented their members, especially in the West, with a plethora of cultures and ideological alternatives. In the course of the twentieth century, the impetus to relativism and a questioning of once authoritative texts has therefore intensified.

Klass notes two current alternatives to science. One is fundamentalism, which proposes an omnipotent deity able to intervene in the world as a real causal force. This is an alternative view, but one that, like science, calls on an established "source of dependable, accurate information about the nature of . . . the universe" (Klass 1995: 156). For this reason, Klass observes, fundamentalists need not be opposed to science but rather can welcome it, if not as authority then at least as tool. Either way, fundamentalism involves a quest for authoritative truth often embodied in a text and in a somatic experience pursued and validated through repeated social practice. Moreover, many conservative Christianities, if not strictly fundamentalist, now sustain this quest for a preestablished and recorded truth with scientistic attributes.

Coleman, Norris, Brown, and Reidhead and Reidhead all describe interesting versions of the quest for authoritative truth. Norris recounts the way in which different types of somatic experience ground different quests for authority. These include full prostration in Sufism, sitting meditation in Zen

Buddhism, and the charismatic Christian swoon, often rendered as "dancing in the Spirit" by Pentecostalists. Her emphasis, however, like Coleman's, is on the social practice that makes this embodied experience real and therefore supports the text. In his account of Swedish charismatics, Coleman underlines the central place that converting others has among the converted. Through a focus on missionizing others, Word of Life believers rely not on a singular somatic experience but rather on the constant telling and retelling of "exemplary narratives" of conversion. They use these to recreate the experience of their own conversion and also to attest to the powers it has brought. Interestingly, in my own work with Jamaican Pentecostalists, I found that saints consistently used such conversion narratives to reinforce their own "in-filling" experience (see Austin-Broos 1997).

Reidhead and Reidhead recount the story of a woman's passage into Catholicism, and ultimately Catholic monasticism, from life as a pastor among Jehovah's Witnesses. This particular case is interesting because their subject describes her Catholic conversion in enthusiastic terms more typical of Pentecostalism. Her body, a "cold, steel milkshake container," was suddenly filled with "fuzzy hot chocolate." Reidhead and Reidhead show how this description of conversion progressively was routinized within Catholicism and then within a monastic setting. Their account is highly evocative of Turner's discussion of existential and routinized *communitas* and the relatively frequent passage in religious life from one to the other (Turner 1969). Brown's very interesting discussion of American Spiritualists portrays a quest for truth grounded more in experience than in text. Yet the vacillation that occurs in the practice of the Spiritualists has its roots in scientistic aspirations. They wish to know whether or not there is life after death, but they often change their conclusions due to the variable experience involved in practices that lack codification. These essays all describe quests for authority mostly embodied in texts and validated by physical experience. Not one but both of these are crucial to the fundamentalist and show how this form of religion can engage with some of the aspirations of science.

Klass points to a second alternative to Western science: the variety of New Age and Neo-Pagan forms he terms "postrationalist." Postrationalists, in Klass's view, reject both fundamentalism and the science that undermined the one God of Judeo-Christian religion. Aware of a larger world and its vast religious possibilities, these practitioners look beyond the West for systems they can engage with. Klass identifies Spiritualism as a forerunner to these developments. Rather than postrationalist, I would describe these quests as essentially romantic. Like the earlier Romantics who first opposed the Enlightenment, these romantics tend to emphasize "the primacy of imagination and the decisive importance . . . of feeling and emotion." Romantics are inclined to see truth not as something preordained but rather as a variable experience "created by the inquirer." Rather than being "a passive recipient of a God-given world," romantics seek to constitute worlds "dynamic, variable and particular."[12] My suggestion is that many peoples involved in conversion, and especially in milieus infused with the West's modernity, vacillate between a quest for scientistic authority and the creativity of a modern romantic. This is reflected in the milieus described by Brown, Norris, and Glazier, but I suspect that it also touches numerous other passages, from those involving Danish Jews and Dani Christians to those of Icelandic spiritists. Rather than mere *bricoleurs*, these various converts quest for a habitus that embraces texts but also accommodates their own capacity for agency. This perhaps is the mark of a transcultural modernity that now informs most of the passages involved in conversion.

CONCLUSION

A major theme in this collection is that conversion is continuing and practiced. The emphasis in the various chapters is not on singular experience, paranormal or otherwise, or on absolute breach with a former life, but rather on the way in which conversion is a passage: constituted and reconstituted through social practice and the articulation of new forms of relatedness. An anthropology of conversion must focus on representation and phenomenology but invariably will return to the practice of social life in which the various embodiments of meaning are sustained in relational ways. This links this collection with broader methodological themes in anthropology concerning social practice and agency. The chapters also reference a turbulent historical setting in which the gamut of nation-states and other nationalisms struggle for salience and stability as cultural milieus. In this context, conversion as religious passage is now a prevalent response to dilemmas intellectual and practical. World religions are being called upon as global economics and secular nationalism offer only uncertain futures to most of their participants. And some of these participants are actively engaged in reinterpreting religion. Possibly this explains why the contributors to this book see conversion as ongoing and partial. Modern developments, both intellectual and political, have freed religion from the corral to which it was assigned by Western Europe. Religion now resides in the world with all its previous entanglements both personal and political, both local and transnational. Studies of conversion, therefore, go to the heart of cultural passage in the world today.

This collection grew out of an invited session at the 2000 meeting of the American Anthropological Association. The panel, "Anthropology of

Conversion," was sponsored by the Society for the Anthropology of Consciousness. I was delighted to participate as one discussant in the panel. The other discussant was the late Morton Klass, who died before this collection of papers could be published. Nonetheless, the collection stands as a tribute to his scholarship and insight within the anthropological study of religion. It also stands as a memorial to his enthusiasm and warmth appreciated by students and colleagues alike.

NOTES

1. My reference here is to Weber's "world religions," including Judaism, Islam, Christianity, Hinduism, Buddhism, and Confucianism (Weber 1991 [1948]). Just as Turner suggests that pilgrimage is a phenomenon of the "historical" or world religions, so it seems that conversion is mainly associated with them. See Turner (1974a, 1978).

2. "Paradigm shift" was the term used by Thomas Kuhn to describe scientific revolution. R. I. Lohmann uses it in this book to describe the changes that occur when autochthonous people are encompassed in a world religion—a revolution for them of equal magnitude.

3. Regarding the term "passage," my debt to Victor Turner is clear (see Turner 1974b). "Turning from and to" is Lewis Rambo's phrase, although I render it in a rather different way (see Rambo 1993).

4. Michael Jackson evokes this notion in his account of Central Australia. See Jackson (1995).

5. "No place" or "nowhere" is the literal translation of the Latin "utopia," which is originally derived from the Greek. "Habitus" is a term used by Marcel Mauss (1979 [1950]: 114) and popularized by Pierre Bourdieu (1967).

6. I intend a deliberate contrast here between religious passage and Clifford's notion of "travel" that possibly addresses too little of the shaping constraints that inform creativity in a modern world. See Clifford (1997).

7. This is simply a brief reference to Hefner's excellent discussion of Max Weber and Christianity as a world religion (see Hefner 1993).

8. Marriott (1976), in describing the Hindu self, first used the term "dividual." His discussion is usefully juxtaposed with Dumont's accounts of European individualism (1986).

9. In a discussion of religious passage, it is always important to note that renderings of self and other in terms of moral surfeit and deficit can be as invidious as "race," especially in sectarianism.

10. Herzfeld links idioms of intimacy to the issue of nationalism (1997).

11. See Klass (1995: 149–62) and de Certeau (1988: 157). The destiny for religion as a social-moral orientation was also canvassed by the evolutionist Tylor (1913 [1871]).

12. See Darcy's excellent short account of Romanticism and its relevance to modern Boasian anthropology (1987).

REFERENCES

Austin-Broos, Diane J. 1997. *Jamaica Genesis: Religion and the Politics of Moral Order.* Chicago: University of Chicago Press.

Bourdieu, Pierre. 1967. *Outline of a Theory of Practice.* Translated by Richard Nice. London: University of Cambridge Press.

Clifford, James. 1997. *Routes: Travels and Translations in the Late Twentieth Century.* Cambridge, Mass.: Harvard University Press.

Comaroff, Jean, and John Comaroff. 1991. *From Revelation to Revolution.* Chicago: University of Chicago Press.

Darcy, Anthony. 1987. "Franz Boas and the Concept of Culture: A Genealogy." In *Creating Culture: Profiles in the Study of Culture*, edited by Diane J. Austin-Broos, pp. 3–17. Sydney: Allen and Unwin.

De Certeau, Michel. 1987. "The Formality of Practices." In *The Writing of History*, translated by Tom Conley, pp. 147–205. New York: Columbia University Press.

Dirks, Nicholas B. 1996. "The Conversion of Caste: Location, Translation, and Appropriation." In *Conversion to Modernities: The Globalisation of Christianity*, edited by Peter van der Veer, pp. 115–36. New York: Routledge.

Dumont, Louis. 1986. *Essays on Individualism: Modern Ideology in Anthropological Perspective.* Chicago: University of Chicago Press.

Geertz, Clifford. 1960. *The Religion of Java.* New York: The Free Press.

Hefner, Robert W., ed. 1991. *Conversion to Christianity: Historical and Anthropological Perspectives on a Great Transformation.* Berkeley: University of California Press.

Herzfeld, Michael. 1996. *Cultural Intimacy: Social Poetics in the Nation-State.* New York: Routledge.

Horton, Robin. 1975. "On the Rationality of Conversion." *Africa* 45, nos. 3–4: 219–35, 372–99.

Jackson, Michael. 1995. *At Home in the World.* Durham, N.C.: Duke University Press.

Klass, Morton. 1995. *Ordered Universes: Approaches to the Anthropology of Religion.* Boulder: Westview Press.

Marriott, McKim. 1976. "Hindu Transactions: Diversity without Dualism." In *Transaction and Meaning: Directions in the Anthropology of Exchange and Symbolic Behaviour*, edited by Bruce Kapferer, pp. 109–42. Philadelphia: Institute for the Study of Human Issues.

Mauss, Marcel. 1979 [1950]. "Body Techniques." In *Sociology and Psychology*, translated by Ben Brewster, pp. 95–119. London: Routledge and Kegan Paul.

Rambo, Lewis R. 1991. *Understanding Religious Conversion.* New Haven, Conn.: Yale University Press.

Sahlins, Marshall. 1976. *Culture and Practical Reason.* Chicago: Chicago University Press.

Tambiah, Stanley. 1995. "The Nation-State in Crisis and the Rise of Ethnonationalism." In *The Politics of Difference*, edited by Edwin Wimsen and Patrick McAllister, pp. 124–43. Chicago: University of Chicago Press.

Diane Austin-Broos

Turner, Victor. 1967. "Communitas: Model and Process." In *The Ritual Process: Structure and Anti-Structure*, edited by Victor Turner, pp. 131–65. Chicago: Aldine.
———. 1974a. "Pilgrimages and Social Process." In *Dramas, Fields and Metaphors: Symbolic Action in Human Society*, edited by Victor Turner, pp. 166–230. Ithaca, N.Y.: Cornell University Press.
———. 1974b. "Passages, Margins and Poverty." In *Dramas, Fields and Metaphors*, edited by Victor Turner, pp. 231–71. Ithaca, N.Y.: Cornell University Press.
Turner, Victor, and Edith Turner. 1976. *Image and Pilgrimage in Christian Culture: Anthropological Perspectives.* New York: Columbia University Press.
Weber, Max. 1991 [1948]. "The Social Psychology of the World Religions." In *From Max Weber: Essays in Sociology*, edited by H. H. Gerth and C. Wright Mills, pp. 267–301. London: Routledge.

I

CONVERSION AND SOCIAL PROCESSES

2

Continuous Conversion?
The Rhetoric, Practice, and Rhetorical Practice
of Charismatic Protestant Conversion

Simon Coleman

In the English town where I live and work, there is an old bridge that spans the river and leads up to the market square. Over the past few years, a middle-aged man has occasionally appeared on the bridge, standing with his back to one of its stone walls. I've always known in advance when he's been there. His voice booms out at passersby, who politely but firmly nudge each other to the other side of the footpath, forming a subtle arc of separation between themselves and the man. Apparently oblivious, he continues to deliver his urgent message: that the world will end soon, that we need to be saved immediately—preferably before we get to the end of the bridge—and that Jesus is our only route to salvation.

I invoke this image partly because it corresponds to common conceptions of conservative Protestantism in much of Northern Europe.[1] To skeptical outsiders, these Christians are associated with unwanted intrusion into neutral, public space. In certain respects, of course, such assumptions are correct. Missionizing is a highly valued activity (cf. Ammerman 1987), and the scorn or indifference of outsiders is often rationalized away by believers as merely indicating the need to increase their proselytizing efforts. When I set out some sixteen years ago to carry out my first stint of research among Pentecostalist and other charismatic groups in Uppsala, Sweden, I remember dreading the thought of explaining to my informants that I hadn't been converted. And indeed, toward the end of the very first Pentecostalist service I attended, an elderly woman spotted me standing next to a senior member of the church. In a voice clearly audible to the rest of the congregation, she hailed me with the words: "Are you saved?"[2]

Much of my fieldwork in Uppsala has in fact been carried out in the main local rival to the Pentecostalist church, a charismatic "Faith" ministry called the Word of Life (*Livets Ord*) that was formed in 1983, three years before my arrival in the town (Coleman 2000a).[3] The new and rapidly growing group has frequently been described by local theologians, other Christians, journalists, and members of the public in terms that invoke classic tropes of brainwashing (Coleman 1989; cf. Barker 1984).[4] Its members, many of whom are in their twenties and early thirties, are alleged to have been converted against their will and made subject to the irresistible charismatic authority of Ulf Ekman, the ministry's founder and leader. Participation is said to involve a highly suspicious surrendering not only of one's personal will but also of one's material resources, alongside a capitulation to brash, overaggressive styles of worship and mission that are assumed to be derived from the ministry's extensive connections with American Faith ministries.

Ironically, Word of Life rhetoric has some affinities with such discourse. Believers generally agree that conversion involves a total surrendering of the self to a higher force, followed by behavioral signs—particularly glossolalia— that indicate a state of ecstasy. Ideally, also, a Christian should be a bold giver of money or other resources to others, on the Faith theory that gifts will return tenfold or hundredfold to the giver. Testimonies from revival meetings and reports from missionaries talk of how thousands of people are being saved in Sweden and abroad. Although, admittedly, brains are not perceived as being "washed," these believers do talk of minds, souls, and spirits being "renewed" by the acceptance of Jesus as Lord.[5] As one preacher I heard at a street meeting put it to passing pedestrians: "You're thinking, 'Oh, it's the Word of Life again, they're mad.' We're not mad; we're saved!"[6]

Conversion as an event and as a practice is regularly articulated by Word of Lifers: through the prayer formulae suggested to nonbelievers that can be deployed as easy-to-use recipes for self-conversion;[7] through altar calls at the ends of services; through radio and television programs, audiocassettes, videos, and websites that apparently reach out to the unsaved; and through numerous accounts of conversions located in personal testimonies, missionary reports, and so on. However, one of my arguments is that there is a disjunction between the frequent charismatic depiction of instant, radical, and total conversion and an ethnographic perspective that indicates a much more gradual and ambiguous socialization into shared linguistic and ritual practices.[8]

Secondly, I want to shift attention away from the most obvious object of conversion discourse, the "unbeliever." A relatively neglected feature of the conversion process concerns the effects it has on the person ostensibly doing the converting.[9] Peter Stromberg (1993: 3; cf. Harding 1987), writing of American evangelicals, has recently argued that the transformational efficacy of the conversion experience is not confined to the original event. For him, telling and retelling conversion stories is a central ritual of faith, framing personal experience in canonical language and recreating that experience in the telling. I want to look at similar narratives of personal conversion but also at other proselytizing activities, verbal and nonverbal, that reignite the symbolic and experiential power of conversionary processes. I argue that reaching out into the world in order to convert others is a self-constitutive act for the charismatics I have studied. Missionization is not merely a matter of attempting to transform the potential convert, but also—perhaps even primarily—a means of recreating or reconverting the charismatic self.

The third part of my argument relates to the kind of people who participate in Word of Life activities. Many have previously belonged to other churches, and some still retain formal membership in churches of a rather different theological hue. Relatively little research has been done on intrareligious shifts in allegiance or identity—a phenomenon Donald Taylor (1999) recently described as "awkward conversion"—and I focus on how shifting de facto allegiance from one church to another is conceptualized by believers.[10]

All of these points contribute to a total picture of what I call *continuous* conversion, in which "continuity" can be understood in a number of related ways. It can imply that movement of the self toward charismatic conviction is an ongoing process, albeit one described by a rhetoric of spontaneous transformation; it indicates a blurring of the boundaries of identity between religious affiliations; and it suggests that analysis of conversion practices should focus not only on the potential neophyte, but also on broader sets of social relations and ideological representations that include and influence the evangelizing believer.

CONCEPTUALIZING CONVERSION

"Conversion" is a fuzzy term. At times, it is tempting to follow the Comaroffs's metaphorical throwing up of hands and their claim (1991: 249–50; cf. Asad 1996: 264) that the word has no meaning as an analytical category because it cannot grasp the highly variable, syncretistic manner in which social identities and cultural styles are transformed in contexts of mission. For them, conversion—if defined as a "transfer of primary religious affiliation" (Peel 1977: 108)—reflects how a Pauline model of conversion, itself resonating with bourgeois ideals of spiritual individualism, has become enshrined in Western thought.

The Comaroffs's unease contributes to broader intellectual chasms that have been evident for the past century. The focus on radical psychological and spiritual transformation on the level of the individual, inherited from William James (1902; cf. Nock 1933),[11] can be contrasted with more sociological and anthropological emphases on economic, cultural, and political contexts that correlate with collective trends in conversion. Stress on the importance of inner transformation is thus challenged by Durkheimian concerns relating to identity and cosmology.[12] Even Horton's (1971, 1975) famous depiction of African conversion to Christianity and Islam, which is frequently accused of intellectualism and lack of connection with political and economic forces (e.g., Fernandez 1978; Hefner 1993: 21–23), is nonetheless an attempt to link macrocosmic, universalist horizons of perception to changing forms of community and new social worlds (Fernandez 1978: 220; Gallaher 1990: 102–3; Meyer 1996).

It is difficult to ignore Hefner's (1993: 23) call for striking a balance between the extremes of intellectualist voluntarism and structural determinism, or Rita Kipp's (1995: 878) proposal of the need for "practice theory" linking microprocesses of consciousness with macropatterns of society and culture. Yet such approaches do not necessarily take us very far toward an understanding of conversion per se because ultimately they apply to *any* aspect of culture, while also perhaps begging comparative questions as to the specific meanings of consciousness, voluntarism, and so on. I prefer to start with the inductive observation that conversion is an ideological category and a set of ritualized practices that are key to Swedish charismatic identity on personal and collective levels. I do not assume that a simple story can be told about the motivations or causes for conversion. My argument is that conversion as a multivalent idea and as a quality of action permeates the charismatic life, and under the right conditions it can help to sustain that life, whether outsiders are persuaded to enter the body of Christ or not.

CONVERSION AS A QUALITY OF ACTION

Let me start my description of Word of Life practices with an ethnographic puzzle. Virtually every service I have attended at the ministry has ended in the classic altar call, the appeal to all who are unsaved in the congregation to come up and choose *this* moment to dedicate their lives to Jesus. Yet at no point have I ever seen anybody actually take up this call during a normal weekday or Sunday meeting.[13] Usually, it is followed by an offer of healing to those who are already saved but who have health or other problems, or by an offer of spiritual reinforcement for those who feel that they have discovered their special calling from God. This latter offer is *always* taken up by some members of the congregation, often in large numbers. Although the conversionist and the healing rituals broadly parallel each other in ritual habitus—with both involving the laying on of hands and the uttering of tongues by the preacher—it is clearly the internally orientated ritual that attracts a greater number of takers.

If Word of Life rhetoric—and that of its critics—is valid and hundreds or thousands are being converted by the group, such transformations are not happening during services in Uppsala. Nor do they seem to be translated into membership of the group. Reliable figures are difficult to obtain, but those that exist (cf. Coleman 2000a: 104) suggest that most Word of Life congregation members—now around 2,500 in number—were already active Christians before they joined, with crossovers from Pentecostalism particularly common.[14] Furthermore, the Word of Life encourages split loyalties by offering spiritual products that do not entail formal membership, including workshops, an extensive Bible School for English-language as well as Swedish-language speakers, national and international media outlets, and even a university affiliated with that of Oral Roberts. In other words, many of the people who engage with the ministry are not members of its congregation, but more temporary consumers of its charismatic resources.[15]

My simultaneous fieldwork within the Word of Life and Uppsala Pentecostalist churches indicates that the "client-like" relationships cultivated by the charismatic ministry help create a distinctive division of spiritual labor in the lives of believers (cf. Flinn 1999: 69). Pentecostalists who are attracted to the Word of Life regard the older congregation as important to them in a social sense, but argue that the newer group has taken over the mantle of promoting revival in Uppsala and indeed Sweden. Pentecostalism represents faithfulness to an almost century-old tradition of noncomformity and is often associated with longstanding kinship or friendship ties; the Word of Life is about dipping into a spirit of revival that is flowing—to use a favorite Pentecostal phrase—"just now." And if the Pentecostal movement has now become respectable in Sweden, the Word of Life retains a notoriety linked to its alleged Americanness and its proselytizing fervor. Thus for Pentecostals, and I suspect for many other samplers of the ministry's wares, the Word of Life provides a liminoid revivalist space within which an identity of deviance—going against the spiritual grain—can ambivalently be embraced by members of established denominations.

It might be argued that what I'm describing here is not "true" conversion, not a "real" turning away from an old life toward a new, but rather a revitalized form of a Christianity gone stale. Certainly, the narratives of "crossover" Christians differ from those belonging to people who have just recently been saved. Among new Christians, the previous life that has been left behind is characterized as one of depression, alcoholism, darkness, lack of direction, and so on. For those who have previously been members of other, very different churches—or indeed still are—contact with the group is translated into self-descriptions that talk more of a "deepening" of faith (cf. Stai 1993), a "closer" relationship with Jesus, or a "revived" understanding of the Bible. Yet, intriguingly, in both cases personal testimonies invoke a charismatic rhetoric that draws on common themes of self-revitalization or even rebirth. Even those previously saved can, in effect, be born "yet again" (cf. Austin-Broos 1981). As with the juxtapositions of ritual conversion and ritual healing at the end of services, identity transformation and identity reinforcement draw on very similar symbolic language.[16]

Thus, although I'm referring to a radically different ethnographic situation, I agree with the Comaroffs (1991: 249) that the moral economy of Protestant conversion, apparently requiring the individual to arrive at a rational choice among religious options, is not always straightforwardly realized in people's lives. However, rather than abandoning the concept of conversion, I prefer to explore its multivalence, even within a single religious organization, by suggesting that it is a quality of action as much as it is a mechanism for bringing outsiders into the group. By this I mean that for all believers, mature or newly saved, participation in the group is likely to involve a huge number of activities that are characterized by a conversionist orientation. In certain cases such action is highly focused and systematic, involving perhaps the training of Bible School students through lectures or knocking on doors around town. Missionary trips abroad are also regularly organized. Exemplary narratives of personal conversion frequently conclude with the convert describing how their newfound charismatic power and evangelical competence has been manifested in a first attempt to convert others.[17] Services contain the altar call, but in addition they may require the congregation to pray for those beyond the church hall who are in need of salvation, and this sense that even local worship is also a form of outreach is reinforced by the fact that services are packaged into videos, audiocassettes, and sometimes radio programs that reach an imagined audience beyond the immediate time and space of the original event. Indeed, the use of media is crucial to the construction of a conversionist quality of action that attaches to so many areas of life: apart from rendering worship available for potentially unlimited consumption, it also indicates the iconic character of all action at the group, the sense that all who are there—particularly preachers but even ordinary members of the audience— may become exemplars for unseen viewers and listeners.[18]

Yet, as with images of the Word of Life that depict it as brainwashing hordes of young, spiritually naïve innocents, all is not as it first appears. Any given Bible School student may only be required to evangelize in Uppsala around once a month. Furthermore, all believers are instructed to avoid argument or self-justification on such occasions. Missionary trips abroad are regularly arranged but may cultivate the experience of having traveled far to spread the Gospel rather than prompting a great deal of direct face-to-face interaction with the unsaved. The program of one such trip given to me by a participant details a five-day journey to Finland, during which time the only prescribed involvement with direct evangelizing occurred on the boat away from and back to Sweden. The use of media technology to spread the Word further divorces the missionary from the missionized, allowing intragroup worship to be regarded as a powerful means of reaching the anonymous Other. Even preaching in the market square attracts an audience that is made up predominantly of Word of Life members themselves, some of whom might attempt to talk to apparently interested strangers but most of whom are likely to contribute to the event by their presence alone. Instructions as to how to convert also imply that a conversionary orientation need not always be expressed in direct confrontation with the unsaved Other. In a newsletter article Ulf Ekman cautions his reader: "If you witness at work remember you are there to work, not witness. 'Let your life be your witness.' Joy, honesty and willingness to work in your life will testify for you."[19]

Thus charismatic convictions about how salvation is actually achieved reinforce the sense that direct and extended social contact is not absolutely key to conversion. It is admitted that some people are "seekers" before they submit themselves to God, and it is certainly emphasized that once somebody has announced their conversion they should be followed up and ushered into church fellowship as quickly as possible.[20] However, the first moment of submission is indeed seen as a moment, an instant, and it can apparently be achieved through the medium of the disembodied Word divorced from human sociality. In Faith rhetoric, reaching out via the electronic media is an effective missionary tool and has the advantage of speaking to potentially unlimited numbers of people at the same time. A confident conversionist orientation and habitus can be cultivated through imagining the unconverted Other as much as meeting him or her face-to-face. Only the *rhetorical* presence of the unsaved person is actually necessary to the system. And although instant results of evangelization are welcomed, these are not always necessary. As one man put it in his testimony, neatly encompassing talk about converting others within a description of his own story: "Even if [nonbelievers] don't receive Jesus immediately, what they hear sticks on to their inside."[21]

These assumptions about conversion should also be viewed in the context of wider Faith ideas about the importance of extending the individual or collective self into a putative "world" (Coleman 2000a, 2000b). Similar notions are evident in many missionizing congregations but are given a particular flavor in Faith discourse. Satirized by outsiders as "Name it and Claim it" theology (cf. Barron 1987), the Faith perspective emphasizes the ability of anointed words—spoken by a believer—not just to *describe* but actually to *become* reality. Similarly, material goods or money that are given to others or contributed to an ambitious enterprise are viewed as investments of the self in a bountiful God, with the assumption that a good rate of return will redound to the person. Conversion practices share with other discursive or physical acts the quality of providing a kind of spiritual accounting of the self through reaching out, articulating powers that must constantly be invoked and reinvoked throughout the whole of life. The personal revitalization that is a feature of Word of Life participation is intimately linked to practices that appear to orient the self beyond parochial and physical limits.[22]

Such action takes on many different referents of meaning. On a personal level, it can imply the adoption of a bold and entrepreneurial character that is not regarded as conventionally Swedish and that is sometimes criticized by outsiders as being typically American. It also implies a criticism of other, older denominations that have let the revivalist spirit die down and become not just institutionalized but also too introverted. More broadly, the Faith rhetoric of outreach can be read as denying the possibility of limiting ambition in cultural, economic, or even political terms, or of submitting to Swedish state bureaucracy. More broadly still, it implies the possibility of feeling part of a global Christian movement whose scope and significance are not confined to one country alone, let alone one that is renowned for its secularity. Indeed, the ministry in Uppsala is only the headquarters of an operation that maintains other offices in Europe, Asia, and the United States and that is in constant and close touch with Faith adherents around the world.

Conversion as I have described it is, therefore, "continuous" in yet another sense: it cannot be isolated as an autonomous mode of action but condenses meanings that are evident in myriad ways of reaching beyond the individual or collective self. Praying for the conversion of unknown others, contributing money to send Bibles to Russia, visiting fellow believers at a conference in Finland, plucking up the courage to witness to a friend, and so on are actions that constitute charismatic identity in the very act of extending it out into the world.[23]

To give an example of how these meanings can be realized and interpreted by the individual believer, let me briefly mention the case of Pamela, a woman in her early twenties who, when I interviewed her in 1987, had been a Word of Life student and an active member in the organization as a whole. Although previously a Christian, Pamela had felt her faith and Christian identity to have been revived after her response to an altar call at a Word of Life service that had resulted in her publicly falling to the ground under the power of the Holy Spirit. Her sense of personal spiritual rebirth was augmented by others' assessments of the degree to which she corresponded to Faith models of behavior. Charismatic friends defined her as markedly outgoing, a "fighter" for the faith; a Swedish pastor informed her that she was destined to save many people through her personal calling; a number of people had actually compared her personality with a well-known American preacher. These labels, combined with her powerful ritual experience and some participation in missionary activities, reinforced in Pamela a conviction of the outgoing self.

I found Pamela's description of herself in the interview to be echoed in the notes she took during attendance at the Word of Life Bible School. She tells herself, "Faith is to connect up to God. He has no limitations," and that "I am growing, faith is in my heart." A further note asserts: "I believe in Jesus and prove it by witnessing about him." In such statements, which are both her responses to lectures and anointed words that will help to create the "reality" they describe, Pamela links some key Faith themes: unlimited growth is connected both to personal faith and to witnessing, the externalized demonstration of faith. Pamela also found a job that resonated perfectly with her newfound identity, involving telephone sales for a firm that was run by a fellow congregation member. Notably *absent* from her conception of herself was any sense of engagement with political issues, indicating that the repertoire of symbolic resonances offered by participation in the Word of Life allows for considerable variations in personal focus.

CONCLUSION

I am not claiming that Word of Lifers *never* convert people through knocking on doors or encountering them in the street. I have simply chosen to point out that conversion is an activity whose significance extends far beyond the question of whether an unbeliever becomes a believer. Most attempts at conversion—in the Word of Life or probably in any other religious group—end in what from the outside looks like a kind of failure since the object of conversion discourse remains unconvinced; but in making such an observation we have hardly said all there is to say about conversion as a practice or a quality of action.[24]

Word of Life claims to be reaching out to the unsaved cannot be dismissed as "mere" rhetoric that is not borne out "in practice." They should be seen, rather, as forms of rhetorical practice that articulate a central and yet multivalent sense of extending the self into the world—they are rituals of identity-marking and formation that can potentially be carried out at any time, at any place. They are also rituals that require an object toward which to reach, even if such an object is imagined. It might, therefore, seem that I am agreeing with Horton that conversion can involve—indeed, can depend upon—a widening of social and intellectual horizons. As I have argued elsewhere (2000a), Word of

Life strategies do provide conservative Protestant appropriations of increasingly global imagery. However, my key point is that Word of Lifers are reaching out into a world that they construct as far as possible, imaginatively and ritualistically, to conform with already established charismatic expectations.

Let me, therefore, finish by returning to my image of the man standing on the bridge in Durham, shouting out a message to passersby who do not appear to be listening to his message. I have not approached the man, and do not know which church, if any, he belongs to. However, if he has anything in common with his Swedish Faith counterparts, his words will not be spoken entirely in vain. They have an audience of at least one, given that the evangelical speaker is also perforce a listener, attending to a message that achieves an important part of its purpose merely by being powerfully and passionately projected out into the world.

NOTES

1. According to van der Veer (1996: 7), the conversion of others has gradually been marginalized in modern Europe and transported to the (often non-Christian), colonized world.

2. Luckily, she hadn't noticed that the service was still going on, so I didn't have time to give a stumbling reply. In this chapter, I have not discussed Pentecostalist attitudes to conversion in any detail.

3. Faith ministries are known for preaching a theology that is oriented toward the gaining of health and material prosperity. The roots of such emphases can be traced to New Thought Metaphysics and postwar healing revivalism. Faith theologies have proved attractive to both working- and middle-class conservative Protestants in many parts of the world, particularly over the past thirty years. The notional head of the movement is Kenneth Hagin, at whose bible school Ulf Ekman (the leader of the Word of Life) studied in the early 1980s.

4. There may be parallels here with Don Seeman's point (made at the workshop from which this book is derived) that processes of conversion raise issues of both authenticity and agency.

5. As is common in Pentecostalist and charismatic groups, the renewed body is seen as a vessel for the Holy Spirit about to conjoin with the broader body of Christ (cf. Austin-Broos 1996: 121).

6. Heard in Uppsala, 1994.

7. A typical prayer might ask Jesus to help the self be "born again" while also confessing that He is Lord.

8. Flinn (1999: 58) criticizes the view that charismatic conversion essentially involves an instantaneous event, and he mentions in evidence the period of "suspension" or indecision that may precede the event itself. Such periods are also common among new converts to the Word of Life.

9. There are parallels here with analyses of overseas missions that emphasize the need to focus on missionaries as well as the missionized (Comaroff 1985).

10. There may be parallels here with the chapter in this book by Glazier (chapter 12) looking at conversion as a syncretist, ambiguous process.

11. See discussions of James (1902) in for example Gallaher (1990: 5), Kipp (1995: 870), and van der Veer (1996: 15).

12. With the two approaches likely to imply rather different understandings of human agency (Kipp 1995: 872) as well as criteria for identifying "authentic" conversion (cf. Keane 1996).

13. It is interesting to compare my experience with that of Austin-Broos, who discusses Jamaican Pentecostal churches (1981: 240). She reports that she never witnessed a service at which two or three persons did *not* respond to the altar call. If it appeared that no unsaved person would come forward, saints themselves would respond, on the grounds that they might be seeking spiritual gifts such as prophecy or the power to heal.

14. In the Norwegian Faith congregation he examined, Stai (1993: 47–48) noted that over half of the members learned about the new congregation through contact with Pentecostalists. Ulf Ekman's background is a former priest in the Swedish Church, but the second pastor of the group, Robert Ekh, is a former Pentecostalist.

15. The provision of such services to "outsiders" is hardly unique. In the UK, the currently popular Alpha Course is aimed both at new Christians and at more experienced believers who desire a spiritual "top-up."

16. Forstorp (1992: 162), describing another Swedish Faith congregation, argues that public healing is a symbolic repetition of salvation, with both manifesting a total giving over of the self to God.

17. Compare with Hawley's point (1998: 4) that the impulse to display sincerity by becoming an enthusiastic apostle of one's new faith typifies the Christian conversion experience. More broadly, he notes (6) that the question of alterity implicit in conversion poses a question about borders: Where is the rupture between self and other to be situated?

18. This sense of potential surveillance, of making the ideal Self available for the Other, is also evident in the way that believers sometimes describe shared biblical language as occupying their bodies.

19. Word of Life Newsletter, November 1985, 5.

20. Small cell groups as well as a "Discipleship School" socialize new members into appropriate linguistic, ritual, and ideological norms.

21. Congregation Newsletter 2, no. 3 (May 7, 1986).

22. Compare with Austin-Broos's discussion (1996: 159) of Csordas (1987) and the notion that *connected* genres of ritual (in Csordas's case, language, involving sharing, teaching, prayer, and prophecy) create an experience of self-affirmation that supports the metaphors and dispositions of a charismatic religion. Compare also with Berger and Luckmann's (1966) emphasis on plausibility structures rather than on conversion events.

23. Ekman notes, in the Word of Life Newsletter, "You shouldn't be afraid to witness. God gives you fantastic openings. You shouldn't be known for being nice, but

for being saved!" (1994 1:10). The same issue carries a pertinent interview with two young Bible School students (Maria and Per-Anders) who have come from an older noncomformist denomination (Örebro Missionsförbundet) and who describe the experience of taking a course at the ministry. The quotation starts with Maria speaking: "'Along with learning to take time with God in prayer, my prayer life has been transformed. Before I was completely absorbed in my own needs, while now I have begun to stretch out to pray for others.'" This sense of reaching out to reinforce a sense of the spiritually empowered self is also articulated through Internet sites (not discussed here).

24. Media evangelism is generally an ineffective means of conversion (cf. Ammerman 1987: 149) if assessed as a method of bringing new people into the church. My experience is that "new" converts to the Word of Life (not examined in any great detail here) come to the group through various, often circuitous routes, most of which involve some kind of previously established social bond to a Faith supporter.

REFERENCES

Ammerman, N. *Bible Believers: Fundamentalists in the Modern World.* New Brunswick, N.J.: Rutgers University Press, 1987.

Asad, T. "Comments on Conversion." In *Conversion to Modernities: The Globalization of Christianity,* edited by P. van der Veer, pp. 263–73. London: Routledge, 1996.

Austin-Broos, D. "Born Again . . . And Again and Again: Communitas and Social Change among Jamaican Pentecostalists." *Journal of Anthropological Research* 37 (1981): 226–46.

Austin-Broos, D. *J'A'maica Genesis: Religion and the Politics of Moral Orders.* Chicago: University of Chicago Press, 1997.

Barker, E. *The Making of a Moonie: Choice or Brainwashing?* Oxford: Blackwell, 1984.

Barron, B. *The Health and Wealth Gospel.* Downers Grove, Ill.: InterVarsity Press, 1987.

Berger, P., and T. Luckmann. *The Social Construction of Reality: A Treatise in the Sociology of Knowledge.* Harmondsworth, UK: Penguin, 1966.

Coleman, S. *Controversy and the Social Order: Responses to a Religious Group in Sweden.* Ph.D. diss., University of Cambridge, 1989.

Coleman, S. *The Globalisation of Charismatic Christianity: Spreading the Gospel of Prosperity.* Cambridge: Cambridge University Press, 2000a.

———. "Moving Towards the Millennium? Ritualized Mobility and the Cultivation of Agency among Charismatic Protestants." *Journal of Ritual Studies* 14, no. 2 (2000b): 16–27.

Comaroff, J. *Body of Power, Spirit of Resistance: The Culture and History of a South African People.* Chicago: University of Chicago Press, 1985.

Comaroff, J., and Comaroff, J. *Of Revelation and Revolution: Christianity, Colonialism, and Consciousness in South Africa.* Chicago: University of Chicago Press, 1991.

Csordas, T. *Language, Charisma, and Creativity: The Ritual Life of a Religious Movement.* Berkeley: University of California Press, 1997.

Fernandez, J. "African Religious Movements." *Annual Review of Anthropology* 7 (1978): 195–234.

Flinn, F. "Conversion: Up from Evangelicalism or the Pentecostal and Charismatic Experience." In *Religious Conversion: Contemporary Practices and Controversies,* edited by C. Lamb and M. Bryant, pp. 51–72. London: Cassell, 1999.

Forstorp, P-A. *Att Leva och Läsa Bibeln: Textpraktiker i Två Kristna Församlingar.* Linköping, Sweden: Linköping University Press, 1992.

Gallagher, E. *Expectation and Experience: Explaining Religious Conversion.* Atlanta, Ga.: Scholars Press, 1990.

Harding, S. "Convicted by the Holy Spirit: The Rhetoric of Fundamental Baptist Conversion." *American Ethnologist* 14 (1987): 167–81.

Hawley, J., ed. *Historicizing Christian Encounters with the Other.* London: Macmillan, 1998.

Hefner, R. "Introduction: World Building and the Rationality of Conversion." In *Conversion to Christianity: Historical and Anthropological Perspectives on a Great Transformation,* edited by R. Hefner, pp. 3–44. Berkeley: University of California Press, 1993.

Horton, R. "African Conversion." *Africa* 41, no. 2 (1971): 85–108.

———. "On the Rationality of Conversion." *Africa* 45, no. 4 (1975): 219–35, 372–99.

James, W. *The Varieties of Religious Experience.* London: Longman, Green & Co, 1902.

Keane, W. "Materialism, Missionaries, and Modern Subjects in Colonial Indonesia." In *Conversion to Modernities: The Globalization of Christianity,* edited by P. van der Veer, pp. 137–70. London: Routledge, 1996.

Kipp, R. "Conversion by Affiliation: The History of the Karo Batak Protestant Church." *American Ethnologist* 22, no. 4 (1995): 868–82.

Meyer, B. "Modernity and Enchantment: The Image of the Devil in Popular African Christianity." In *Conversion to Modernities,* edited by P. van der Veer, pp. 199–230. London: Routledge, 1996.

Nock, A. *Conversion.* Oxford: Oxford University Press, 1933.

Peel, J. "Conversion and Tradition in Two African Societies—Ijebu and Buganda." *Past and Present* 76 (1977): 108–41.

Stai, S. "'Omvendelse og Nettverk': Et sosiologisk perspektiv på den virkningen omvendelsen har på nettverstilknytningen for medlemmene i 'Trondheim Kristne Senter.'" Master's thesis, Religionsvitenskapelig Institutt (Trondheim, Sweden), 1993.

Stromberg, P. *Language and Self-transformation: A Study of the Christian Conversion Narrative.* Cambridge: Cambridge University Press, 1993.

Taylor, D. "Conversion: Inward, Outward and Awkward." In *Religious Conversion: Contemporary Practices and Controversies,* edited by C. Lamb and M. Bryant, pp. 35–50. London: Cassell, 1999.

Van der Veer, P. "Introduction." In *Conversion to Modernities,* edited by P. van der Veer, pp. 1–21. London: Routledge, 1996.

3

Agency, Bureaucracy, and Religious Conversion: Ethiopian "Felashmura" Immigrants in Israel

Don Seeman

Purity of heart is to will one thing.

—Søren Kierkegaard

There is a moral and epistemological dilemma at the intersection of conversion, state bureaucracy, and social experience in Israel today. Namely, how can divergent claims about agency in religious conversion (on which access to certain state benefits depend) be adjudicated? The focus of this dilemma is a community of migrants who can best be described as twice-converted, because they are members of a Beta Israel (Falasha) community whose ancestors converted to Christianity in Ethiopia but who are today clamoring for the right to "return to Judaism" in the context of mass migration to the State of Israel. The dilemma posed by these "Felashmura," as they have been called (it is a term that they themselves reject), points to a common and probably insoluble conundrum faced by conversionary religions, modern state bureaucracies, and ethnographers alike. To put it simply, all of us are engaged in the ancient but problematic quest for purity of heart.

This is clear enough with respect to the gatekeepers of religious identity and state citizenship (in this case, rabbis and immigration officials). As institutional gatekeepers, they are empowered both to monitor and to manage processes of social transformation that include immigration and conversion, and to do so by employing often nebulous criteria that include estimations of human agency like "purity of heart." Does a potential convert have ulterior motives for joining the faith? Should a potential asylum seeker be designated as a political or as an economic refugee, and how is his or her legally determinant motivation to be ascertained in a world where many migrants can be plausibly said to be both scared *and* hungry? These are weighty questions, on which life and death can sometimes hang. Like religious gatekeepers (but perhaps less explicitly), the agents of the state construct plausible narratives of human motivation and circumstance in order to determine who benefits, and how, from the protective network of state and international law that governs movements of people across borders. Necessarily, these gatekeepers prefer simplistic narratives in which subjects can be said to "will one thing" and can be classified with ease. Their dilemma is that this is rarely if ever the case.

Like bureaucrats, ethnographers and historians also work to construct plausible narratives of human agency in settings of social change, and it should be noted that these narratives too can have profound or even catastrophic consequences in the lives of the people they depict. Scholars eager to demonstrate the "relevance" of their findings to social policy may for instance borrow unreflectively from the same narrow cultural taxonomies that underlie bureaucratic exclusion, with its endless myopic quest for monocausal explanations of human behavior. The case of the Felashmura is arresting in this regard precisely because of the synergy between bureaucratic, religious, ethnographic, and historical accounts of agency that have contributed over time to this community's burden. Conversion of the Felashmura in Israel is bound up with a larger set of bureaucratic practices and ideologies that are directed toward the alchemy-like transformation of migrants into citizens for which the modern nation-state is renowned (cf. Herzfeld 1992). In the Israeli case, this dynamic is compounded by the close relationship between religious and bureaucratic adjudication of personal status issues and by the state's willingness to solicit input by scholars. The result is a complicated set of sometimes-conflicting criteria by which potential Ethiopian immigrants must be judged, including genealogy and membership in a distinctive confessional community. For Felashmura, the dilemma is to demonstrate a sincere "return" to the religion of their ancestors (i.e., Judaism), which is not somehow predicated on their desire to leave Ethiopia, which would disqualify that return in the eyes of immigration authorities. Understanding the experience of religious conversion requires an appreciation for these kinds of social and political constraints. It also requires attention to the cultural idiom (in this case, "return") in which religious transformation is framed.

THE POETICS AND PRACTICE OF "RETURN TO JUDAISM"

A converted Jew named Henry Aaron Stern became the first agent of the London Society for the Promotion of Christianity amongst the Jews (popularly known as the LJS or London Jewish Society) to reach the highlands of Ethiopia in 1860. Although Stern acted on the basis of his presumed ethnic affinity with the Beta Israel in order to persuade them to become "Christian Israelites," his efforts also ironically brought Beta Israel for the first time to the sustained attention of Jews in Western Europe. Some of these European Jews took an interest in "rescuing" Beta Israel from missionary inroads and ultimately from Ethiopia itself, and to this end they begin to send emissaries and "counter-missionaries" to Ethiopia in order to assess the situation there. These Westerners took differing views as to the Jewishness of the Beta Israel, and they set in motion a series of contests over cultural and religious authenticity that continues unabated to this day (Kaplan 1987; Seeman 1999; Seeman 2000).

Although missionary inroads among the Beta Israel were initially quite limited in number, their social influence was significant. They accelerated the decline in traditional authority among Beta Israel religious leaders, and contributed to a growing sentiment among Beta Israel that they should begin for the first time to view themselves as members of an international Jewish diaspora. Most of those Beta Israel who resisted conversion to Christianity eventually came within the orbit of Western Jewish emissaries like Jacques Faitlovitch, who attempted to reform Beta Israel religious practice so that they could be more effectively "reunited" with distant brethren. Faitlovitch's relative success may be due to the fact that whereas Christian missionaries deployed a trope of radical rebirth and transformation in Christ, he spoke of a return to common origins obscured by persecution and exile, which resonated with many Beta Israel. Faitlovitch worked to develop a cadre of young Beta Israel "culture brokers" (Messing 1982) who would work with him to promote social change in their own communities, and it can be argued that these "culture brokers" were the first "Ethiopian Jews" in the modern sense of the term.

A good example is the story of Tamrat Emmanuel, a Beta Israel boy of 16 who had been studying at a Swedish missionary school when Faitlovitch persuaded him to accept Jewish sponsorship instead. Faitlovitch sent Tamrat abroad to study in the hopes that he would later return to become a teacher of Beta Israel in Ethiopia. When Tamrat indeed returned and became the principal of the first Beta Israel school under Jewish auspices, he insisted that it be opened near Addis Ababa so that he could reach out to long-assimilated Beta Israel Christians living in that region and influence their "return" (Tamrat 1984). This interest was not shared by most of the foreign Jews who would come to be involved in Ethiopia and who largely ignored the question of Beta Israel Christians until it became clear after 1991 that significant numbers of the descendants of converts would continue seeking to join their relatives who had by now emigrated to Israel. Although Beta Israel Christians had played an important role in the whole history of contact between Ethiopian and non-Ethiopian Jews, this seemed to come as a surprise to the Israeli and American Jewish publics. In the closing hours of the Ethiopian Dergue regime's hold on power in 1991, over 14,000 Ethiopian Jews were airlifted to Israel, but several thousand more were left behind at an Addis Ababa transit camp because they had been designated Felashmura, or descendants of converts, by the Israeli government. This was the community among whom I conducted ethnographic fieldwork between 1992 and 1996, and although it took three years of political and bureaucratic wrangling to achieve, they did eventually arrive in Israel under a plan that gave their stated desire to "return to Judaism" official sanction and form.

The Return to Judaism program under which Felashmura were permitted to immigrate was officially sanctioned for the first time in 1994 under a deceptively simple plan. An interministerial committee had been convened to deal with the related crises of Felashmura refugees and of family reunification for new Ethiopian immigrants who had left relatives behind. The committee concluded that applicants with first-degree relatives in Israel should be admitted to the country on a humanitarian basis. This was less than Felashmura advocates had sought, since it did not recognize them as Jews and would not allow all of them to immigrate at once. However, a compromise was reached according to which immigrants who had arrived under family reunification could then participate in an accelerated Return to Judaism program administered by Israel's Chief Rabbinate. They would secure their own recognition as Jews first and then would be able to apply for family reunification of their own relatives who remained in Ethiopia. Although the program was in theory optional, failure to participate meant among other things that relatives in Ethiopia might not be brought to Israel, so that in the end only a few among the thousands of individuals who immigrated between 1994 and 1996 actually refused.

Return to Judaism was never described by its advocates as a program for conversion. It was officially open only to persons of Beta Israel (i.e., Jewish) descent who wished to return to their religious roots. At the same time, however, it is important to note that all of the procedures adopted by the program—an accelerated (three-month) course in basic Judaism, circumcision for men, and immersion in a *mikveh* for both men and women—were derived from normal Jewish conversionary practice in Israel. The primary differences between "return" and normal conversion as practiced in Israel at the time were that the program took only three months (as opposed to a year or more) to complete and that no one who was eligible was ever discouraged from participating in the program or turned away.

The program was administered by Rabbi Menahem Waldman, who boasted a long history of activism on behalf of Felashmura immigration to

Israel. He insisted that the program was penitential rather than conversionary, and this claim was crucial to his attempts to garner support from a religious establishment that was, to say the least, suspicious of anything that sounded like mass conversion. On the other hand, Rabbi Waldman did acknowledge that the format of the program allowed for some flexibility, since it did in fact meet all of the religious requirements for conversion to Judaism, thereby obviating the need for foolproof genealogical screening of program applicants. Although he always maintained that participants in the Return to Judaism program were "pure" in a genealogical as well as an intentional sense, therefore, it can also be said that the success of the program relied heavily on his careful but unspoken pragmatism.

In political terms, the Return to Judaism was subject to attack from a number of different directions, all of which began from more or less plausible, though not necessarily correct, arguments about the agency exercised by program participants. For officials at the Ministry of Immigrant Absorption, which was controlled at the time by a party identified with the secular left in Israeli politics, Felashmura were unwanted "economic refugees" whose Beta Israel descent should not be used in cynical attempts to gain Israeli citizenship. At the same time, powerful voices in Israel's religious establishment expressed doubt that Felashmura could be described as sincere penitents, since their manifest desire to leave Ethiopia was so strong. In 1996, rumors about the insincerity of program participants actually led to the suspension of the entire Return to Judaism for a period of several months and consequently to a hiatus in Felashmura immigration from Ethiopia. Ritual observance among participants in the program varied a great deal during this period, but all understood that the public face of the program must be one of unqualified commitment to Orthodox Judaism, and immigrant leaders spoke about this need frequently.

In a very real sense, the whole Return to Judaism can be seen as an imperfect tool for the suppression of anxiety about the religious agency of new immigrants. This anxiety focused on two distinct historical moments that were constantly juxtaposed in public debates, including the formal deliberations of the 1994 interministerial committee. The descendants of converts were described alternately in Israeli media as *anusim*, or forced converts (evoking the fifteenth-century Iberian *conversos*), or as *mitnazrim*, voluntary Christianizers. Ultimately, the avowedly neutral term "Felashmura" was settled upon thanks to a fanciful Hebrew derivation from *felasha she-hemir et dato* ("Falasha who exchanged his religion") that was bandied in the press.

This significance of the debate over nomenclature should not be underestimated. The difference between *anusim* and *mitnazrim* is a difference between victims of catastrophe, who are in principle deserving of "Jewish solidarity" (in the words of one expert witness to the 1994 interministerial committee), and traitors for whom the State of Israel bears little or no responsibility. Conversion to Christianity was framed in this debate primarily as a national and ethnic defection beyond any specifically religious meaning it may have held. Converts and their descendants were portrayed as individuals who had abandoned their people for personal gain during periods of persecution. This was significant because although apostasy as a religious sin may be canceled by repentance ("An Israelite remains an Israelite even though he sins," according to the accepted Jewish religious norm), this kind of secular apostasy is a stain from which converts and their descendants may never recover. The historical question of past conversion and its motivation is, therefore, rarely treated as a purely historical problem but rather as a determining element in the moral calculus that underlies contemporary social policy and through which bureaucratic categories are determined and maintained. For the new immigrants, it was important to frame their history as one of suffering so great that it could serve to mitigate the claim of infidelity with which they were charged.

Initially, therefore, Rabbi Waldman angered Felashmura leaders when he refused to accept their claim that all converts to Christianity in Ethiopia had done so on pain of death and should be considered "forced converts" under the terms of Jewish law. On the other hand, he worked hard to deemphasize the importance of this initial apostasy by focusing on the Return to Judaism that was already underway unofficially in Addis Ababa. He argued that apostasy was a religious category that could be repaired through heartfelt repentance and that this was precisely what the Felashmura were prepared to offer. "The 'Beta Israel' community in Addis Ababa has repeatedly demanded of Israel and its representatives," he wrote in 1996, "'We are Jews. We have abandoned our past. Accept our regret. Teach us the way of Torah and mitzvot'" (Waldman 1996). By locating the problem of agency in a context under his own control (i.e., the Return to Judaism program rather than earlier apostasy), Rabbi Waldman became a powerful and effective advocate of Felashmura immigration. His view should be contrasted with that of a Ministry of Absorption spokeswoman, who was publicly cited in a deportation case arguing, "They [the immigrants] are always trying to fool us [regarding their identities and motivation for coming to Israel]. . . . We cannot allow them to go on fooling the people of Israel."

Of course, neither of these depictions of agency among Beta Israel converts and their descendants won unqualified success in the political battle over Felashmura immigration. And neither managed to transcend the narrow sectarian interests in whose service it had been constructed: immigrant advocacy on the one hand or opposition to immigration on the other. Wherever one positions oneself in that debate, the discourse on purity of heart tends to erase from view the lives of the people whom it purportedly describes.

THIN DESCRIPTIONS

On a morning in November 1995, some sixty recent immigrants from Ethiopia boarded a bus at the Neve Carmel absorption center near Haifa for the short ride to a nearby school where they would complete the formal requirements of their Return to Judaism. Some had immigrated as recently as three months before and had enrolled in the program even before learning Hebrew. New immigrants typically lived in trailer homes at Neve Carmel, and here they were subject to a great deal of formal and informal scrutiny by educators, immigration officials, and representatives of the religious establishment. Because each of these groups wielded some degree of power over new immigrants but did not necessarily see eye-to-eye on the Return to Judaism or its goals, participants were subject to a great number of contradictory pressures during their first months. They were also subject to a profound politics of distrust, in which their motives and behavior were analyzed and parsed by competing, not necessarily sympathetic parties.

The mood on the bus was subdued but not anxious. Participants in the Return to Judaism program tended to accept the need for participation but to avoid discussion of what that acceptance might imply. At public rallies or in encounters with the Israeli media, they still largely rejected the whole Felashmura designation as senseless and stigmatizing, arguing that they had never been Christians at all or that their ancestors had only converted to Christianity under duress. In private, more complicated realities surfaced obliquely. "I've eaten many things in my lifetime," one mother of five named Rachel told me, referring to her family's complicated religious history—but "now all we want is to raise our children as Jews and get on with our lives." I will return to her story shortly.

The unwillingness of most immigrants to discuss the intimate details of their religious histories may have been a reasonable strategy under circumstances in which such information could easily be used to cause them harm. But it also contributed to a sentiment expressed by many academic researchers, politicians, and members of the public that the entire Return to Judaism program was a fraud that should be discontinued. During the period of my fieldwork at Neve Carmel, rumors began to circulate in the news media that many participants in the program were engaging in Christian missionary activity, further compromising public support. These rumors were never substantiated and were in my judgement false, but accusations of missionary activity also began to surface in social disputes between immigrants themselves, with the same force and destructive potential that has been ascribed to witchcraft allegations in other settings. As in witchcraft allegations, these accusations followed the contours of social fissures within the community, demarcating lines of jealousy or malice that set local relationships in stark relief. Immigrants' attacks on one another's religious motivations and agendas mirrored those to which the community as a whole was subject in its dealings with the state.

In this setting, of course, the question of agency in religious life arises both as an ethnographic and as a political conundrum. To avoid raising the question at all on the grounds that it is subjective or falls outside of the anthropologist's purview is to bracket one of the most important social facts constraining the lives of new immigrants. But how does one ask or write about agency in religious conversion without falling into the same rhetorical habits as the political actors described above, for whom ideological needs determine not only the questions asked but also to a large extent what answers may be given? One way is to try to account for the diverse social institutions and political actors who have an interest in the outcome of questions about agency and who contribute to its social articulation. Most of these actors had only the barest firsthand knowledge of the Felashmura community, but I found it surprisingly difficult to articulate any more responsible alternative for bureaucratic or political use. I have come to believe that this has something to do with the recalcitrance of social experience to the politically expedient "pure hearts" discourse on which state bureaucracies rely.

Consider the ritual aspect of the Return to Judaism. As participants disembarked from the bus, they were divided into groups by sex. All of the participants had already passed a perfunctory exam on Jewish law and practice, and the men had already undergone either circumcision or a kind of symbolic re-circumcision known as *hatafat dam brit*, in which a drop of blood from the penis is drawn. Now, in same-sex groups of about twenty, all the immigrants were led to a ritual pool, or *mikveh*, where they would remove their clothes (women donned loose-fitting robes) and immerse. This took place under the watchful eyes of the *bet din*, an informal court of three adult males needed to ratify conversion. The participants stood in line afterwards to receive the paperwork that confirmed their new status, and then got back on the bus for Neve Carmel.

These proceedings were conducted in a spirit that can only be described as bureaucratic efficiency. This was hardly the "total transformation of the person by the power of God" that scholars like Lewis Rambo (1993) identify as "genuine conversion." The most consistent feature of the rituals themselves was probably the demand for submission to bodily scrutiny by the state apparatus. During immersion, men and women submitted their unclothed bodies to the shaming gaze of outsiders who were empowered to affirm or to reject the "return" they sought to enact. Shame was an even more explicit feature of the *hatafat dam brit* procedure, in which men waited in line to have a drop of blood drawn from their bodies under the gaze of a ritual court. The procedure was relatively painless, a mere pinprick, but that pinprick had to be witnessed by the individual members of the court. The *mohel* (circumcision expert) who conducted the procedure spoke little with participants but kept up a lively commentary for the witnesses on the quality of the circumcisions that many men had had performed in Ethiopia, the way an experienced diamond cutter might appraise another professional's work.

Although most recent immigrants submitted to the procedure as just one more indignity, participants who had been in the country somewhat longer were often openly resentful and clearly shamed. For the members of the court, *hatafat dam brit* was a purely technical requirement of Jewish law to be conducted as quickly and dispassionately as possible. But for participants in the Return to Judaism program, submission to the drawing of blood and to its scrutiny by the court was a visceral enactment of their whole compromised subject position vis-à-vis the state. Through these rituals of domination, as well as the formal and informal scrutiny of daily life at the immigrant center, they learned that the taint of apostasy could only be repaired through the repeated baring of hidden intimacies to public view, and, worse, that even this submission might never be pronounced "enough."

We tend to believe as anthropologists that "thick" enough description of cultural and social context can elucidate any problem, and this is not a commitment I am prepared wholly to undermine. We do need to distinguish between all the different kinds of winks and nods that Geertz (1973) describes, and not just in our professional lives. But perhaps the problem of agency is less transparent than most of our interpretive models seem to suggest. We tend to focus on the shared, public, and communicative "web" of culture to the detriment of its strategic, idiosyncratic, and sometimes deliberately mystifying uses in lived experience, where culture is a contributory but never determinative factor of what it means to be human. It may be possible to thickly describe the sheep and cows in a plausible account of social action, as Geertz recommends, yet to nevertheless fail to recognize the indeterminacy of human presence that animates and transcends social action in its every move.

Let me return to the story of Rachel, the woman who told me she had "eaten many things" during the course of her religious life. Like most intimate revelations, this one came not as the result of an interview or an interrogation, but in the course of daily life some months after I had become a functional member of her household. Rachel and her husband came to Israel with an unusually high level of education and had ambitions to become schoolteachers. Her grandfather had converted to Christianity long before Rachel was born, but he nevertheless demanded that his offspring memorize the genealogies that linked them to a number of important Beta Israel families who eventually came to Israel during the 1980s. By chance, I knew some of these extended kin and was able to verify their links to Rachel's grandfather, as well as the fact that they wanted little to do with his grandchildren "because they went off and became 'Felashmura.'"

Perhaps because Rachel and her husband were educated and relatively successful economically, and perhaps also because an ethnographer from America had been spending so much time in their household, rumors began to spread that they were among the Pentecostal missionaries allegedly receiving money from foreign sponsors. I had already conducted interviews and attended prayer meetings with the four or five Pentecostals who were active at the absorption center, and I knew that Rachel and her husband had no real connection with them, but still the rumors intensified. I felt sure that I could not have missed the signs of something so fundamental as Pentecostal activity, given our proximity and friendship, but decided after some trepidation to confront Rachel and find out what she thought. Apparently, one of the rabbis from the Return to Judaism program had also confronted her the week before, and she was still angry. "He came to the door and said 'I know you are Pentecostal. You can be thrown off the program.' I told him it wasn't true and shut the door in his face. I swore I would never enter his synagogue again."

Rachel's anger, bordering on despair, was also directed toward her neighbors and fellow immigrants who had spread the rumors about her. "We just have to finish [the program] and leave here," she told me, and in fact hers was one of the first families to leave Neve Carmel for permanent housing several months later. This is when she grew thoughtful and said, "I have eaten many things in my life. . . . But it was our grandfather's mistake, not ours. What do they want from us?"

A few days later, Rachel brought up this incident again and made essentially the same comments. But she continued this time with an odd story about the everyday experience of the Return to Judaism with which I want to draw this chapter to a close. On the previous Saturday, Rachel told me, she had been suffering with a terrible headache. Like other Beta Israel women, she typically participated in communal coffee-drinking sessions up to three times a day with family and neighbors. This was an important part of social existence at Neve Carmel, and only Pentecostals (for whom coffee was addictive and hence Satanic) typically refrained from participating. The problem for women in the Return to Judaism program, however, was that the use of fire for cooking is prohibited on the Jewish Sabbath, and this effectively meant that Saturdays would have to pass without coffee. For some, this meant extreme headaches and withdrawal throughout the day. When Rachel's headache got so that she could hardly stand it, she decided to make some instant tea of coffee for relief—anything that the neighbors wouldn't be able to smell from their own immigrant trailers, just across the road. But when her then nine-year-old son saw her doing so, he interrupted her in obvious distress. "If you make coffee," he asked, "where will they bury you?" Rachel's decision to share this story with me marked a turning point in our relationship, but its meaning was only partly transparent. Concern that one will be buried amongst one's kin and coreligionists is an ever-present anxiety among members of the Felashmura community and also has deep roots in Beta Israel culture as a whole. It had been a topic of some discussion in the rumor mill at Neve Carmel that month that failure to complete the Return to Judaism program might be grounds for denial of burial in a Jewish cemetery, which if true would be a harsh punishment indeed. This was an especially bitter subject for Rachel, who blamed Israeli authorities for having held up her family's emigration from Addis Ababa while her father grew ill and was ultimately buried there as a refugee. I had visited his unmarked grave when I first met Rachel in Ethiopia in 1992, so I knew why her son's question hit her with such force. She told me that she had cried when she heard his question and promptly gave up her plans for coffee that day. Later, she repeated the story to her husband, who also cried, and then took some of the limited savings they had collected in order to buy an electric heating tray that could keep water hot throughout the Sabbath. In technical terms, Rachel's problem was solved, but this episode also points to the more insoluble elements at the heart of Felashmura experience in Israel.

The emotive significance of this story to Rachel and her family far outstrips its seeming importance in objective terms, but it is key to my understanding of agency in the story of her "return." She told me this story partly in order to assert her sincerity and to demonstrate the groundlessness of the missionary accusations that had been levied against her and the whole Felashmura community by extension. She had gone so far as to give up preparation of coffee in order to reassure her son that her return was complete, and that she would be buried among her own people in the land of Israel. But this account is ultimately very different from the purity of heart narratives offered by bureaucrats, rabbis, and some academics. Its "moral," if it may be said to have one, is more opaque, because it opens onto a life-world in which the Return to Judaism takes place under severe constraint and in which the social pressures generated by bureaucratic taxonomies extend even to private interactions between a nine-year-old boy and his mother.

Rachel emerges in this story as neither cynically utilitarian nor single-mindedly devoted to an abstract ideal of "return." Anthropologists in a variety of settings have argued that religious conversion sometimes has more to do with strategies of social or ethnic affiliation than with frankly confessional notions of interior spirituality (Kipp 1995), and that seems at least in part to be the case here. Sagi and Zohar (1994) have shown that the traditional Jewish responsa literature also emphasizes conversion as affiliation, as in "Your people shall be my people, your God my God", while leaving the latter more open to interpretation than the former. But I do not want to exchange one set of reductionist stories about religious agency here for another by arguing that Rachel's conversion experience is somehow essentially Jewish for that reason.

Rachel's Return to Judaism clearly involves a desire to benefit from citizenship in a relatively prosperous welfare state. But it also involves deep sentiments of loss and recovery, of the return to origins, and of a decidedly communal sense of relation to the God of Israel. Despite her bitterness toward some aspects of the Return to Judaism program, all of Rachel's children now attend religious schools and conduct what in Israel is described as a "traditional," though not strictly Orthodox, lifestyle. The contours of her agency in conversion can only be mapped obliquely from within an unfinished life story in which various things are invariably at stake simultaneously so that no "one thing" can ever be willed to the exclusion of all others. By focusing in part on the bureaucratic institutions and processes that impose themselves on Rachel's experience, I am not trying to shift attention from religious experience to social structure, but to convey a sense of the texture of an inhabited world. This may be the most—and the best—to which ethnography can aspire. We ought to escape bureaucratic habits of mind that focus on abstracted "identities" and the seamless movement between them as the proper subject for ethnography of religious conversion.

This is not an argument for less precision in ethnographic writing but for much greater precision in our descriptions of lived experience, and for humility in the face of attempts to represent human agency more fully. We can approach that goal asymptotically through "thicker" descriptions and more inclusive theoretical models. Depictions of social and religious transformation that exclude the constraining institutions and strategic interventions of powerful social actors should, for instance, be rejected out of hand. So, too, should accounts that fail to explicitly account for our constructions of plausibility *and what they exclude*, or that exclude without reflection the voices of those whose lives we have undertaken to represent. But even the very thickest of descriptions will inevitably remain thin by comparison with what they must describe. We should be honest about the limitations of our craft and analytical about where those limitations lie. The very best accounts of conversion and other transformational experiences may well remain those that manage to convey the irreducible "abundance" (cf. Feyerabend 2000) and indeterminacy of social life, an abundance that exceeds our grasp.

REFERENCES

Emmanuel, Tamrat. "The School for Falasha Children in Ethiopia at the Time of the Italian Invasion." *Pe'amim* 58 (1994): 98–103.
Feyerabend, Paul. *The Conquest of Abundance.* Chicago: University of Chicago Press, 2000.
Geertz, Clifford. *The Interpretation of Cultures.* New York: Basic Books, 1973.
Herzfeld, Michael. *The Social Production of Indifference.* Chicago: University of Chicago Press, 1992.
Kaplan, Steven. "The Beta Israel Encounter with Protestant Missionaries." *Jewish Social Studies* 49 (1987): 27–42.
Kipp, Rita Smith. "Conversion by Affiliation: The History of the Karo Batak Protestant Church." *American Ethnologist* 22 (1995): 868–882.
Messing, Simon D. *The Story of the Falashas: "Black Jews" of Ethiopia.* Brooklyn, N.Y.: Balshon Printing and Offset, 1982.
Rambo, Lewis R. *Understanding Religious Conversion.* New Haven, Conn.: Yale University Press, 1993.
Sagi, Avi, and Zvi Zohar. *Conversion to Judaism and the Meaning of Jewish Identity* (in Hebrew). Jerusalem: Bialik Institute, 1994.
Seeman, Don. "One People, One Blood: Public Health, Political Violence and HIV in an Ethiopian-Israeli Setting." *Culture, Medicine and Psychiatry* 23 (1999): 159–95.
———. "The Question of Kinship: Bodies and Narratives in the Beta Israel-European Encounter (1860–1920)." *Journal of Religion in Africa* 30 (2000): 86–120.
Waldman, Menahem. "The Return to Judaism of the Felashmura" (in Hebrew). *Techumin* 16 (1996): 243–272.

4

Converted Innocents and Their Trickster Heroes: The Politics of Proselytizing in India

Kalyani Devaki Menon

In January 1999, the Australian missionary Graham Staines and his two young sons were brutally murdered in the eastern Indian state of Orissa. This was not the first incident of violence against Christians in India. The fatal attack on Staines and his sons came in the wake of two months of attacks on Christians,[1] Christian missionaries,[2] and Christian churches.[3] However, this event captured the attention of the world's media and highlighted the urgency of understanding the escalating tension between Hindu nationalists and the minority population of Christians in India.

Hindu nationalists claim that people convert to Christianity either because they have been tricked by missionaries or because they have been seduced by offers of material remuneration. By effectively linking conversion with issues of national security and cultural actualization, they argue that proselytizing is part of a conspiracy to destroy "Indian" culture and to destabilize the "Indian" polity. These objections have led to numerous protest rallies and speeches and, in some specific instances, to violent confrontations between Hindus and Christians. However, Hindu nationalist criticism of conversion and proselytizing is fraught with contradictions in both theory and practice. For instance, the movement has been actively "reconverting" Christian tribals to Hinduism, yet asserts that Hinduism does not engage in conversion.

The dissonance between the rhetoric and actions of the movement suggests that what is at issue is not simply the act of conversion from one religion to another, but rather what conversion implies. Conversion to Christianity challenges Hindu nationalist definitions of India as a Hindu nation and threatens the mass base of the movement. Thus, underlying these dissonant acts and rhetoric are the struggles to contain the perceived challenges to Hindu nationalism implied by conversion to Christianity.

HINDU NATIONALIST CRITICISM
OF CONVERSION AND PROSELYTIZING

The Hindu nationalist movement in India has existed in various forms for over a century, but at no time has it been more powerful in the sociopolitical landscape of India than it is today. The movement is united by the common desire to purge the country of all "foreign" (i.e., Muslim and Christian) influences and to establish India as a Hindu nation. Although violence between Hindu nationalists and Muslim communities in India has a long history, large-scale violence between Hindus and Christians is relatively unprecedented. I begin by analyzing the charges leveled against missionaries by Hindu nationalism, or *Hindutva*, in order to contextualize the escalating tensions between the two groups. I then present some of the contradictory practices of *Hindutva* to argue that the movement uses conversion to create subjects of a nationalist Hinduism that privileges Brahmanical values and the scriptural prescriptions embodied in Vedic texts over the myriad local articulations of Hinduism (Hansen 1999: 66–67).

The following story, related to me by an elderly male member of the movement, effectively captures the criticism that *Hindutva* has of Christian proselytizing in India. It recalls the popular Hindu epic about the god-king Ram, now an icon of *Hindutva*. In this epic, Ram's wife Sita is kidnapped by the demon-king Ravana and taken to Lanka, from which Ram, with his army of monkeys, must rescue her. In most versions of the epic, Sita emerges as the embodiment of purity and virtue despite attempts by Ravana to seduce her. The story suggests the contrary:

> These missionaries, they go to villages and hoodwink innocent and uneducated villagers. There was a missionary who took three magnets on which he had pasted pictures of Ram, Sita and Ravana. The uneducated villagers knew nothing about magnets. The missionary had cleverly placed the picture of Ram and Sita on magnets with a positive charge while the picture of Ravana was on a negative charge. He then showed it to the villagers and asked them: why is Sita always going towards Ravana and not to Ram, her husband. He said that Hinduism was such a corrupt religion to worship Sita when she was so low as to be attracted to Ravana and to turn away from her husband.

In this version of the story, the missionary uses his devious tricks to "hoodwink" innocent villagers and cast aspersions on Sita's chastity in order to denigrate Hinduism. The story embodies many criticisms that *Hindutva* has against Christian proselytizing: the trickery of missionaries, the duping of "innocent" Hindus in order to convert them, and the disrespectful denunciations of Hinduism. Urvashi Aggarwal told me another story that, like the one above, suggests the naïveté of the convert while portraying missionaries as devious and calculating. She said: "These Christians mix medicines like Aspirin into water and say this is holy water. Then they give this water to sick Hindus and they get cured." According to Urvashi, the missionaries then claim that the recovery was a divine miracle and tell the person that it was the holy water blessed by Christ that cured them. Urvashi asserts that this is how missionaries establish the power of Christianity and trick unsuspecting and ignorant Hindus into converting from Hinduism to Christianity. She contends that missionaries also give money and food to convert people.

These stories reflect the belief in *Hindutva* that nobody converts of his or her own free will. Converts are innocents who have either been duped, as the above stories demonstrate, or seduced by material inducements offered by missionaries. As Jayant Chandra remarked to me, "If someone converts because he wants to that is his outlook. But here . . . there is inducement. Conveniences are offered. If your child does not have a job then one will be given. A person who does not have bread to fill his stomach does not worry too much about his religion. He says, ok, I must fill my stomach."

Equally important to all these stories is the assumption that the convert was originally a Hindu who was tricked out of the fold. A woman called *Taiji* (aunt) by members of the movement, who has devoted over fifty years of her life to *Hindutva*, said, "Before they became Muslims and Christians they were Hindus weren't they?" She told me a story about a person in Varanasi who had become a Christian. Even after his conversion, he would go to the River Ganga to worship the Sun God every morning, as he had done ever since he could remember. The local padre told him that he must stop doing this. The man refused, saying that even though he was a Christian, he could not give up what was part of his culture.

This story reflects an idea that is key to *Hindutva*, namely that Hinduism is not simply a religion but is rather a culture or a way of life. Christianity is seen as a threat to this unified Indian/Hindu national culture. During one of many protest rallies against the Pope's visit to India in November 1999, one prominent male member of the movement used rape as a metaphor for conversion, arguing that the practice raped people of their culture. The cultural threat of Christianity is often constructed upon women's bodies, suggesting, as many scholars have shown, the gendered nature of nationalist discourses (Yuval-Davis and Anthias 1989). Vimla, a twenty-eight-year-old woman in the movement, had this to tell me about Christianity and women:

An unmarried girl gave birth to Jesus. So Christians do not believe that it is a matter of shame if someone gives birth to a child while they are still unmarried. They say, never mind, the lord Jesus is being born, this is how the lord Jesus was born. So since the day that the Christian faith first set foot in this country, since that day there has been rape and oppression of women in India. . . . In our culture girls cannot even see their husbands before marriage. Without veiling they cannot go outside their homes. And after they are adults girls cannot even sit next to their fathers or their brothers. But today they wander around with strangers. All this should not happen. Whatever filth has spread in our nation it has been spread by Christians.

A major concern expressed by members of the movement has to do with allegiance to the nation. This concern is one that suggests the problematic use of religion to construct nationalist subjectivity. According to *Hindutva* logic, since India is Hindu, all Hindus swear allegiance to the Indian nation. However, since Muslim and Christian gods are located elsewhere, the same cannot be said for them. Although some Indian Christians trace their conversion to the arrival of St. Thomas on the Malabar Coast in 52 C.E., for those in the *Hindutva* movement Christianity is a "foreign" religion forever associated with the Western world.

Although the Christian population in India is barely 3 percent of the total population (Philip 1999: 8), many in the movement fear that conversions to Christianity pose a threat to the stability of the Indian polity. By publicly linking these fears to the powerful memories of the partition of the subcontinent into India and Pakistan, nationalists effectively convey the need for mobilizing against conversion and against those who would spread Christianity in India. Nandini Bharati, a leader of the women's wing of Sewa Bharati, a branch of the movement, told me that conversions from Hinduism are part of a larger world conspiracy to divide India along religious lines. She told me that this was how Pakistan was "taken away" and how "they" tried to take away Punjab by calling for the separate Sikh state of Khalistan. Aditya Trivedi made an important connection between conversion to Christianity and the violent rebellions in many of the northeast states of India, saying, "The terrorist organisations in the north-east are getting support from international Christian missionaries." Echoing the sentiments of Nandini, Trivedi asserted (in English):

> Their strategy is such that we will concentrate on certain pockets and those certain pockets will be made anti-Hindu. And anything which becomes anti-Hindu becomes anti-India. We believe that once somebody changes his religion he changes his nationality also. Solid proofs are Kashmir where Islam is the dominant factor. They say we don't want to live with India. Here the dominant factor is Christians. They say we are a different country.

The use of the northeast as an example to demonstrate the antinationalism of Christianity is problematic in many respects. Paul Brass asserts that, in fact, language and religion were not primary to the tribal peoples of the northeast, but rather that "the main argument for separation and secession was that tribal peoples were simply not Indians at all" (Brass 1994: 202). A. J. Philip notes that in the northeast, "The church has in many ways stood for national integration. The Meiteis, the Tripuris, the Bodos, and the Assamese ULFA cadres are not Christian. In Nagaland and Mizoram, the church has helped in restoring peace within the Indian framework" (Philip 1999: 8). Brass contends further that ULFA, a violent secessionist movement in the northeastern state of Assam, grew out of already existing movements by Hindu Assamese expressing their resentment of the loss of jobs and land to non-Assamese, particularly Bengalis, who had been migrating to the northeast and dominated the government since the British period when Assam was part of the Bengal presidency (1994: 204–5). The problems of the northeast are multiple, are very complex, and cannot be reduced to the simple manipulations of a few Machiavellian missionaries. In his analysis of the multiple violent secessionist movements in the northeastern states of India, Brass argues that the problems of the northeast should be understood as deriving in large part from the relationship that the central government has had with these regions in recent years. Brass suggests that the problems of the northeast arise "from the tensions created by the centralizing drives of the Indian state in a society where the predominant long-term social, economic, and political tendencies are towards pluralism, regionalism and decentralization" (1994: 227).

When violence broke out between Hindus and Christians in Gujarat in 1998 and was followed by attacks against Christian missionaries and Christian churches in 1999, many observers wondered why Christians had suddenly become the target of Hindu nationalist attention. Christians, after all, despite a presence in India for 2,000 years, have been fairly removed from all the major upheavals that have marked the relationship between Hindus and Muslims through history. Stories like those recounted above became critical tools through which to create a sense of public outrage and mobilize people against Christians in India. For those who may remain unmoved by suggestions that Christianity, because it is inherently Western, poses a threat to the Indian/Hindu way of life, the movement presents cases of more tangible threats, such as those presented by forced conversions, massacres, or national security. Linking Christianity to violence in the northeast is a powerful means to create that sense of outrage, particularly because it taps into an already existing sense of discomfort about the randomness of violence in the northeast. It also suggests that such violence is a threat to the sanctity of India's borders just like the Kashmir issue or the Khalistan issue—again tapping into fears and threats that are already part of public consciousness. In recent years, much has been written about the power of collective memory to mobilize communities for collective action (Swedenberg 1995). These stories can be understood as part of an effort to shape public memory about Christians in India that portrays a nation under siege and makes the Hindu nationalist political agenda compelling to ordinary people.

CONTRADICTORY PRACTICE

Although *Hindutva* is very critical of missionaries offering inducements in order to convert people, its members see no logical contradiction in their own efforts to prevent conversions by offering similar inducements. Ela Mishra told me, for example, that one of the main aims of Sewa Bharati in starting schools in slums and amongst tribal populations is to prevent conversions. The purpose of these schools is not only to prevent the tribals from converting to Christianity, but also to teach them that they are Hindus and that their tribal religions are simply a local, and therefore corrupt, expression of Hinduism (Hansen 1999). Missionaries, by contrast, are criticized for converting people under the guise of helping the poor by setting up schools and hospitals.

Others in the movement, although clearly situating the social work of the movement as a response to conversions, place the blame on Hindus rather than on the missionaries. *Taiji* asserted, "We [Hindus] are the ones who have shunned the poor and the lower castes while the Christian missionaries have embraced them. If we do not want people to convert, we must make sure that they are well taken care of within our own communities. Otherwise how can you blame them for converting?" She said that the movement's work is directed at ensuring the uplift of poor and backward-caste communities. She said that this is why when the cyclone hit Orissa, "Our girls went running there. They distributed steel plates, bowls and glasses because these people had nothing left." The movement sent in its troops to demonstrate to cyclone victims that they were part of a larger, benevolent Hindu community. Neither *Taiji* nor others I spoke to saw this as duplicity on the part of the movement. More disturbing, perhaps, was their failure to question the ethics of capitalizing on the tragedy of cyclone victims. Ironically, missionary activity is accused of immorality for exploiting the misfortunes of the poor and for using schools and hospitals to proselytize.

Ela vehemently condemned missionaries, saying, "I like everything about Christianity except for this hidden aim underlying all their activities to convert under the guise of helping." At the same time, she too sees no duplicity in the *Hindutva* movement's attempts to circumscribe the power of missionaries to convert people. The movement is not above offering direct material rewards to establish community and to prevent people from converting. Although the movement has condemned the payment of dowry for a girl upon her marriage, I was told of several occasions when the movement stepped in and paid a girl's dowry in order to prevent her from converting to Christianity. Vimla told me of an occasion when she prevented an entire family from converting to Christianity because, unable to afford the dowry being demanded, they had found it impossible to marry their only daughter. For them, conversion would mean not having to pay this dowry. Vimla convinced the family not to convert by promising that the movement would pay the required dowry. Although she is critical of missionaries who offer material rewards to converts, Vimla does not question the ethics of purchasing allegiance to the nation through material remuneration.

Many nationalists assume that conversion takes people out of the Hindu fold. They assert that unlike "foreign" religions, people cannot convert into Hinduism, and thus the religion can never replace those who convert. These arguments do not take into account such as efforts as the Arya Samaj Movement, spearheaded by Swami Dayanand Saraswati. In response to conversions to Islam, particularly in the Punjab region in the latter part of the nineteenth century, Arya Samaj was responsible for mass "re-conversions" to Hinduism (Madan 1996). Nationalists also do not recognize the recent mass reconversions to Hinduism, organized by their own movement (particularly amongst Christian tribals), as the practice of conversion. (In an interesting parallel to Christian conversions, those who agreed to reconvert in Ahwa, Gujarat, were made to take a dip in the hot springs of a nearby village. Then the officiating priest tied a locket with the picture of the monkey-God Hanuman with black string around the neck of the newly reconverted.)[4]

Few have challenged the use of the term "reconversion" by the movement, so that the question of whether these tribals were Hindu before they became Christian has remained largely unaddressed. Sumit Sarkar argues that the use of the term reconversion is a form of "semantic aggression," for it suggests the natural reorientation of people back to their "original" state (Sarkar 1999). In addition, Hindu tribals are also being converted to another form of Hinduism through the "civilising mission" that animates the movement's educational institutions in tribal areas. Thomas Hansen describes this as the project of "nationalist sanskritisation," which appropriates the "little traditions" of Hinduism into the "Brahmanical great tradition" of nationalist Hinduism (Hansen 1999: 104–7).[5] "Sanskritisation" is a term coined by M. N. Srinivas to refer to the process by which lower castes (especially those belonging to the intermediate strata) attain higher positions in the caste system by adopting (allegedly) Sanskritic values (Srinivas 1952: 65). Hansen argues that "the syncretic platform, the recruitment of the religious establishment, and the paternalistic reconversion strategies all point to the equation of a brahmanical

'great tradition,' seeking to heal up and cover over the many disparate, contradictory, and fragmented 'little traditions' of dispersed Hindu practices under a simplified, 'thin' national Hinduism, largely defined in terms of san-
skritised practices" (Hansen 1999: 107).

THE POLITICS OF CONVERSION

The dissonance between the actions and rhetoric of the movement suggests
that what is at issue is not the act of conversion itself, but rather the challenge
that conversion to Christianity presents to *Hindutva*. Conversion to Christianity threatens the construction of India as a nation for Hindus. Hindu nationalists regard Christianity as a foreign religion that is seducing people
away from their original faith, Hinduism.

Christianity has been an integral part of the religious landscape of India for
centuries, particularly in states like Kerala which have a significant Christian
population. While the assertion that Syrian Christians in Kerala were converted by St. Thomas in 52 C.E. cannot be supported or invalidated by historical evidence, Corrine Dempsey argues that historical data establishes the existence of Christian communities by the fourth century (Dempsey 2001: 5). The
construction of Christianity as "foreign" to India, despite this lengthy presence
in the subcontinent is part of a larger trend of nationalist discourses in which
cultures (in this case, Hinduism) are "unproblematically" inscribed onto territory (Gupta and Ferguson 1992). Conversion becomes a metaphor for the invasion of national territory by "foreign," and indeed illegitimate, religions.

Conversion to Christianity threatens the "competitive logic of numbers" introduced by the colonial census that established the numerical division of the
population by religious grouping and fueled the majoritarian impulses of the
modern nation-state (Sarkar 1999). Peter van der Veer asserts that because
"numbering is an intrinsic part of the modern nation-state," constructions of
majority and minority groups are centrally implicated in the debates over
conversion (1996: 14).

Conversion to Christianity also threatens the very essence of Hindu nationalist subjectivity, thus prompting the movement to engage in its own form
of conversion, or "re-conversion." Conversion can be understood as what
Nicholas Dirks calls "the project of translation" (1996: 134) necessary to incorporate "others" into the metanarrative of the nation. Dirks contends that
conversion is "a sign of the epistemological violence implied by myriad efforts to know, domesticate, name, claim, and ultimately inhabit 'the other'"
(1996: 121). Conversion places individuals within a new epistemological uni-

verse, one that requires, as Robert Hefner claims, a "commitment to a new kind of moral authority and a new or reconceptualized social identity" (1993: 17). *Hindutva*'s attempts to counteract the actions of missionaries can be understood as the practice of conversion to "translate" both Hindus and non-Hindus into a new kind of Hindu nationalist subject.

CONCLUSION

To conclude, Hindu nationalists have protested against conversion and proselytizing, arguing that missionaries either trick innocent Hindus into converting to Christianity or that they bribe them by offering material remuneration. Although this may often be the case, I argue here that *Hindutva* is not above engaging in these very practices either to prevent people from converting to Christianity or to incorporate them into the metanarrative of the Hindu nation. The re-conversion of Christian tribals, their sanskritisation in *Hindutva* schools, and the appropriation of Hindus into the "imagined community" (Anderson 1983) of the Hindu nation through social work or financial help can be read as the practice of conversion by *Hindutva*. These practices are part of a larger process of translation (Dirks 1996: 134), whereby the individual is inserted into the hegemonic narrative of the nation. The appropriation of the "other," the domestication of difference (Dirks 1996: 121), and the curtailment of defection are all key to understanding the supremacy of *Hindutva* in the cultural and political landscape of India.

The dissonance between *Hindutva*'s criticism of the conversion practices of Christian missionaries and their own practices of conversion suggests that it is not the concept of conversion that is at issue but rather the challenge to *Hindutva*, both numerical and semantic, implied by conversion to Christianity. Conversion to Christianity is portrayed as an act that threatens the integrity, security, and cultural essence of the nation. By vilifying Christians, Christianity, and Christian missionaries not only as morally suspect but also as a threat to the sanctity and integrity of the Indian polity, the movement is able to project its agenda as the moral and patriotic duty of all Indians, thereby establishing its own legitimacy and mobilizing support for its political platform. Conversion is not seen as simply an individual expression of faith but rather as a political choice that necessarily implicates questions of national allegiance, patriotism, and cultural determination. Conversion to Christianity threatens the very raison d'être of Hindu nationalism: that India is, and has always been, a Hindu nation in which Hindu values, culture, and beliefs must be privileged.

NOTES

Funding for this project was provided by the American Institute for Indian Studies. I would like to thank Susan Wadley, Ann Gold, John Burdick, Arlene Davila, Sudipta Sen, Keri Olsen, Mark Hauser, Andrew Buckser, and Stephen Glazier for their suggestions. I have used pseudonyms to protect the identity of my informants.

1. See *Times of India*, 30 December 1998, 1; and *Times of India*, 31 December 1998, 8.

2. See *Times of India*, 26 January 1999, 11. For more on the Staines incident, see *Times of India*, 25 January 1999, 1; *Times of India*, 25 January 1999, 3; and *Indian Express*, 28 February 1999, 4.

3. See *Times of India*, 28 December 1998, 1; and *Times of India*, 29 December 1998, 8.

4. See the description in *Hindustan Times*, 16 January 1999, 1.

5. Hansen, *Saffron Wave*, 107.

REFERENCES

Anderson, Benedict. *Imagined Communities: Reflections on the Origin and Spread of Nationalism.* London: Verso, 1983.

"Archbishop Condemns Missionary's Murder." *Times of India*, January 25, 1999, 3.

"Attack on 4 More Churches in Gujarat." *Times of India*, December 29, 1998, 8.

"Attacks on Christians Signals VHP-BJP Rift." *Times of India*, December 30, 1998, 1.

Brass, Paul. *The Politics of India since Independence.* New York: Cambridge University Press, 1994.

"Central Team to Submit Report on Dangs Today." *Times of India*, December 31, 1998, 8.

"Dangs Tribals Snared in Communal Tussle." *Times of India*, December 31, 1998, 8.

Dempsey, Corinne. *Kerala Christian Sainthood: Collisions of Culture and Worldview in South India.* New York: Oxford University Press, 2001.

Dirks, Nicholas B. "The Conversion of Caste: Location, Translation, and Appropriation." In *Conversion to Modernities: The Globalisation of Christianity*, edited by Peter van der Veer, pp. 115–36. New York: Routledge, 1996.

"Four Missionaries Attacked in Allahabad." *Times of India*, January 26, 1999, 11.

Gupta, Akhil, and Ferguson, James. "Beyond Culture, Space, Identity and the Politics of Difference." *Cultural Anthropology* 7, no. 1 (1992): 6–24.

Hansen, Thomas Bloom. *The Saffron Wave: Democracy and Hindu Nationalism in Modern India.* New Delhi: Oxford University Press. 1999.

Hefner, Robert W. "Introduction: World Building and the Rationality of Conversion." In *Conversion to Christianity: Historical and Anthropological Perspectives on a Great Transformation*, edited by Robert W. Hefner, pp. 3–44. Berkeley: University of California Press. 1993.

Hindustan Times, 16 January 1999, 1.

Indian Express, 28 February 1999, 4.

Jaffrelot, Christophe. *Hindu Nationalist Movement and Indian Politics: 1925 to the 1990s.* New Delhi: Penguin Books India, 1999.

"Killings a Monumental Aberration." *Times of India*, January 25, 1999, 1.

Madan, T. N. *Modern Myths, Locked Minds: Secularism and Fundamentalism in India.* New Delhi: Oxford University Press, 1996.

"More Attacks of Churches, Schools in Gujarat." *Times of India*, December 28, 1998, 1.

Philip, A. J. "The Missionary and the Paranoid: Who's Afraid of Conversion?" *Indian Express*, 12 January 1999, 8.

Sarkar, Sumit. "Conversions and Politics of the Hindu Right." *Economic and Political Weekly* 34, no. 26 (June 26, 1999): www.epw.org.in/showArticles.php?root=1999&leaf=06&filename=2763&filetype=html.

Srinivas, M. N. *Religion and Society among the Coorgs of South India.* London: Asia Publishing House, 1952.

Swedenburg, Ted. *Memories of Revolt: The 1936–1939 Rebellion and the Palestinian National Past.* Minneapolis: University of Minnesota Press, 1995.

Van der Veer, Peter. "Introduction." In *Conversion to Modernities: The Globalisation of Christianity*, edited by Peter van der Veer, pp. 1–21. New York: Routledge. 1996.

Yuval-Davis, N., and Anthias, F. *Woman-Nation-State.* New York: MacMillan. 1989.

5

Comparing Conversions among the Dani of Irian Jaya

Charles E. Farhadian

This chapter compares two types of conversion: the first a conversion from a local religion to Christianity, and the second a conversion from a Western missionary understanding of Christianity to a reformulation of Christianity using putatively Melanesian categories. The social context of the first conversion is the Dani upland located in the district of Jayawijaya, which is in the central mountains of Irian Jaya. The second social context is the metropolitan center of Jayapura, which is located on the north coast of the island.

THE FIRST CONVERSION: HIGHLAND DANI

Evangelical Protestant missionary endeavors in Irian Jaya (West Papua) were permeated by a deeply felt spiritual vision about humanity and its purpose within the created order and heavenly realm. In Kenelm Burridge's words, the goal of missionaries "to build a Christian community in a virgin field never was simply a social or personal challenge and adventure but a divine instruction, why they were born."[1] Evangelical missionaries in Irian Jaya were explicit about their desire to work for the evangelization of the world as a precursor to Christ's Second Coming. Early missionary endeavors were motivated by a spiritual vision to tell Dani that Jesus "shall save you from your sins."[2] Great emphasis was placed on telling the story of the gospel in order to invite hearers to join Christians on a journey toward heaven.

For the Dani, Western mission activities encompassed much more than a single communicative act of proclaiming the gospel. As one college-educated urban Dani put it to me, "The missionaries built up their evangelism post by bartering salt and steel axes and shovels. By that way, the missionaries brought the gospel." Christian and Missionary Alliance (CMA) missionaries went to Irian Jaya to share a spiritual gospel unencumbered by worldly entrapments, but they were seen as possessing unbelievable material wealth. Nearly every early contact story features an instance in which gifts of food and tools were given by the missionary to the local group. Gifts were often a crucial medium of contact.

As missionaries built airstrips and received copious goods delivered by Mission Aviation Fellowship (MAF) Cessnas and helicopters, Dani associated material blessings with Christian missions. From the missionary perspective, all contact materials such as salt, planes, and airstrips were a means to attain one goal: the religious conversion of the Dani. From the perspective of the Dani, however, material contact was inseparable from the message of the newcomers. Displays of material wealth shored up the potency of the missionaries' spiritual message.

A significant outcome of missionary contact with the highland Dani was the demise of the traditional warfare and the concomitant celebration of peace between formerly warring clans. Discussions were initiated among Dani leaders concerning the benefits of accepting the new knowledge. Occasionally, Christianity's reception was backed directly by village big men who reprimanded those unwilling to convert.

It should be noted that although thousands of Dani identified with Christianity, there were also resistance movements that were often led by powerful chiefs. Moreover, conversion to Christianity challenged the authority of traditional systems of magic, attempting to displace magic with a commitment to Christ. Official missionary reports suggest that "if a group resists the Gospel, they should be roughed up, and they will then 'find their hearts' and embrace the Gospel . . . several of our people were killed."[3]

Constructing the New Jerusalem

Driven by an urgency to share the gospel in the Dani vernacular, early missionaries became students of local languages and cultures. Myron Bromley and Gordon Larson, missionaries with the CMA, began evangelizing along the eastern and western borders of Daniland, respectively. Translation of the Bible into local languages, medical care, education, and literacy were geared toward getting the evangelized ready for the modern world.[4] Dani expectations of a better world burgeoned as a new world was literally constructed in their presence.

Bodily habits and practices were modified through missionary influence; for example, upland Dani began cutting their long hair and washing with soap. Missionary-initiated health clinics administered medicines that are mentioned prominently in early conversion narratives. Like Western material goods, the efficacy of Western medicine was interpreted as a potent symbol of the power of the Western missionaries' God.

The initial conversion of highland Dani to Christianity is recorded in the anthropological literature as well as in missionary accounts. The Highland Dani interpreted mission Christianity in terms of their own concept of *nabelan kabelan*, a concept of salvation that is shared by small-scale communities throughout the highlands. *Nabelan kabelan* describes a quality of life in which death and mourning cease. It is a state where Dani experience the reunification with their dead ancestors and a return to life as it had been lived in the past.[5] *Nabelan kabelan* was an abstract ideal, but it was measured concretely through an increase in food supply, betterment of health, and general prosperity. Highland Dani interpreted mission Christianity as a fulfillment of *nabelan kabelan* because missionaries emphasized that converts would receive eternal life and abundance if they accepted the message of the gospel.

According to a Dani informant, one reason for large-scale conversions to Christianity was the belief that *nabelan kabelan* had arrived on Earth in the message and persons of the missionaries. For some, the missionaries were closely associated with God; this association legitimated their call for change, even in the most mundane aspects of life. One missionary report reads, "The missionary is the mouthpiece of God; therefore this is a command from Him! Failure to build the little house [i.e., toilet house] behind the village will call forth the anger of God."[6]

Natives believed that accepting the message of the gospel was tantamount to receiving eternal life on Earth. It was a guarantee that their skin would be regenerated, disease would end, and their fields would yield large and plenteous sweet potatoes. Accompanying missionaries were material goods that the Dani saw as evidence of having entered the time of *nabelan kabelan*. A Papuan leader put it to me this way: "For our people, the very presence of the missionaries, the airplanes, which they had never seen, the clothes, even their bodies were part of [salvation]. Everything was new. . . . Why not accept it?"

The Burning Movement

The Dani responded to invitations to become Christians with large-scale conversions and spontaneous "burning movements" in which, in the words of missionaries, ancestor charms and weapons of war were burned, signifying that the Dani were going to follow "the Jesus way." These burnings occurred in most highland Papuan communities. Participants, numbering in the tens of thousands, believed that the end of the world was near and that soon Jesus was going to return.

Western missionaries and local Dani perceived each other through onto-genic categories. Some missionaries, who had been trained in evolutionary anthropology, saw the Dani as uncivilized. The Dani saw missionaries as ghosts and ancestors. Each, therefore, questioned the humanity of the other. Conversion to Christianity contributed significantly to social tensions among the Dani. The first generation of Dani Christians assumed that a state of hu-man perfection and fulfillment would immediately follow their conversion, but death, disease, and other marks of human finitude persisted. Missionary Christianity introduced a new system of knowledge and morality based on biblical passages, church authority, and peculiar evangelical convictions con-cerning human beings, sin, and salvation.

The Christian message was not universally accepted within highland com-munities, but it engendered a large-scale, interregional community who shared a common hope that *nabelan kabelan* had indeed arrived. The unify-ing power of this shared vision enabled local communities that were once primarily self-sufficient to become subject to a similar transethnic confidence.

THE SECOND CONVERSION: A SUBJUGATED PEOPLE

The second Dani conversion occurred within the context of metropolitan Jayapura during the late New Order regime. It represented a conversion from a privatized form of religion to a view of religion that sought active engage-ment in the public sphere. Established by President Suharto in 1966, the New Order regime implemented an aggressive development scheme coupled with policies designed to bring about economic stability. But the New Order's vi-sion of a unitary nation-state resulted in numerous human rights violations against the Dani, as well as a massive military presence in metropolitan cen-ters of Irian Jaya. The province resembled an occupied territory.

The Indonesian military's "integrative political power"[7] directly promoted its vision of a New Society through direct (and often harsh) execution of the national ideals of the *Pancasila* and the 1945 Constitution. For most of the New Order regime, the dual function (*dwifungsi*) of the military establish-ment, whereby "Indonesian armed forces have permanent responsibilities in the fields both of national security and of social-political-economic develop-ment" dominated the sociopolitical landscape of the entire archipelago.[8] This symbolized both the unity of a national vision and the growth of a state ap-paratus that announced and maintained the New Society.

Given that the military was deeply embedded in civilian life, it was the most prominent image of Indonesian national unity in Irian Jaya.[9] Papuans were frequent victims of human rights violations perpetrated by Indonesian armed forces. Their *sejarah sunyi* (silent history)[10] deeply impacted their self-understandings and visions of the future. But Dani fear was shrouded in a cloak of silence. Many Dani preferred to live with trauma rather than die at the hands of the Indonesian armed forces. They seldom told their stories publicly.

During the New Order regime, stories of trauma were often confined to individual families and communities. They lacked a common institutional apparatus or written articulation that would have served to notify distant tribes of each other's shared suffering. The Dani remained sequestered in their personal lives. During pastoral visits to the districts of Jayawijaya and Paniai in the mid-1990s, a Dutch Roman Catholic priest used the term *sejarah sunyi* (silent history) to describe to me the trauma experienced by people in these regions. He claimed that during pastoral visits he heard comments like, "This is where my husband was taken away and they tortured him over there," "My father died there, by that tree," and "This is where I was raped." These stories were not included in official textbooks but were carried in people's minds and often inscribed on their bodies.

THE BISHOP'S REPORT

On August 3, 1995, Bishop H. F. M. Munninghoff, OFM, of the Roman Catholic Diocese of Jayapura, released a summary report, *Violations of Human Rights in the Timika Area of Irian Jaya, Indonesia: A Report by the Catholic Church of Jayapura.* Munninghoff's report eventually led to a conscientization of diverse Papuan groups throughout the province. The report detailed executions, murders, disappearances, arbitrary arrests, detentions, tortures, surveillance, and destruction of property, and it provided specific names, dates, and surrounding events of human rights violations. Some abuses were perpetrated on those who were considered supporters of raising the Morning Star (*Bintang Kejora*) flag—a sign of Papuan political independence. Others were brutalized for unsubstantiated suspicions of having had connections with the *Operasi Papua Merdeka* (Free Papua Movement, or OPM).[11]

It is significant that stories of abuse and intimidation came from members of both Roman Catholic and Evangelical churches (i.e., GKII) and brought to light the experiences of various Papuan groups (e.g., Amungme, Dani, Me, and Damal).[12] In addition to Bishop Munninghoff's report, the Conciliar Protestant church (Gereja Kristen Injili, or GKI) produced a report chronicling Irian Jaya's thirty years under Indonesian rule.[13] Both reports were written originally in Bahasa, Indonesia. In early August 1995, Bishop Munninghoff sent his report via the Indonesian Bishops' Conference to the Indonesian National

Commission for Human Rights. The report was later obtained by various non-governmental human rights organizations (e.g., Human Rights Watch), and it was posted on the Internet. Australia used the document to challenge Indonesia's earlier reports denying human rights violations. When Papuans read Bishop Munninghoff and the GKI's reports on the experience of living under Indonesia, a new awareness and solidarity among Papuans developed.

The Rise of "Papuanness"

In the late 1990s, the term "Papuan" was reintroduced into the public discourse. Reports from the Roman Catholic and GKI churches gave disparate Papuan groups awareness of their common predicament. As some put it, learning of Bishop Munninghoff's report made all Papuans of "one heart." Their common experience in suffering fostered a construction of Papuan identity and transtribal commonality that spanned beyond highland communities. A revalorized concept of "Papuanness" began to overcome the pejorative and humiliating connotations formerly attached to the term: uncivilized, "cultureless," black natives. With the distribution of missionary reports, people began to feel that, in the words of one of my highland informants,

> We're just like others . . . they've been killing us all these years, but we've been silent. We thought this is how we are supposed to live. Then, this report changed things. If we open up ourselves, putting these issues on the table and making a good report, then there will be people who will listen to us and help us. . . . Yes, it's all of us. We've all been affected. Yes, they've been doing that among the Amungme and Dani, but they've also been doing that to us too.

Various tribal groups recognized their own stories reflected in ecclesial reports. Even the methods of torture and intimidation seemed similar. The experience of "unity in suffering" led to a widespread new feeling of Papuanness. This concept became the vehicle for a reconfigured Dani self-understanding.

An Absence of Outlets

Even after human rights violations became widely known, there was no institution to address Papuan discontent. The GKII's evangelical tradition, which focused primarily on doctrinal matters and church growth, categorically disallowed political involvement. Based on their reading of Romans 13, evangelical missionaries frequently argued for the support of government authorities. Church elites justified themselves by appealing to evangelical mission theology and policies that had been introduced by Western missionaries, allowing little room for new expressions of Christian faith or the voices of the afflicted. Moreover, the New Order regime provided no institutional outlet for the distressed in Irian Jaya, and Papuans held the government responsible for oppressive measures and corruption. The Dani traditionally dealt with suffering through religious means, using the ritual of pig sacrifice. Within this tradition, suffering and sickness were believed to have a prior cause, stemming from problems with relations with humans, spirits, or the environment.

The Repoliticization of Private Spheres

With no institutional channels available for expressing Papuan discontent, a new discourse of action arose in the late New Order period that repoliticized private spheres. Raising of the Morning Star flag, for example, a putatively Papuan cultural symbol of political independence, became a public form of resistance that occurred frequently throughout the province. Protest and resistance had long been a part of the Papuan response to foreign domination, going back to the Dutch occupation.[14] What is most significant in the late New Order and post–New Order periods is the degree to which resistance consisted of multi-Papuan voices and the emergence of an inchoate institutional apparatus to channel Papuan political aspirations. Increasingly, highland Dani hopes for human fulfillment were subsumed within a larger pan-Papuan vision that came to define Dani resistance and protest. The social carriers of this vision of political independence were Papuan intellectuals (i.e., educators, pastors, and government employees) who advocated a new — and distinctly Papuan — vision of the future.

"Onward Christian Soldiers"

Songs of protest were a particularly poignant example of how conversion to Christianity bolstered identity conservation and political aspirations. The performative structure[15] of Papuan discourse is a result of an encounter among Papuan cultural logic, Malay *pendatang* (outsiders, non-Papuans), and the culture of Western missionaries. Public displays of resistance and the choruses of chants and songs functioned as a counter-statement to the attempted colonization of Papuan identity. In the late and post–New Order period, for example, urban Dani students gathered in public places to protest against human rights violations. This was a different approach from the small-scale guerrilla activities of the OPM, whose tactics involved raiding transmigration villages, attacking mining facilities, and kidnapping people. The hymn "Onward Christian Soldiers" (*Maju Laskar Kristus*) was adopted by Dani protestors and recast as a vehicle for the insertion of Papuan political will, thereby casting a political message in religious terms. Beginning in the late 1980s and early 1990s, diverse Papuan groups adopted "Onward Christian Soldiers" as a rallying cry.

The hymn was so closely associated with political independence that it was no longer sung in some churches; when the predominately American evangelical community of the mission station called *Pos 7* sang "Onward Christian Soldiers," its members stressed that the words expressed highly spiritualized sentiments—the fight was between God and Satan, good and evil, not between "flesh and blood." Among Papuans, however, the social use of this hymn was infused with political meaning. What was axiomatic for Papuans was not so much church performances as public performances. Following traditional Dani practice, religion becomes authentic by performance. There were few common non-Christian songs, apart from Indonesian nationalistic ones. Many third- and fourth-generation Dani Christians protested. In Jayapura, the voices of highland Christian Dani, whose conversion dated only to the 1960s, merged with that of coastal Papuans, whose conversion to Christianity dated back more than a hundred years. They formed a unified Papuan awareness. "Onward Christian Soldiers" provided a new language for the Dani. Using it in public protest suggested that Christian language could be used as a cultural vehicle to communicate Papuan frustration. Protesters sang "Onward Christian Soldiers" while they marched, making it difficult to distinguish between verbal and physical modes of protest.

An example of how songs were utilized occurred in 1989, when a large garden was being organized by Papuans to commemorate the Morning Star flag raising by Kotowangai a year earlier. People came from all over the district of Jayapura. One of my informants remembered that the police stopped traffic in Kota Raja, a small town east of Jayapura. All *pendatang* were allowed to proceed through to Jayapura, but all Papuans were instructed to stop and turn around. The police determined whom to stop on purely racial grounds, based on skin color and hair type (brown or black skin, curly or straight hair). My informant continued,

We couldn't go through. So, the Papuans started singing, "Onward Christian Soldiers." This helped people realize that they were different from the *pendatang*, the Indonesians, and a feeling of "we-ness" was created.

THE DEPRIVATIZATION OF CHRISTIANITY

Since the demise of the New Order regime, Dani conversion to Christianity has become more public. It became "deprivatized." Christianity in the 1990s was no longer contained within a particular ecclesiastical structure. Rather, conversion to Christianity led to a reconfiguring of Papuan identity. This reconfiguration was at once discontinuous and continuous with Papuan traditions. It was continuous because conversion to Christianity entailed a partial fulfillment of Papuan religious yearnings. It was discontinuous with Papuan religious traditions because it introduced a standardized scripture, the Bible, which was seen as the final authority on all matters ranging from personal ethics to political theory. The "Word" became an authority that transcended the authority of local tribal chiefs, government officials, and Western missionaries. In that process, new voices arose, articulating and challenging the notion that what were at odds were not sectarian truths, but *public* truths.[16] Christianity as a force for social change and a new vision of hope combined with Papuan traditional religion, and religious truths, which could not help but be public and performative, became real. Papuans accepted missionary pronouncements about heaven and eternal life, but did not accept the Cartesian split inherent in post-Enlightenment Western epistemology.

COMPARING CONVERSIONS AMONG THE DANI: THE OBJECTIFICATION OF CULTURE

The first conversion introduced a transtribal, transcendent authority and new social structure among a previously disparate highland people. Traditional boundaries once supported by alliances and kinship patterns gave way to religiously based identities. This created greater social cohesion and social divisions (see Hayward, 1997). A distinct transtribal church emerged from readjustments of social and religious boundaries. Church dioceses were initially formed by faith missions according to their comity agreements rather than along confederacy lines, which frequently necessitated holding a series of peace treaties among warring tribes prior to a diocese's establishment.[17]

The second conversion was characterized by moving from Western mission—highly privatized—understandings of Christianity to a view marked by a pragmatic Melanesian notion of public performance. In the late and post–New Order periods, Christianity among the Dani and other Papuans provided a robust vocabulary of democratic idioms that could be injected easily into the public sphere. An irony is that the public use of religion was discouraged by the very persons who had introduced Christianity to the Dani. Political intervention was rejected by Western evangelical mission officials who characterized public engagement as "worldly." Yet the publicness, that is, the performative structure, of Dani religiosity invigorated Dani cultural confidence.

Stimulating Reflexivity

On the heels of Western missions, a new discourse within the Dani community emerged. On the one hand, it threatened the persistence of traditional authority structures and cosmologies. On the other hand, it provided answers to the Dani longing for eternal life, human fulfillment, and hope for a better world. Although not wholly determinative, there are connections between Dani religious conversion and social change. Mission Christianity influenced traditional Dani lifeways by its "deroutinization" of existing practices. It placed traditional practices within a larger social and religious universe and enabled its content to act upon those practices in a way that was at once continuous and discontinuous with Dani desideration. Dani reflexivity centered on an analysis of the validity of mission Christianity and its promises within the local context. The concept of *nabelan kabelan*, reconfigured along the lines of biblical affirmations, served as a channel to articulate an alternate vision and provided a medium in which to channel Dani political aspirations.

In its uneven appropriation mission, Christianity grew to be a significant boundary marker between those inside and outside the faith (see Buckser, chapter 6). Yet for the majority of Dani, Christianity was an appealing alternative to previous ways. Much like the medieval church, the mission church in the Dani highlands provided a host of human services beyond simply preaching. It advanced a unified vision of social advancement that integrated physical, intellectual, and spiritual ministries, and it did so with surprising success given the relative paucity of Western missionaries.

Conversion to Christianity required membership in a new organization with new rules and social expectations. It was often precipitated by contact materials (e.g., salt, clothes, food, gramophones, airplanes, and airstrips), use of missionary high status within the village, healthcare, education, and literacy. Sunday became a day of rest, and virtually all villagers attended church services that closely followed an evangelical Protestant model. Monday through Saturday were days for work and school. Numerous Dani cultural particularities—such as polygamy, men's long hair, greasing with pig fat, finger cutting, bride price, and pig sacrifice—were discouraged because they were part of the "former life," while idioms reflecting the new creation were introduced.

Western missionaries offered a highly rationalized religious perspective, reflecting established theological emphases within American evangelicalism and as well as ushering in incipient modern conditions. They introduced "standardized, literacy and education-based systems of communication."[18] They pioneered the standardization, dissemination, and "rationalization" of mission Christianity as well as other spheres of life through record keeping. They introduced modern economic social conditions by stipulating that access to education required payment of either cowry shells or national currency. In addition, Western missionaries supplied a "readily accessible reservoir of meanings" through the process of religious rationalization.[19] Papuans sought to use the Bible not just as a spiritual guide but for their whole lives. Religious truths incarnated in Melanesian lives could not help but be public, made real by performance. As noted, Papuans received the Word about heaven and eternal life, but not the Cartesian split inherent in post-Enlightenment Western epistemology. Whereas Western Evangelical mission theology highlighted personal transformation stemming from a personal relationship with Jesus, Papuan Christians emphasized Jesus' religious pragmatism in feeding the multitudes, healing the sick, and turning the tables in the temple. This same religiosity would animate their public use of Christianity. In the case of Papuan Christians of Irian Jaya, conversion to Christianity led them to challenge the very moral foundations of the New Society that was being formed by Indonesian political authorities.

NOTES

1. Kenelm Burridge, *In the Way: A Study of Christian Missionary Endeavors* (Vancouver: University of British Columbia Press, 1991), 240.

2. Russell T. Hitt, *Cannibal Valley* (New York: Harper and Row, 1962), 14.

3. James Sunda and Doloras Sunda, "Conference Report of Pyramid Station," unpublished manuscript, 1964, 3.

4. Frank L. Cooley, *Indonesia: Church and Society* (New York: Friendship Press, 1968), 61.

5. See Douglas Hayward, "Time and Society in Dani Culture," *IRIAN: Bulletin of Irian Jaya* 11, nos. 2–3 (June and October 1983): 42; Jan A. Godschalk, "Cargoism and Development among the Western Dani," paper presented at the Seminar on Development in Irian Jaya and Research of Indonesian East Section II, Jayapura; Universitas Cenderawasih, Jayapura, Irian Jaya, 1988, 2–5; and Jan A. Godschalk, "How Are Myth and Movement Related?" in *Point Series 2*, ed. Wendy Flannery (Goroka, Papua New Guinea: Melanesian Institute, 1983), 68–69.

6. James Sunda, "Your Skin My Skin: A Quest for Eternal Life," unpublished manuscript, 62.

7. Christine Drake, *National Integration in Indonesia* (Honolulu: University of Hawaii, 1989), 53.

8. Benedict Anderson, *Language and Power: Exploring Political Cultures in Indonesia* (Ithaca, N.Y.: Cornell University Press, 1990), 115.

9. See Christine Drake, *National Integration in Indonesia* (Honolulu: University of Hawaii, 1989); and Adam Schwarz, *A Nation in Waiting: Indonesia in the 1990s* (Boulder, Colo.: HarperCollins).

10. J. Budi Hernawan, OFM, and Theo van den Broek, OFM, "Dialog Nasional Papua, Sebuah Kisah 'Memoria Passionis,'" *Tifa Irian* (week three, March 1999): 8.

11. *Operasi Papua Merdeka* (Free Papua Movement) is the pan-Papuan indigenous independence movement of Irian Jaya.

12. GKII, or *Gereja Kemah Injil Indonesia* (Evangelical Tabernacle Church of Indonesia); also known as KINGMI.

13. Gereja Kristen Injili, "Irian Jaya Menjelang 30 Tahun Kembali ki Negara Kesatuan Republik Indonesia. Untuk Keadilan dan Perdamaian. Laporan Disampaikan kepada MPH-PGI dari GKI di Irian Jaya" (Jayapura, Irian Jaya, April 1992).

14. See Nonie Sharp, *The Rule of the Sword: The Story of West Irian* (Malmsbury, Victoria, Australia: Kibble Books in association with Arena, 1977).

15. See Marshall Sahlins, *Islands of History* (Chicago: The University of Chicago Press, 1985).

16. See George Weigel, "Roman Catholicism in the Age of John Paul II," in *The Desecularization of the World: Resurgent Religion and World Politics*, ed. Peter Berger (Grand Rapids, Mich.: Eerdmans, 1999), 25.

17. Douglas Hayward, *Vernacular Christianity among the Mulia Dani: An Ethnography of Religious Belief among the Western Dani of Irian Jaya, Indonesia* (New York: American Society of Missiology and University Press of America, 1997), 94.

18. Ernest Gellner, *Nations and Nationalism* (Ithaca, N.Y.: Cornell University Press, 1983), 54.

19. Robert W. Hefner, "World Building and the Rationality of Conversion," in *Conversion to Christianity: Historical and Anthropological Perspectives on a Great Transformation*, ed. Robert W. Hefner (Berkeley: University of California Press, 1993), 18.

REFERENCES

Anderson, Benedict. *Language and Power: Exploring Political Cultures in Indonesia.* Ithaca, N.Y.: Cornell University Press, 1990.

——. *Imagined Communities.* New York: Verso, 1998.

Berger, Peter, Brigitte Berger, and Hansfried Kellner. *The Homeless Mind: Modernization and Consciousness.* New York: Vintage Books, 1974.

Boland, B. J. *The Struggle of Islam in Modern Indonesia.* The Hague: Martinus Nijhoff, 1982.

Bromley, Myron. *The Grammar of Lower Grand Valley Dani in Discourse Perspective.* Ph.D. diss., Yale University, 1972.

Burridge, Kenelm. *Mambu: A Study of Melanesian Cargo Movements and Their Social and Ideological Background.* New York: Harper & Row, 1960.

Casanova, Jose. *Public Religions in the Modern World.* Chicago: The University of Chicago Press, 1994.

Cooley, Frank L. *Indonesia: Church and Society.* New York: Friendship Press, 1968.

Drake, Christine. *National Integration in Indonesia.* Honolulu: University of Hawaii Press, 1989.

Gellner, Ernest. *Nations and Nationalism.* Ithaca, N.Y.: Cornell University Press, 1983.

Gereja Kristen Injili. *Irian Jaya Menjelang 30 Tahun Kembali ke Negara Kesatuan Republik Indonesia. Untuk Keadilan dan Perdamaian. Laporan Disampaikan kepada MPH-PGI dari GKI di Irian Jaya.* Jayapura, Irian Jaya, April 1992.

Godschalk, Jan A. "Cargoism and Development among the Western Dani, Irian Jaya Seminar. Maklah Seminar Pembangunan Irian Jaya dan Penelitian Indonesia Bagian Timur II" [Working Paper for the Seminar on Development in Irian Jaya and Research of Indonesian East Section II, Jayapura]. Universitas Cenderawasih, Jayapura, Irian Jaya, 1988.

———. "How Are Myth and Movement Related?" In *Religious Movements in Melanesia Today*, edited by Wendy Flannery, pp. 62–77. Goroka, Papua New Guinea: Melanesian Institute, 1983.

Hayward, Douglas. *Vernacular Christianity among the Mulia Dani: An Ethnography of Religious Belief among the Western Dani of Irian Jaya, Indonesia.* New York: American Society of Missiology and University Press of America, 1997.

———. "Time and Society in Dani Culture." *IRIAN: Bulletin of Irian Jaya* 11, no. 2–3 (June and October 1983): 31–55.

Hefner, Robert W. "World Building and the Rationality of Conversion." In *Conversion to Christianity: Historical and Anthropological Perspectives on a Great Transformation*, edited by Robert W. Hefner, pp. 3–44. Berkeley: University of California Press, 1993.

Heider, Karl G. *The Dugum Dani: A Papuan Culture in the Highlands of West New Guinea.* Chicago: Aldine, 1970.

Hernawan J. Budi, OFM, and Theo van den Broek, OFM. "Dialog Nasional Papua, Sebuah Kisah 'Memoria Passionis.'" *Tifa Irian* (week three, March 1999): 8.

Hitt, Russell T. *Cannibal Valley.* New York: Harper and Row, 1962.

Hoskins, Janet. "Entering the Bitter House: Spirit Worship and Conversion in West Sumba." In *Indonesian Religions in Transition*, edited by Rita Smith Kipp and Susan Rodgers, pp. 136–60. Tucson: University of Arizona Press, 1987.

Hutchison, William R. *Errand to the World: American Protestant Thought and Foreign Mission.* Chicago: University of Chicago Press, 1987.

Keyes, Charles F., Helen Hardacre, and Laurel Kendall. "Contested Visions of Community in East and Southeast Asia." In *Asian Visions of Authority: Religion and the Modern Societies of East and Southeast Asia*, edited by Charles Keyes, Helen Hardacre, and Laurel Kendall, pp. 1–16. Honolulu: University of Hawaii Press, 1994.

Kipp, Rita S. *Dissociated Identities: Ethnicity, Religion, and Class in an Indonesian Society.* Ann Arbor: The University of Michigan Press, 1996.

Lijphart, Arend. *The Trauma of Decolonization: The Dutch and West New Guinea.* Yale Studies in Political Science, vol. 17. New Haven, Conn.: Yale University Press, 1966.

Linnekin, Jocelyn, and Lin Poyer. "Introduction." In *Cultural Identity and Ethnicity in the Pacific*, edited by Jocelyn Linnekin and Lin Poyer, pp. 1–16. Honolulu: University of Hawaii Press, 1990.

Martin, David. *Tongues of Fire: The Explosion of Protestantism in Latin America.* Oxford: Blackwell, 1990.

Munninghoff, H. F. M., OFM. *Violations of Human Rights in the Timika Area of Irian Jaya, Indonesia: A Report by the Catholic Church of Jayapura.* Report 6. Irian Jaya, Indonesia: The Diocese of Jayapura, August 1995. Available at www.cs.utexas.edu/users/boyer/fp/bishop-irian-jaya.

Osborne, Robin. *Indonesia's Secret War: The Guerilla Struggle in Irian Jaya.* Boston: Allen & Unwin, 1985.

Rambo, Lewis R. *Understanding Religious Conversion.* New Haven, Conn.: Yale University Press, 1993.

Sahlins, Marshall. *Islands of History.* Chicago: The University of Chicago Press, 1985.

Sanneh, Lamin. *Translating the Message: The Missionary Impact on Culture.* New York: Orbis Press, 1989.

Schwarz, Adam. *A Nation in Waiting: Indonesia in the 1990s.* Boulder, Colo.: HarperCollins, 1994.

Start, Daniel. *The Open Cage: Murder and Survival in the Jungles of Irian Jaya.* London: HarperCollins, 1997.

Weigel, George. "Roman Catholicism in the age of John Paul II." In *The Desecularization of the World: Resurgent Religion and World Politics*, edited by Peter Berger, pp. 19–35. Grand Rapids, Mich.: Eerdmans, 1999.

6

Social Conversion and Group Definition in Jewish Copenhagen

Andrew Buckser

Studies of religious conversion have often focused on conversion's experiential dimensions. Scholars have produced rich analyses of what goes on in the minds of converts (e.g., James 1929; Lofland and Stark 1965; Rambo 1993; Snow and Phillips 1980), as well as of the social texts and circumstances that shape the conversion process (e.g., Cohen 1986; Finn 1997; Hefner 1993; Whitehead 1987). Much less has been said about conversion as a social event, a phenomenon with meanings and consequences for the social groups within which they occur. Conversion to a religion is an irreducibly social act; one does not merely join a faith, but one enters into a set of new relationships with members of a religious community. Conversion, therefore, changes not only the individual, but also the groups that must assimilate or give up the convert. In addition, it raises a set of questions that the communities must address—how to socialize the new convert, how to establish the authenticity of conversion, which internal factions the new convert will support or undermine, and so on. Answers to these questions affect the internal politics, social organization, and self-understanding of religious groups. These social dimensions of conversion have not been a focus of anthropological research (though see Hefner 1993: 27–31; Viswanathan 1998).

Some of the most sensitive questions surrounding conversion relate to definitions of religious community. Conversion suggests ideas about the nature of group and other, and especially about the boundaries between the two. For groups assimilating converts, therefore, conversion creates an occasion for debating and negotiating the contours of community. Even in relatively cohesive groups, differences exist on such issues, and these oppositions affect attitudes toward taking in new members. Conversion is not merely a site of celebration and a reinforcement of group beliefs, but also a site of conflict, a point at which competing notions of group and other directly confront one another. In groups for which boundaries are highly contested, where factions have deep and enduring antagonisms over what the group should be and whom it should include, conversion can become one of the most inflammatory and divisive moments in community life. The intensity of conflict will be greater, and the position of the convert more fraught, the more disagreement and ambivalence attend the definition of the group's nature and boundaries (cf. Barth 1969; Cohen 1985).

This chapter looks at these dynamics in a group for which the nature of community is highly contested and in which conversion is a site of continual dispute and political tension: the Jewish community of Copenhagen, Denmark, where I have conducted fieldwork since 1996. Within this group, the vast majority of conversions are social conversions, stemming in one way or another from mixed marriages. The experiences of those of who seek to convert to Judaism become points of conflict over the nature of Jewish community, authority, and religiosity. This conflict makes conversion one of the most explosive issues in congregational politics, and it subjects those who have gone through it to ongoing suspicion and scrutiny. This chapter discusses the forms these conflicts take, and it suggests some implications for our understanding of the social aspects of conversion more generally.

BACKGROUND

The Jews of Copenhagen comprise the oldest and best-established minority group in the small Scandinavian nation of Denmark.[1] The community dates back to the early seventeenth century, when Jewish merchants from Germany and Holland first began settling in the capital. Isolated and alien in its early years, the community began to integrate with the larger society around 1800, and its members achieved full citizenship in 1814. In the years since, Copenhagen's Jews have created a substantial institutional and cultural tradition in the city. Their institutions include a stately synagogue in the center of town, a large administration building near Christiansborg Palace, an active Jewish school, and such institutional adjuncts as day care centers, kosher delicatessens, alternative synagogues, and a museum. Jews also operate a wide variety of voluntary associations, including cultural societies, journals, social clubs, Zionist associations, musical societies, and youth groups. The size of the community has varied over the decades, hovering between 5,000 and 7,000 for much of the twentieth century; membership has fallen in recent years, but the group still represents one of the most active and engaged religious groups in contemporary Scandinavia.

Most of this activity falls under the authority of a single official organization, the Jewish Community of Copenhagen (*Det Mosaiske Troessamfund*, or MT). The MT owns and operates the main synagogue, as well as most of the other Jewish institutions in the city. It also funds and provides offices for most of the Jewish voluntary associations. The MT bills itself as an inclusive organization, a "unity congregation," and it tries as far as possible to include all Jews within its borders. Doing so can be difficult; the Jewish community in Copenhagen is deeply fragmented, and factions built around religious and social differences have existed since its inception. Some of these differences derive from the waves of immigration that have brought Jews to Denmark over the centuries, as newly arriving groups have found themselves at odds with the established communities. Other differences relate to disagreements over ritual practice, with an Orthodox minority struggling bitterly with the more religiously liberal majority. Still others derive from arguments over the meaning of "Jewishness," language, the community's relationship to Israel, issues in Danish politics, and a host of other issues. Such divisions color almost all Jewish activity in Copenhagen, including the politics and administration of the MT itself. The MT has endured nonetheless, in large part due to its flexible approach to defining Jewish activity and practice. It funds groups with very different outlooks on Judaism, and it allows any Jewish resident of Denmark to join or run for office. Likewise, it maintains strictly Orthodox ritual practice within the synagogue, for the stated purpose of allowing members of all branches of Judaism to participate. As a result, although not all Danish Jews belong to the MT, none dispute its centrality to Jewish life in the city.

One distinctive feature of the Jewish world in Denmark is its deep engagement with the surrounding culture. Danish Jews encounter very few barriers to full participation in the larger society; the anti-Semitism so endemic to much of European culture has never gained a strong foothold in Denmark, and in recent decades it has disappeared almost entirely. This acceptance found dramatic expression in 1943, when thousands of resistance members and ordinary Danes combined to rescue almost the entire Jewish community from the occupying Nazis.[2] For their part, most Jews have entered deeply and enthusiastically into Danish culture. They dress, talk, and act entirely like other Danes. They work in regular Danish occupations and have contributed important figures to Danish politics, media, and popular culture. Because they are so few in number, most Jews live their daily lives in non-Jewish settings. Most Jewish children attend regular Danish schools for much of their education, most adults have largely non-Jewish social circles, and almost all Jews work in non-Jewish workplaces. For most members of the MT, therefore, Danish identity is as central to self-perception as Jewish identity.

Bringing these two identities together can be a difficult task (Buckser 2000). Danish Jews tend to think of Jewishness in primordial terms, as something inscribed in the body and blood as well as in heritage and religion. Most feel that Jews have a distinctive manner and appearance, even if they cannot say exactly what those are. At the same time, however, most Jews identify heavily with Danish culture, a culture that tends to stress homogeneity and belonging and to stigmatize difference. Danish popular culture defines Danish commonality through some of the same practices that Jewish culture uses to define Jewish distinctiveness, including foodways, affective style, humor, and tradition (see Buckser 1999; Jokinen 1994; Knudsen 1996). Being a Danish Jew, therefore, requires the combination of two distinctive and often contradictory identities. Many of my informants describe the process as difficult, unending, and emotionally painful. Their resolutions vary with their particular circumstances, and they entail a variety of understandings of what Jewishness and Danishness consist of. Decisions about what it is to be a Jew, and by extension what is meant by Jewish community, are not arrived at by community consensus but through a profoundly individual project of reconciling two dimensions of self that stand in fundamental conflict.

These circumstances make the precise boundaries of the Jewish community extremely difficult to establish. Who is a Jew? Who should decide who counts and does not count? Are some Jews more real, more authentic, closer to a primordial essence than others? Danish Jews answer these questions in widely differing ways. Some disagreements run along factional lines—liberal Jews, for example, tend to favor a more inclusive definition of Jewry, but the more Orthodox favor a narrower one—but others do not. As noted, the MT has survived by avoiding these questions as much as possible, by taking a "big tent" approach that allows a variety of different understandings of Judaism to participate and interact. With its Orthodox ritual and inclusive membership, the MT allows the meaning of Jewishness to be resolved at an individual—not a community—level.

CONVERSION IN JEWISH COPENHAGEN

The flexibility of the MT is tested when it faces the problem of conversion. Conversion is an unavoidably communal issue; it implies not merely a change in one person's self-identification, but also the ratification and recognition of that change by the wider community. The issue carries a particular importance in Denmark because it arises so often there. In comparison to other world religions, Judaism does not generally seek converts, and indeed it tends to discourage them. For much of Jewish history, conversion to Judaism has been relatively rare and has had little social impact. In Denmark, however, the close engagement of Jews with the surrounding culture has made conversion a much more important issue. This is not because Danes have been widely attracted to Judaism—few Danes have any detailed knowledge of Jewish beliefs or practices—but because Jews have intermarried with non-Jewish Danes at extremely high rates. Most estimates put the current rate of mixed marriages in the Jewish community at 75 percent or higher. This pattern is not new. Although intermarriage rates have risen and fallen repeatedly over the past 200 years, such unions have made up a significant portion of the total since the early 1800s (see, for example, Arnheim 1950a; Arnheim 1950b; Arnheim 1950c; Balslev 1932). For most of its modern history, and increasingly over the last several decades, intermarriage has constituted a basic feature of the social world of Danish Jewry.

By some standards, Copenhagen Jews treat intermarriage quite leniently. Intermarried Jews remain part of their families of origin and the MT. They are not regarded as having left Judaism except on the very rare occasions when they explicitly do so. The Orthodox interpretation of Jewish law, however, imposes constraints on the recognition of mixed marriages. Partners must have a civil wedding, not a religious one, and they may not conduct it in the synagogue. A non-Jewish spouse may not be buried in the Jewish cemetery or participate in certain Jewish social activities. Perhaps most importantly, traditional Jewish law, known as *halakhah*, reckons Jewish descent through the maternal line; accordingly, if a man intermarries, the MT will not regard his children as Jewish. (Judaism has no particular term for such children; for convenience, I will call them "patrilineal Jews.") These problems make conversion an appealing prospect for many intermarrying couples, as well as for some children of intermarried Jewish men. Most Jewish marriages, therefore, raise the issue of conversion, either for their participants or their offspring, and decisions about conversion touch almost every Jewish family.

It is possible, of course, to convert out of strictly religious motives, without Jewish ancestry or plans for a Jewish marriage. But such instances are rare, and they tend to be regarded with suspicion by members of the community. In most cases, conversion is not a matter of religious insight, a validation of a transformation of consciousness, but a means of reckoning with the consequences of a particular social action.

The question of conversion can raise a variety of questions involving differing notions of ethnicity, religiosity, and the connection of the Jewish community to the larger world. Here, I focus on two: the questions of the definition of community raised by conversions at marriage, and the issues of authority that attend the conversion of patrilineal Jews.

Marriage Conversion and the Meaning of Jewishness

Anna Jensen, now a 28-year-old psychology student in Copenhagen, was a 20-year-old undergraduate when she began dating a Jewish boy named Oskar Goldschmidt. Anna did not regard herself as religious, having seldom attended church since her confirmation; Oskar, likewise, seldom attended religious services, and he regarded himself as an atheist. During a year-long stay in Israel as a teenager, however, Oskar had become deeply conscious of his Jewish identity, and at age 20 he was actively involved in Jewish youth and sports associations. When the couple began discussing future possibilities of marriage and children, Oskar expressed concern about the difficulties of a mixed marriage. He was very anxious that his children be Jewish, and he wanted his sons to identify with the Jewish traditions and social networks that meant so much to him. He therefore asked Anna if she would consider converting. The idea struck her as strange at first—she associated conversion with a kind of religious experience that was utterly foreign to her—but as she learned more about it, she found the prospect appealing. Converting would give her and Oskar something in common, an ability to participate together in Jewish rituals and keeping a Jewish home. It would mean a great deal to Oskar and to his parents. She didn't foresee any problem with her own family, none of whom were religious. Indeed, they, like her, saw something vaguely exciting in the distinctiveness of a Jewish identity, something temptingly unusual amidst the bland homogeneity of Danish culture. She found the exotic and intricate requirements of Jewish ritual practice fascinating, a puzzle of sorts, to work out in the process of daily life. As their marriage approached, conversion appeared to her as a straightforward and interesting way of solidifying her relationship with Oskar and the identities of their children.

For the Jewish community, by contrast, Anna's conversion and others like it raised some very difficult questions. Was this kind of motivation a sufficient justification for conversion? Could anyone convert to Judaism who fell in love with a Jew, or did there have to be some sort of independent interest in being Jewish? Could a convert be accepted who had expressed neither belief nor interest in the tenets of Jewish theology? If the answer was yes, what sort of requirements should be expected of such a convert? Surely, she would have to commit to living as a Jew—but what does living as a Jew involve, and how could her sincerity be proven? And what would happen if her marriage to Oskar were to fail, as so many marriages do? Answering such questions is a subject of serious dispute among the city's Jews, as it has been for the past century.

Answers tend to fall into two categories. One position sets high barriers to conversion. Conversion, it is argued, should be restricted to those who possess a deep connection to Jewish religion and culture, not to those who find it a convenient way to simplify a marriage. People like Anna should be required to show a spiritual interest in Judaism over a long period of time and to undergo extensive instruction in Jewish life and ritual before being considered as candidates for conversion. Intermarriage is, after all, a serious transgression of Jewish law, and allowing easy conversions amounts to condoning it. Moreover, a marriage convert like Anna cannot be expected to become truly Jewish. She may call herself a Jew, and she may observe some of the rituals, but she will remain at heart a gentile. She will raise her children with Danish customs and a Danish worldview, not Jewish ones. Though the conversion will make them halakhic Jews, it will not make them spiritual Jews, and they are likely to shed their Judaism when they grow up. If she and Oskar divorce, experience suggests that she will return with the children to the family and church of her childhood. This view of conversion finds its strongest support among the deeply religious members of the MT, many of whom have close connections to Orthodox Jewish communities elsewhere in Europe. In many cases, they turn to such communities for spouses for their own children. Better to find a real Jewish spouse in London or Antwerp, they argue, and maintain the traditions and beliefs of Judaism than to pick a convenient Danish wife and call her a Jew.

The second position finds its strongest adherents among the less observant, Danish-identified members of the congregation and argues that the Orthodox approach is unrealistic. As noted, Danish Jews intermarry at extraordinarily high rates, and one cannot expect the situation to change; the decision to be made is not whether intermarriage should occur, but how to deal with it after it has occurred. In that context, an easier and even routine conversion offers the best possibility for maintaining Jewish community and culture. Anna's ability to pass on Jewish tradition may be limited, but conversion can only increase her knowledge of Jewish tradition. Surely, she would not raise better Jews if she were still a Christian. Her conversion also admits her children to Jewish education and rituals. And if she is not a perfectly observant Jew, how many Jews are? Most Danish Jews are very lax in synagogue attendance, kosher housekeeping, and other forms of Jewish religiosity. Converts, who consciously commit to a Jewish life, arguably practice better Judaism than the majority of the congregation. If Jews worry that converts are insufficiently committed, that they will return to Christianity in the event of a divorce, then they should make converts more welcome. Rather than keeping people like Anna outside the community, the argument goes, Jews should pull them in.

The differences between these two positions reflect a deeper split in the constitution of the Danish Jewish community itself. On the one hand, the community is built upon a structure of law, ritual, and ideology derived from a premodern tradition (cf. Di Bella, chapter 7); *halakhah* and much of Orthodox theology were formulated before 1800, when Jews constituted an organic and largely self-contained community. To be a Jew, according to this body of law, is to be part of such a working social entity. In daily life, however, Danish Jews experience Jewishness in the context of late modern ethnicity, a type of ethnic affiliation Herbert Gans (1979) describes as "symbolic ethnicity." Today, Jews are integrated into a number of communities, through occupation, interests, and family, none of which constitutes more than a small portion of their world. Ethnicity in such a context is not so much a connection to social entity as a feature of self, defined individually in the context of a largely Danish social experience. As Jews work out individual resolutions to the problem of Jewish identity, they tend to use one or the other of these contexts for defining the Jewish community to which they belong. The most Orthodox turn to halakhic model, examining conversion in the light of its effects on an integrated and distinct Jewish society. Their opponents, on the other hand, turn to the symbolic model and focus on conversion's effects on the fragmented social world of the individual.

Opposition emerges in the ways in which people on the two sides articulate issues of conversion. When I asked Orthodox members about cases like Anna's, they responded in terms of the meaning of Jewishness and the Jewish community. Jewishness, I was often told, is not something one just puts on like a suit of clothes; it requires a commitment to be a Jew, to follow Jewish law, and to regard the Jewish community as one's home and reference group. Orthodox members took care to distance themselves from particular cases—"Mejnar is a nice man," an ultra-orthodox leader told me about one case, "I don't have any problem with him. But one has to think about what being Jewish means." Liberals, by contrast, usually focused on the specific case at hand, emphasizing the hardship or emotional hurt imposed by a stringent policy toward conversion. Was it fair, they asked, that this or that person who was willing to contribute to the Jewish community was turned away? What is, for the Orthodox, a question of community definition is for the liberals a question of individual pragmatics—how to deal with the given fact of intermarriage in a world defined by immersion in Danish society.

Fortunately for Anna, her conversion took place during the last years of Rabbi Bent Melchior's tenure. This was one of the easier periods in which to convert in Denmark, and her conversion went very smoothly. Melchior required her to attend conversion classes for almost a year, together with Oskar. There she learned the basic information necessary for leading a Jewish life: the ritual calendar, the logistics of kosher housekeeping, the rules of the Sabbath, the format of the Jewish service, and so on. Anna then underwent a conversion ceremony, complete with immersion in a ritual bath. She became a Jew; in fact, she became quite an observant Jew, considerably more religiously active than Oskar, who told me that he finds some of her scrupulous ritual observance annoying. He's glad that she's Jewish now and thinks it will make things easier for their children when they have some, but it's been hard giving up roast pork.

Descent Conversion and the Construction of Authority

Conflicts over conversion entail not only definitions of community, but also constructions of authority. They involve not only concerns about what the Jewish community should be, but also who should be allowed to make that decision. These questions emerge with particular force in the other main occasion for conversion in Denmark, that involving patrilineal Jews. Although precise statistics are difficult to establish, clearly only a minority of non-Jewish spouses convert. For the majority, the issue of conversion moves into the next generation, to the children of Jewish fathers and non-Jewish mothers. Such individuals face a very different sort of transformation than Anna. For those who seek conversion, the process represents a formalization of a Jewish identity, not its creation; they decide to convert because they consider themselves Jewish, not because they wish to become Jewish. Often, they have a thorough Jewish education and extensive Jewish social networks, and in most cases they have a more conscious commitment to the community than the majority of its members. From a halakhic standpoint, however, they have no more claim to Jewish identity than any other Dane, and the rabbi often requires them to undergo a lengthy conversion process. Conversion thus privileges formal MT institutions over personal experience in establishing Jewish identity, a distribution of power that raises opposition and resentment from many of those affected by it.

This dynamic is characterized by Esther Herzog, a 26-year-old bank administrator who converted in 1996. Esther's parents divorced when she was 10 years old, and afterward she lived with her non-Jewish mother. Her relationship with her father was somewhat distant, especially after he moved back to his native Israel a few years later. Esther grew up with connections to Judaism, however, and her mother had tried to foster Esther's Jewish interests after the divorce. She sent Esther to the Jewish school for several years and encouraged her to socialize with Jews. On her graduation from gymnasium, Esther lived with her father in Israel for about six months. She looks back fondly on that time and says that she often considers moving to Israel permanently. On her return to Copenhagen, she decided that Jewishness was her true identity. She went to the rabbi and told him that she wanted to convert. She expected the rabbi to welcome her immediately and was shocked and hurt when he did not. Rather, the rabbi suggested that she begin going to services for a while and get involved in Jewish activities, and he would let her know when he thought she was ready. She followed his advice, throwing herself headlong into the Jewish world. She attended services, observed holidays, and joined a youth group and a Zionist organization. She checked in with the rabbi occasionally, making sure he knew of her involvement, but he remained noncommittal about admitting her to conversion. He hinted that it would help matters if she had a Jewish boyfriend, a suggestion that led to several short and unhappy romances. After almost a year of anxiety, the rabbi finally decided to admit her to conversion instruction, and within a few months she was formally converted.

The conversion process brought Esther face-to-face with the dual nature of Jewish identity in Copenhagen. To be a Jew is both to belong to a particular community and to hold a particular understanding of self. Like most Copenhagen Jews, Esther thought of Jewishness primarily in terms of personal ethnic identification; she regarded herself as a Jew because she felt Jewish, irrespective of her tenuous ties to Jewish worship or her distance from Jewish community. The MT, by contrast, regarded such feelings as irrelevant. Jewish identity, in its view, depended not on the subjective assessments of individuals but on a common religious and legal framework. For Esther, conversion represented the primacy of this community law over individual experience. The rabbi who required it, who set the conditions upon which Esther could "really" be a Jew, embodied the power of the group to shape personal identity.

Esther resented this power enormously. Her bitterness over the ordeal, even several years later, is plainly evident. She was angry at being forced to attend services, at having to make a show for the rabbi to prove her own identity. The anxious waiting period and the possibility of rejection struck her as a cruel means of forcing her to acknowledge the rabbi's power over her. It felt arbitrary and archaic, she says, and she says it showed how out of touch the community was with contemporary Jewish life. Even their criteria seemed sexist and absurd. Why should she need to go through all this, she asked, just because her mother, not her father, was a non-Jew? Esther's ire has led to active involvement in the MT, where she champions the cause of mixed couples and women in committee work and community journals.

I met similar reactions to the conversion process not only among patrilineal converts but also among many other liberal Jews. The notion that a set of arcane traditional laws should determine who is a Jew, rather than the felt experience of living people, clashed with liberal understandings of the nature of Jewish ethnic identity in contemporary Denmark. In cases like Anna's, these understandings have led to calls for easier access to conversion; in cases like Esther's, they have led to anger at the authority structure of the congregation.

POLITICAL IMPLICATIONS OF CONVERSION

In a fragmented community like that of the Copenhagen Jews, many congregational disagreements lie simmering for years. The group has survived in large part by avoiding outright confrontations, letting a variety of viewpoints on Jewishness and Jewish religiosity coexist alongside one another. Issues of conversion, however, require clear choices. The community, through its representatives, must make an unambiguous statement of who does and who does not belong, and it must apply that statement to specific individuals seeking entry to the group. Such decisions have concrete and immediate consequences. Individuals may or may not be allowed to marry in the synagogue, to circumcise their sons, or to send their children to Jewish institutions. Such consequences touch not only the individuals but also larger family and social networks. As a result, conversion presents one of the most politically fraught moments in the life of the Jewish community—a moment in which the congregation must declare its position on the nature of Jewishness—and the answer will have a widespread effect.

This situation imbues conversion with both danger and possibility for a religious leader. As in most Jewish communities, the Chief Rabbi of Copenhagen holds final authority over the conduct of ritual in Denmark; since he alone is able to perform the conversion ceremony, he decides who will be allowed to convert and the terms under which they can do so. In some cases, his decisions have unleashed revolts within the congregation. In 1903, for example, the traditionalist Rabbi Tobias Lewenstein decided to change the conditions by which patrilineal Jews could enter the community. Earlier rabbis had routinely converted patrilineal Jews as long as they had been raised as Jews. Lewenstein tightened requirements sharply, demanding that converts be raised in kosher homes and attend religious school throughout childhood. His action provoked an outcry from congregational liberals, who after an extended, public, and very bitter battle, had him dismissed from office. A reverse case occurred in the 1970s and 1980s, when the liberal Bent Melchior earned the enmity of traditionalists through what they saw as his rubber-stamp approach to conversion. In 1981, by aligning with another disaffected group, the traditionalists managed to terminate Melchior's contract. The current rabbi, Bent Lexner, has pushed his congregation in a more Orthodox direction and has worked hard to woo liberals to his position. Although many of those I interviewed liked him very much, his restrictive views on conversion remain a powerful barrier to their supporting him. The intensity of feelings surrounding conversion make it a recurring danger to the political tenure of rabbis.

At the same time, conversion policies also can be a source of strength. Lewenstein's stance on conversion made him a hero to the congregation's traditionalist wing. After his dismissal from the MT, supporters established a second synagogue for him to lead, a synagogue that remains in operation today. Likewise, although Melchior's conversion policy made him enemies among the Orthodox, it also made him friends among liberals. After the board terminated his contract in 1981, an energetic campaign by these supporters managed to replace the board and reinstate Melchior in 1982. When carefully managed, conversion policy can provide a source of allies as well as antagonists, and most rabbis tread a delicate line on the subject.

The political valence of conversion also touches the lives of converts. Intense feelings surrounding the process have led a number of converts to become more active in congregational affairs. Converts like Esther, for example, frequently appear in the leadership of the congregation, especially in its social clubs and intellectual societies. Tensions surrounding conversion also shape their perception by other Jews in daily life. A number of converts told me of a lingering sense of illegitimacy, a feeling—in many cases quite justified—that other Jews regard them as frauds or interlopers. Esther complained that she constantly had to prove her Jewishness, and it was never enough; through a snide reference here or a cryptic comment there, people in the MT repeatedly cast doubt on whether she was a genuine Jew. As a result, she says that she has to follow Jewish law with far greater care than would a born Jew. Most Jews can eat a nonkosher meal, work on Saturday, or go out with a non-Jewish man, and no one thinks anything of it. But if Esther does these things, people will question the sincerity of her conversion. Jewishness is a conscious identity she has deliberately chosen, but it is one in which she never feels entirely secure.

Conversion, in this sense, does not make one a regular Jew. It makes one a convert, a distinctive status that carries ongoing symbolic and practical consequences. Converts exemplify basic conflicts in the construction of Jewish identity: individual versus group, choice versus obligation, objective law versus subjective experience. Conversions thus become not merely evanescent rites of passage but permanent features of the self.

CONCLUSION

The association of religious conversion with theological insight has deep roots in the Western Christian tradition. It stands at the center of the tradition's key narratives, including the cathartic transformations of saints like Paul and Augustine. In such stories, conversion involves a fresh vision of the truth, a realization that the new religion represents a higher understanding of the world. Such conversions are echoed in Protestant revival movements and in "born-again" churches, where even longtime members seek to experience a new consciousness of the meaning of their faith. This notion also informs much of the social scientific work on conversion, which has focused on the processes through which radical changes in religious worldviews take place. While acknowledging the influence of social dynamics on conversion, scholars have trained their gaze largely where Christianity has trained it: on changes in belief and experience of the world that Christian conversion demands. Like born-again Christians, they have tended to overlook conversions that lack that sort of change; they have regarded them as less than "true" conversions and classified them as political or social rather than religious phenomena. Consequently, they have said relatively little about the effects of such conversions on either the experience of converts or on the religious communities that they join.

Yet the social and experiential correlates of social conversion are no less complex or wide-ranging than conversions motivated by belief. In Copenhagen, conversions lay bare a variety of tensions concerning the nature of Jewish identity, authority, and religiosity, and they force individuals to come to terms with their own views on these issues. Converts provide a focus for community debate as well as symbols of ambivalence and tension afterward. The nature of these conflicts reflects the particular social and cultural position of Jews in contemporary Denmark; the organizational stresses surrounding the incorporation of the community into the modern state, and the stresses involved in secularization, push the debate over conversion in a specific direction and place specific actors on either side of the issue. In other groups, conversion reflects different strains on social organization or the construction of identity. But even in groups that value belief-conversion more than the Danish Jews, and even in groups that deny the validity of purely social conversion, the social dimension of conversion offers a revealing window into group ideas about identity and community.

We should not assume, moreover, that social conversions are somehow less authentic or less complete than those based on religious inspiration. Membership in a religious community derives from more than a set of beliefs; it also involves a set of relationships with other members, a set of practices and habits, and a set of aesthetic orientations and discursive styles (Hefner 1993: 27–28). Converts are able to assimilate such elements without the corresponding beliefs, and indeed these elements may provide a better index of a person's conversion. During the partition of the Indian subcontinent, for example, social workers often met fierce resistance when they tried to return women who had been forcibly converted to Islam to their original Hindu homes (Menon and Basin 1993; Viswanathan 1998: xii–xiv). Having married Muslim men, raised Muslim children, and lived Muslim lives, they had effectively become Muslims, whatever their religious beliefs or the circumstances of their conversion. The social and practical dimensions of conversion, that is, had significance beyond and above that of faith. A similar case could be made for converts in Jewish Copenhagen. Orthodox Judaism places greater weight on practice than on belief; although it is good to believe in God, it is essential to carry out the commandments of *halakhah*. An atheist can be a perfectly observant Jew, and indeed many are. To evaluate the completeness of a conversion on the extent to which it is rooted in faith, therefore, rather than on the extent to which a convert is immersed in Jewish practice and social networks, is to impose a false standard of authenticity.

Indeed, it might well reverse the real situation on the ground. I did meet a religiously inspired convert in Copenhagen, a pleasant young woman who had fallen in love with Judaism while on a visit to an Israeli kibbutz. She had studied the Jewish scriptures intensively and could discuss Jewish theology with considerable sophistication. She was, above all, forthright concerning her belief in God and the divine foundations of Jewish ritual. Her belief was obviously a comfort to her, and it justified an impressively stringent regime of ritual practice. However, her belief did not make her more authentically Jewish than other converts I met. If anything, it made her less so. Most Copenhagen Jews do not walk about in a state of theological certitude; like most other Danes, they have serious doubts about the existence of God and balance their interest in religious observance against their participation in a decidedly secularized culture. Their attitude toward religion is ridden with ambivalence and skepticism, making the observance of *halakhah* a complicated decision. Arguably, it is not the true believer but someone like Esther who is closer to the Jewish experience. Brought into the group by family connections, conflicted about her own beliefs and identity, unsure of her place in the community and angry at its leadership, Esther may little resemble the classic picture of the successful convert—but she certainly exemplifies the experience of a great many of the Copenhagen Jews.

NOTES

1. For general historical studies of the Danish Jews, see Bamberger (1983), Borchsenius (1968) and Feigenberg (1984). For a discussion of the contemporary community, see Buckser (1999a, 1999b, 2000).

2. For studies of this event, see Buckser (2001), Sode-Madsen (1993), Goldberger (1987), and Yahil (1969).

REFERENCES

Arnheim, A. (1950a). "Jøderne i Danmark—Statistisk Set." *Jødisk Samfund* 24, no. 1: 18–19.

———. (1950b). "Jøderne i Danmark—Statistisk Set." *Jødisk Samfund* 24, no. 2: 20–21.

———. (1950c). "Jøderne i Danmark—Statistisk Set." *Jødisk Samfund* 24, no. 3: 18–19.

Balslev, B. (1932). *De danske Jøders historie.* Copenhagen: Lohse.

Bamberger, I. N. (1983). *The Viking Jews: A History of the Jews of Denmark.* New York: Shengold.

Barth, F., ed. (1969). *Ethnic Groups and Boundaries: The Social Organization of Culture Difference.* London: Allen & Unwin.

Borchsenius, P. (1968). *Historien om de Danske Jøder.* Copenhagen: Fremad.

Buckser, A. (1999a). "Keeping Kosher: Eating and Social Identity among the Jews of Denmark." *Ethnology* 38, no. 3: 191–209.

———. (1999b). "Modern Identities and the Creation of History: Stories of Rescue among the Jews of Denmark." *Anthropological Quarterly* 72, no. 1: 1–17.

———. (2000). "Jewish Identity and the Meaning of Community in Contemporary Denmark." *Ethnic and Racial Studies* 23, no. 4: 71-734.

———. (2001). "Rescue and Cultural Context during the Holocaust: Grundtvigian Nationalism and the Rescue of the Danish Jews." *Shofar* 19, no. 2: 1–25.

Cohen, A. (1985). *The Symbolic Construction of Community.* London: Tavistock.

Cohen, C. L. (1986). *God's Caress: The Psychology of Puritan Religious Experience.* New York: Oxford University Press.

Feigenberg, M., ed. (1984). *Indenfor Murene: Jødisk liv i Danmark 1684–1984.* Copenhagen: C. A. Reitzel.

Finn, T. M. (1997). *From Death to Rebirth: Ritual and Conversion in Antiquity.* New York: Paulist Press.

Goldberger, L., ed. (1987). *The Rescue of the Danish Jews: Moral Courage under Stress.* New York: New York University Press.

Hefner, R. W., ed. (1993). *Conversion to Christianity: Historical and Anthropological Perspectives on a Great Transformation.* Berkeley: University of California Press.

James, W. (1929). *The Varieties of Religious Experience: A Study in Human Nature.* New York: Random House.

Jokinen, K. (1994). "Cultural Uniformity, Differentiation, and Small National Cultures." *Cultural Studies* 8, no. 2: 208–19.

Knudsen, A. (1996). *Her går det godt, send flere penge.* Copenhagen: Gyldendal.

Lofland, J., and R. Stark (1965). "Becoming a World-Saver: A Theory of Conversion to a Deviant Perspective." *American Sociological Review* 30, no. 6: 862–75.

Menon, R., and K. Basin (1993). "Recovery, Rupture, Resistance: Indian State and Abduction of Women during Partition." *Economic and Political Weekly:* 2–11.

Rambo, L. R. (1993). *Understanding Religious Conversion.* New Haven, Conn.: Yale University Press.

Snow, D. A., and C. Phillips (1980). "The Lofland-Stark Conversion Model: A Critical Reassessment." *Social Problems* 27, no. 4: 430–47.

Sode-Madsen, H. (1993). *"Føreren har Befalet!": Jødeaktionen Oktober 1943.* Copenhagen: Samleren.

Viswanathan, G. (1998). *Outside the Fold: Conversion, Modernity, and Belief.* Princeton, N.J.: Princeton University Press.

Whitehead, H. (1987). *Renunciation and Reformulation: A Study of Conversion in an American Sect.* Ithaca, N.Y.: Cornell University Press.

Yahil, L. (1969). *The Rescue of Danish Jewry: Test of a Democracy.* Philadelphia: Jewish Publication Society of America.

7

Conversion and Marginality in Southern Italy

Maria Pia Di Bella

The relationship between language, ritual, and liminality in the act of conversion will be highlighted, in this chapter, by two examples, one historical and one ethnographic. The first example shows how a marginal social figure—in this case, a criminal condemned to death—is reintegrated into society after having experienced a particular ritual focused on conversion or reconversion. The second shows how conversion to Pentecostalism in a rural setting marginalizes the faithful due to their use of glossolalia. Although these two examples are taken from different regions of Italy—Sicily for the first case, Apulia for the second—and from different time periods—the early modern era for the first and the contemporary era for the second—their comparison sheds light on the ways in which conversion not only plays a major role in inserting the individual in (or separating him or her from) a collectivity but also determines the pragmatics of the language that converts are allowed to use or are capable to develop.

CRIMINALS' CONVERSIONS

The first example is from archival materials (Di Bella 1999a, 1999b). It concerns tasks performed by a Sicilian company, The Company of the Saintly Crucifix (*Compagnia del Santissimo Crocifisso*), better known as the *Bianchi* (White Ones). The *Bianchi*, constituted in Palermo in 1541, was composed mainly of aristocrats. Their tasks consisted of comforting, for three days and three nights, all persons who had been condemned to death for criminal offenses.

85

From 1541 to 1820, the *Bianchi* assisted 2,127 persons, forty of whom were women (Cutrera 1917). The period 1541 to 1646 was a very cruel one for the condemned, especially commoners, for they were usually carried to the gallows on a tumbrel, where an executioner racked them with hot pincers, cut off their right hands, and burned their feet; their limbs were tied to horses in order to pull them apart; and they were quartered alive. After 1642, hands were cut only from the corpses, and only corpses were quartered.

The condemned were handed over to four members of the company and isolated in a section of the prison that was set aside for such occasions and designated as the chapel, where the *Bianchi* assisted them morally and spiritually by following a specific ritual. Thus, the "health of the souls" of those to be executed was entrusted to the *Bianchi*, who instructed the condemned on "how to die a good Christian death." Three liminal days of seclusion were spent preparing the condemned to accept fully his fate and convince him to die bravely. Any earthly sufferings that his body would endure were considered to be the *sine qua non* condition of salvation, for sufferings gave access to an afterlife that would otherwise have eluded him. The psychological preparation provided by the *Bianchi* thus enabled the condemned to accept the "separation of soul and body" with religious detachment (Di Bella 1999a).

A brief description of the prescribed ritual followed by the *Bianchi* is necessary in order to show the relationship between language, ritual, and liminality. When the prisoner was brought in front of the four hooded *Bianchi*, they first informed him of the place, the day, and the hour of execution. After a few words of comfort, they declared him a member of the company and, to signify his full integration, they lifted their hoods in order to show him their faces. Then they led him in front of the *Ecce Homo* and the statue of Our Lady of Sorrows (*Addolorata*), whose hands he had to kiss. Next was an inquiry into his person, the circumstances of imprisonment, and his feelings about it. If he gave signs of resistance, he was firmly exhorted to accept his fate. After being escorted to his cell (*dammuso*), the four *Bianchi* embraced him and kissed his feet as a sign of humility. For any material or spiritual comfort during the night, he could summon the *Bianchi* by pulling on a rope.

Over the remaining two days, the condemned was taken, first, to the oratory of the chapel to pray with a lighted candle in front of the *Ecce Homo*. This occurred both before and after the several masses in which he had to assist. Next, he was taken for confessions and communions and, last, to rehearse the ladder exercise (*esercizio della scala*), that is, the gestures and the words to perform during the procession from the prison to the scaffold. If requested, the *Bianchi* also allowed the condemned to dictate a "discharge of conscience" (*discarico di coscienza*), which enabled him to die without sin of false accusation on his conscience.

On the day of his execution, the condemned left the prison blindfolded and was taken in procession to the scaffold. He was attended by the four *Bianchi* who had assisted him and was followed by the fifty-two remaining members of the *Bianchi*, who recited litanies or chanted *Miserere* or *De profundis.* When the procession arrived at the place of execution—usually the central Marina square—it halted. Here, the condemned knelt in front of the *Bianchi*'s priest to receive absolution. To the question whether he wished to die like a Christian, he answered in the affirmative. The priest began to recite the Apostle's Creed, and at the words *passus et sepultus est*, the hangman put the rope around his neck. When the prayer was over, the condemned kissed the hangman's feet and the steps of the scaffold. A small chain representing Our Lady of the Dying (*Madonna degli Agonizzanti*) was given him for comfort. Finally, the hangman pulled the rope and launched him into the air.

Manipulation of the bodies of the condemned was at the core of these spectacles of justice offered to vast audiences in the streets of Palermo, reminding everyone of the martyrs' and, most of all, of Jesus's sufferings. The official discourse, on the other hand, stressed the care of souls of condemned persons, while the body was left to its expected resurrection. Theological references gave the people of Palermo a basis that made their compassionate actions appropriate. Since Christ's sufferings—endured to save humanity as a whole—were constantly present in Christian conscience, all the social spectrum of Palermo participated by material help or by prayers, either to save the condemned soul or to send it, in the worst of cases, to purgatory. Thus, the expiation of the crime became the collective concern of all members of the community.

The epilogue of reintegration of the condemned into the Christian community took place in the church of the beheaded bodies' souls. From 1795 on, the corpses of the condemned were buried in the nearby cemetery, and the faithful attached to the beheaded bodies' souls a status that was typical of canonized saints. Sicilian priests accepted the fact that parishioners addressed themselves to the beheaded bodies' souls as if the latter were beatified or canonized, and, most strikingly, permitted ex-votos to hang in the churches in their charge.

CONVERSIONS TO PENTECOSTALISM

The second example is based on small Pentecostal groups that began to appear in southern Italy at the end of World War II. Ethnographic research on the impact of this new doctrine in a rural milieu was carried out principally in Accadia in the Apulia region, as well as in other places where the Unitarian doctrine developed (Gesualdo, Villanova in Campania; San Fele in Basilicata; Randazzo, Marsala in Sicily). Unitarian doctrine was then compared to certain neighboring Trinitarian Pentecostal groups (Anzano and Monteleone, also in Apulia).

The introduction of Pentecostalism and its growth in rural settings followed roughly the same pattern. Three distinct phases can be discerned: the conversion phase, followed either by the consolidation or rupture phase, and the institutionalization phase. Only the first phase will be considered: the phase of conversion, which is characterized by the arrival of a missionary in the village, vigorous proselytizing to his or her extended "family," the first baptisms (often collective), and persecution of the embryonic group by villagers, local clergy, and police.

For all Pentecostal groups studied, missionaries shared similar backgrounds: they were village natives who emigrated to the United States or Latin America at an early age and later converted to Pentecostalism. By its frequent use of glossolalia (speaking in tongues), Pentecostalism removes the obstacle of language among its faithful, and this has been shown to foster immigrants' integration into new environments (Wilson 1970). Pentecostal converts believe they are "saved" thanks to a new baptism and by the presence of the Holy Ghost within their bodies. As they become conscious of this different status, they return home to "save" their families.

After returning to their native villages, families react to the new doctrine according to their personal evaluation of the missionaries: if they have developed a reputation of "succeeding" in the United States or Latin America, the whole family converts. If, on the other hand, missionaries have a reputation of failure, they will be rejected. Moreover, missionaries seek to expand their circle of converts, but they do not search very far since their ambition is limited to converting persons with whom their family has ties. Nevertheless, their personal reputation and the social origin of their families determine the degree of success in native villages: the more modest the family origin, the more limited the success.

From the perspective of the convert, conversion is seen as following a "personal" calling—usually contained in a dream or after a long sickness—which they feel incapable of resisting. The "calling" is thereafter confirmed by a "gift" from the Holy Ghost, which, in southern Italy, is manifested mainly by glossolalia. In Accadia, the faithful who receive the gift of glossolalia display it prominently during prayers. Prayers are offered twice at every service and usually last twenty minutes or more (Di Bella 1982). During these prayer interludes, converts are on their knees, extemporizing aloud, or singing long litanies, punctuated by a collective "gloria, gloria, Gesù, Signore, halleluia."

Missionaries are not considered to be responsible for a believer's conversion to Pentecostalism; they are only carriers of Jesus' message. Glossolalia determines a convert's adherence to the faith. This involuntary emission of a message that in the speakers' regular language has no meaning (Di Bella 1988) is interpreted as a sign of the Holy Ghost's presence in their body or mind. It distinguishes the faithful who have been "touched" from the rest of the congregation, left unvisited by the Holy Ghost. Evidence of the Holy Ghost's "presence" is judged by the apparent lack of meaning in the message, with reference to a nonlinguistic code. Nonsense takes on a precise significance. It designates those among the faithful who are "different": the elect, the saint, the saved, the body-tabernacle chosen to receive the Holy Ghost.

Glossolalia establishes a difference between those who are "saved" and those who are not. At the same time, it establishes equality among the faithful who have been "saved" by the Holy Ghost. Whereas baptism separates the believer from the rest of the village, speaking in tongues differentiates the elect from the non-elect. This "gift" of tongues can raise significant barriers among adepts. For example, a marriage between a believer who has the "gift" of glossolalia and a believer who does not is frowned upon. Members who make no effort to receive the gift are ostracized, and those who do not receive it, despite many efforts, are pitied.

DIFFERENCES IN THE CONVERSIONS' RESULTS

Both examples focus on marginals (criminals in the first example, poor peasants in the second), but outcomes of their respective conversions are diametrically different. In the first example, ritual conducted by the *Bianchi* during the liminal period of three days and three nights becomes a necessary precondition to stage a theater of public consent in the streets of Palermo. It is the acquiescence of the condemned—to play dutifully the Christic role—that reintegrates him into the community, while his bodily sacrifice brings about sanctification.

In the second example, poor peasants who convert to Pentecostalism are doubly marginalized: first from their community of origin on the day they decide to leave the Catholic church, and second in their own group if they do not speak in tongues. Although converted or reconverted criminals acquire an enhanced status, provided they expire on the scaffold in the prescribed way, Pentecostal converts find themselves expelled from their original social positions and are confronted only by the presence of Jesus.

The social reintegration that follows conversion of the criminal is symbolic for it happens after death. For this reason, criminals were not allowed to say anything personal during the procession from the prison to the gallows so as not to disturb the symbolic order. For this same reason, criminals had to content themselves with repeating prescribed formulas learned by heart during the ladder exercise. Pentecostal believers, on the other hand, are left alone, but alive, in a dialogue that allows them to express freely their personal religious feelings and experiences, but in a way that limits communication with outsiders.

CONCLUSION

Language, ritual, and liminality are important elements in the study of conversion (Csordas 1997). In the two examples, the centripetal or centrifugal direction was illustrated by showing how, in the first case, acts were determined by the aims and processes of conversion, whereas in the second one the aims and processes of conversion were preceded and determined by acts. In both cases, language is seen as a disruptive force. The *Bianchi* confraternity managed to subdue disruption by convincing criminals to refrain from public language, whereas Pentecostals legitimize language through a nonlinguistic code that is understood only by the Holy Ghost. Ritual thus ranges from control to the encouragement of disruptive forces of self-expression. Finally, liminality highlights the transformation the converted has gone through by a sign easy to interpret: either by making the convert lose his capacity to talk or to see—as in the case of the criminal going to the gallows—or by encouraging the convert to speak in tongues—as in the Pentecostal case.

NOTE

I would like to thank Robert Anderson (British Museum) and the editors of this book for their help in looking over my English.

REFERENCES

Cassin, H. 1956. "Quelques facteurs historiques et sociaux de la diffusion du protestantism en Italie méridionale." *Archives de Sociologie des Religions* 2: 55–72.
———. 1960. "La Vie religieuse." In *La Calabre: Une région sous-développée de L'Europe méditerranéenne*, edited by J. Meyriat, pp. 225–61. Paris: Colin.
Castiglione, M. 1972. "Aspetti della diffusione del movimento pentecostale in Puglia." *Uomo e Cultura* 9: 102–18.
Courtine, J-J., ed. 1988. "Les glossolalies." *Langages* 91: 5–124.

Csordas, Thomas J. 1997. *Language, Charisma, and Creativity: The Ritual Life of a Religious Movement.* Berkeley: University of California Press.

Cutrera, A. 1917. *Cronologia dei giustiziati di Palermo 1541–1819.* Palermo: Scuola Tip. Boccone del povero.

De Certeau, M. 1980. "Utopies vocales: glossolalies." *Traverses* 20: 26–37.

Di Bella, M. P. 1982. "Un culte pentecôstiste dans les Pouilles." *Les Temps modernes* 435: 824–33.

———. 1988. "Langues et possession: le cas des pentecôtistes en Italie méridionale." *Annales ESC* 4: 897–907.

———. 1999a. *La Pura verità: Discarichi di coscienza intesi dai "Bianchi" (Palermo 1541–1820).* Palermo: Sellerio Editore.

———. 1999b. "L'*omertà* pietosa dei condannati a morte in Sicilia." *Prometeo* 68: 98–104.

Lewis, I. M. 1971. *Ecstatic Religion. An Anthropological Study of Spirit Possession and Shamanism.* Harmondsworth, UK: Penguin.

May, C. 1956. "A Survey of Glossolalia and Related Phenomena in Non-Christian Religions." *American Anthropologist* 58: 75–96.

Miegge, G. 1959. "La Diffusion du protestantisme dans les zones sous-dévoloppées de l'Italie méridionale." *Archives de Sociologie des Religions* 8: 81–96.

N.A. 1975. "Glossolalie". In *Encyclopaedia Universalis*, vol. 19, pp. 790–791. Paris: Encyclopaedia Universalis France.

Samarin, W. J. 1972. *Tongues of Men and Angels: The Religious Language of Pentecostalism.* New York: MacMillan.

Scotellaro, R. 1952. "Vita di Chironna evangelico." *Contadini del sud.* Bari: Laterza.

Seguy, J. 1972. "Les Non-conformismes religieux d'Occident." In *Histoire des Religions*, edited by H. C. Puech, vol. 2, pp. 1229–1303. Paris: Gallimard-Pléiade.

Wilson, B. R. 1959. "The Pentecostal Minister: Role Conflicts and Status Contradictions." *American Journal of Sociology* 64: 494–502.

———. 1970. *Les Sectes religieuses.* Paris: Hachette.

II

CONCEPTUALIZING CONVERSION:
ALTERNATIVE PERSPECTIVES

8

"I Discovered My Sin!": Aguaruna Evangelical Conversion Narratives

Robert J. Priest

Ducitak, a grandmother, began:

> I used to be *tudau* ("sinful"), *pegkegchau* (bad). I did many bad things *Apajui* (God) does not like. When I heard the word of *Apajui*, I discovered (*dekawami-ajai*) my sin (*tudau*), what I am. I said, "truly I am going to the place of fire (*ji-inumap*)." Thinking of this, I wept much. And so I "contracted myself" (*suju-mankamiajai*) to *Jisucristui*. Then I began to obey the word.

In the 1970s, many Aguaruna-Jívaro villages of northern Peru temporarily saw a majority convert to evangelical Christianity under the influence of Aguaruna evangelists. By the time of my field research (1987–1989), the number of active converts had stabilized at 10 percent to 30 percent in many villages. Aguaruna assistants helped me tape, transcribe, and translate thirty-four conversion narratives that form the base for this chapter.

The concept of sin seems to play a key role in Aguaruna conversion to Christianity. William James (1902) argued that a "sense of sin" accompanies a certain kind of personality characterized by a "sick soul" or a "divided" self. This sense of sin predisposes people to religious conversion but is itself simply a personality trait, apparently unconditioned by prior beliefs, symbols, and discourses. Others (e.g., Proudfoot 1985) argue that belief is prior to and constitutive of experience, and that only where people have been fully socialized to Christian beliefs is it possible to have a fully Christian conversion experience, complete with a "sense of sin." Indeed, anthropologists have sometimes implied that indigenous peoples, lacking such prior socialization, are unlikely to be moved by "sin discourses" (Kroeber 1948: 612; Mead 1949: 126, 164, 277; Sahlins 1996: 425)—and thus unlikely to experience genuine religious conversion to Christianity.

"Sin" does play a part in Aguaruna conversion narratives—with most narratives containing the same basic elements found in Ducitak's account above. However, they typically present preconversion lives as ones without prior socialization to Christian ideas and without a sense of sin. Puanchig, in his fifties, says, "In the times before following *Apajui* . . . I did not sense myself (*dakaptsaijai*) to be a sinner (*tudau*) and did not feel that what I did was bad." The idea of self as sinner is presented as an emergent understanding triggered by hearing the "word of *Apajui.*" Nuwakuk, in her forties, says: "[When] they announced the word of Apajui, I discovered about myself (*dekagmamawami-ajai*) that I was a sinner." Old man Wampagkit says that upon hearing "the word of Apajui . . . I saw/discovered (*wainmamkamiajai*) my sin (*pegkegchaujun*)." The theme of lacking a sense of sin is followed by an emergent discovery of self as sinner and by vigorous affirmations of the self as sinner: "Truly I am a sinner (*tudaunuk*)!" "I was very much of a sinner!" "I was very evil (*katseknuk*)!" "I am going to tell you how I worked badness (*pegkegchaun*)!" "I used to work much sin."

A sense of sin is emergent immediately prior to, or as an accompaniment to, conversion. It does not appear to have preexisted as a core personality trait or to have been structured by extensive prior socialization to Christian beliefs and practices. It is this emergent sense of self as sinner that I explore in this chapter. How are we to understand the statement "I discovered my sin"?

THE VOCABULARY OF SIN

When Aguaruna Christians characterize themselves as *pegkegchau*, *tudau*, *katsek*, *yajau*, *antuchu*, or *tsuwat*, they are using everyday vocabulary. Anything ugly, deformed, dirty, bad-tasting, damaged, or worthless is *pegkegchau*—"bad." Applied to people, it is a term of moral condemnation. Those who are thieves, adulterers, slanderers, stingy, lazy, or incestuous are labeled *pegkegchau. Tudau* carries exclusively moral connotations and is used to characterize anyone engaged in active transgressions like incest, bestiality, wife-beating, adultery, sexual exhibitionism, theft, and, above all, complaining about food one's wife or mother has prepared. It is not used for stigmatized but less active character traits like stinginess, gluttony, or laziness. *Katsek* has the underlying idea of "damage." It is used when one breaks a pot or burns down a house, whether accidental or not. But it is also used for adultery, theft, slander, homicide, fighting, and most disapproved behaviors—with the implication that these are socially damaging. *Yajau* is used of those who are cruel, brutish, malicious, or without normal moral sentiments. One who is *yajau*, I was told, maliciously kills his neighbor's animals, offers his sister to a passing stranger, molests women, carves images of female genitals along paths, and beats his mother, wife, child, or dog when angry. *Antuchu* means "doesn't listen" but is used to characterize anyone rebelling against right order. *Tsuwat* literally means "dirty" but is continually invoked in moral discourse. Slander is *tsuwat chicham* ("dirty speech") and the slanderer *tsuwat wenintin* ("one with a dirty mouth"). *Tsuwat anentaintin* ("one with a dirty heart") is someone who outwardly pretends good moral sentiments but is inwardly malevolent. One who "works filth" (*tsuwat takaamu*) is committing adultery or stealing.

"Discovery of sin" for Aguaruna is not a result of new vocabulary being learned. Contemporary Aguaruna Christians, like Old Testament Jews and New Testament Christians, employ multiple words from everyday moral discourse to speak of moral defect and failure. No Aguaruna, Hebrew, or Greek term has the distinctively religious connotations of our English word "sin." Theirs are everyday terms of moral disapproval that are also employed in religious discourse. The prior existence and deployment of such vocabulary in everyday moral discourse is a necessary, but not sufficient, precondition for the "sense of sin" found in Aguaruna conversions.

THE CONTENT OF MORAL IDEAS

But if the "discovery of self as sinner" is not contingent on new vocabulary, might it not be contingent on new moral ideas that reframe formerly innocent behaviors as sinful?

Conversion narratives touch on various sins. Sexual transgression is often mentioned: "I, with women, have worked much sin." Homicide figures prominently: "I killed two people, and then another, and another and another. Altogether I have killed five." Slander, mockery, and threat are often mentioned: "I mocked other people." "I spoke many bad words!" Sometimes bad thoughts are mentioned: "I thought many bad thoughts!" Wife-beating and theft are periodically referred to. And the sin of drinking or getting drunk from manioc beer is a constant refrain. As these are described, narrators occasionally voice the idea that formerly they did not see these as sinful. In the context of describing his own homicides, one Christian says, "I saw the killing which we Aguaruna do, and I thought it was good." In the context of listing his sins ("Drinking manioc beer, I beat my wife, and was a killer."), Puanchig stressed, "I did not understand that what I did was evil."

The sins converts referred to tended to be ones already traditionally disapproved. There are two clear exceptions to this. Traditionally manioc beer was a core staple, drunk from childhood. Mamai claimed that, as a child, she was told, "When we *nampeamu* (drink/party) without fighting, this makes Apajui happy." Although no other informant attributed such a sentiment to God, Mamai accurately captures the traditional emphasis. Manioc beer is a source of joy and pleasure. Moral warnings were against fighting, slandering, and pursuing affairs while drinking, not against drinking per se. Here, the moral message of evangelists, under the influence of Nazarene missionaries, was a teetotaler message. Drinking was reconfigured as core to other evils.

Dati, a leading Aguaruna evangelist, told a story of Satan (*Iwanch*) sacrificing a turkey, jaguar, and pig and pouring their blood over the plants from which alcoholic beverages derive. Satan's curse was that people who drink too much will get puffed up and proud like a turkey, then mean and bad tempered like a jaguar, and finally lie unconscious in their own filth on the ground. The audience laughed uproariously, and the story was retold all afternoon. Clearly, it was felt to reflect experienced realities. Aguaruna Christians describe preconversion lives where they frequently awoke after a *nampet* (drinking party) with shame, anger, and fighting. My observations and Harner's (1972: 110) support this description. But although most mark their conversion, in part, by their break with manioc beer, many subsequently modified their emphasis to an ethic of limited consumption—claiming to preach only what the ancestors taught: "Don't get drunk and fight." On another occasion, I heard Dati translating for a mestizo preacher. When he preached against the sin of drinking beer, Dati stopped translating and said forcefully, "We don't preach that here! You can preach against getting drunk, but not against drinking." Dati, himself a teetotaler, no longer preaches a teetotaler message. Many pastors have followed his lead. And yet conversion narratives usually treat the break with manioc beer as core.

The second marked contrast with preconversion morality concerns attitudes toward *ikmat*—"revenge." Traditional moral discourse focused on a rhetoric of *diwi*, or "debt." Every death had to be avenged, thereby canceling the debt. Under Aguaruna ideology, adult deaths were due either to physical violence or to witchcraft (witches in this culture being male). And since every death had to be avenged, homicide rates were high among Jivaroan groups. According to Michael Brown's (1984: 197) study, 37 percent of adult male deaths were due to homicide—which he says is lower than in the past. Jane Ross's study of the less acculturated Achuar-Jívaro found that 59 percent of adult male deaths were due to homicide, significantly higher than rates (21 percent and 41 percent) reported for the Yanomami (Ross 1980: 46). When an Aguaruna Christian says, "I saw the killing which we . . . do, and thought it was good," he accurately reflects traditional sentiment. Aguaruna homicide is motivated by indignation and justified as a righteous act of righting a prior wrong. Every killer's narrative begins with some other person's unjustified homicide, which the killer is rectifying through a fully righteous act of *ikmat*—which cancels the *diwi*. Since homicides were normally carried out by a group of men, each spearing or shooting into the body and sharing credit for the killing, and since male standing was directly dependent on participating in such violent acts, most older men have participated in multiple killings. (For fuller treatment of Aguaruna homicide, see Priest 1993: 244–353.)

Conversion narratives stress radical renunciation of a retaliatory ethic. As evangelists stressed, "Unless you forgive others, Apajui will not forgive you." Wishu comments, "I did not know forgiveness until I followed Apajui. Those who do me harm, I know Apajui will punish, so I do not worry." And again, "When my wife was unfaithful, and when they killed my brother, I made no threats. I just told it to Apajui alone." Dawai says, "My wife had an affair . . . but I did not beat her. I treated her well." Albino describes a man beating him up for an imagined offense: "I did not retaliate. I only said, 'brother, I reply in the name of Apajui. In vain you do this, but I forgive you.'" Some traditionalists complain bitterly that pastors "protect witches" from being killed. Pastors defend accused witches not because they disbelieve the witchcraft charge, but because God alone has the right to avenge a death. When one old man, Wampagkit, went blind, others attributed it to witchcraft and asked his authorization to retaliate against the witch. He refused, saying, "If my enemy has harmed me, Apajui will defend me when he comes."

When Aguaruna converts identify *nampet* (drinking/partying) or homicide and other retaliatory acts as sins they have repented of, it appears that the "discovery of self as sinner" is at least partially based on a recoding as sinful of what was formerly approved. This does not fully explain the emergent sense of self as sinner, however, since a majority of confessed sins are of a sort already disapproved of within traditional culture.

BEFORE GOD

Elderly converts report minimal knowledge of Apajui prior to conversion. Mamai says, "In former times we did not know of Apajui. The old ones just said, 'Apajui made the earth, and he lives. He will destroy it.'" Apajui is featured in two traditional myths. In one, Apajui and Kumpanam lived on opposite cliffs where the Marañon River cuts through the last ridge of mountains. Apajui forbade Kumpanam from looking at his daughter. When Kumpanam disobeyed, thus impregnating Apajui's daughter, Apajui left in anger for the sky. In another myth, Apajui comes to Earth, dirty and hungry, seeking lodging. He is mocked and turned away. In anger, he announces a flood. One family extended hospitality, so he told them to build a balsa raft, put dirt on it, plant crops, and build a house. The incestuous and those who killed "in vain" (without justification) were excluded. Contact with the rain by any who committed incest resulted in their flesh liquefying. Adults were not to look at the sky, lest they die. As the water rose, threatening to crush them against the sky, children who were sexually innocent were told to put a staff through the roof and tap three times on the sky—at which point Apajui caused the waters to recede.

The first of these myths corresponds to myths reported around the world of a high god who withdraws from humankind after some transgression. The second corresponds to similar flood myths reported in traditional societies around the world. Whether or not such stories antedate or reflect European influences, they were deeply entrenched as traditional stories prior to the first sustained presence of missionaries in the late 1920s.

Missionaries initially rejected Apajui as a term for God and used "Tatayus"—a hybrid from Spanish and Quechua. But in the early 1960s, when converts were observed addressing Apajui in prayer, missionaries concluded that Apajui was an acceptable term for God. By the time of my fieldwork, Tatayus was seldom mentioned.

The emergent sense of sin reported by Aguaruna converts is directly dependent on discourses about Apajui, discourses reporting on "words" understood as those of Apajui. Wampagkit describes his early life,

> I lived in vain. . . . I was a *nampen* (drinker/partier), and a fighter. When someone would be killed I would participate. My one desire was to be *Kakajam*. I would mock other people. Living like this, I was happy. . . . I was not following Apajui. Why? Because there was no one yet announcing the word of Apajui. At that time I heard those who were announcing the word of Apajui, a good word. And so I too followed Apajui. There I saw/discovered (*wainmamkamiajai*) my sin (*pegkegchaujun*). I said, "It is true. I have done that which Apajui does not like." And so I followed *apu Jisusan.*

REVERSING THE DIRECTION OF MORAL ACCUSATION

If one compares traditional moral discourses against those of Christian converts, there does not appear to be a significant increase in the sheer number of times that words of moral accusation occur. But there is a shift in *where* accusation is directed. Traditionally, it is almost always directed against an "other," virtually never against "self." Some cultures encourage the individual to attribute misfortune to one's own moral failure ("moral causal ontology"), whereas others ("interpersonal causal ontology") locate the source of misfortune in another's evil (Shweder, Much, Mahapatra, and Park 1997:

120–23). Aguaruna culture exemplifies the latter. That is, virtually every misfortune triggers the quest for a guilty "other."

Under Aguaruna ideology, a witch may be unaware he is a witch. But his envy, hatred, anger, resentment, jealousy, and animosity toward another have the mystical power to inflict sickness and death. In a typical scenario, when someone is dying, a diagnostic process commences that includes social assessments of the sentiments of neighboring men toward the dying person. Of course, in a face-to-face community, where neighboring men have competed for the few marriageable women, where individuals have cuckolded one another, where some consistently have abundant food while others suffer with less, and where gossip stirs resentments, animosities, and remembered grudges, there will often be many whose known or suspected sentiments make them prime suspects. And since every death must be avenged, every impending death triggers a diffuse anxiety over who will be blamed as witch and killed. A few weeks earlier, many may have clearly demonstrated envy, anger, or resentment toward a healthy individual. As illness brings this person close to death, however, the whole community shifts dramatically into a mode of absolute solidarity with the victim, with vigorous pronouncements of righteous indignation against the evil witch and a proclaimed willingness to avenge the death of "my brother." Each individual denies any witch-like sentiments within the self, adopts a moral stance of righteous indignation, and joins in a communal act of identifying some other individual as the sole repository of evil who must be eliminated by a righteous act of homicide. People kill witches for the very traits often exemplified in their own lives.

Although witch discourse is only one part of moral discourse, it exemplifies a consistent tendency of traditional Aguaruna discourse to apply terms of moral evil to "others" and almost never to "self." "I discovered my sin!" is notable, not for its moral vocabulary but for directing the accusing words against the self. Conversion narratives, in agreement with the judgment of Apajui, direct words of moral accusation against the self in a fundamental divergence from patterns in the traditional culture. Conversion narratives name the sins of the self in a context of repentance, confession, and renunciation.

FEAR AND TREMBLING BEFORE GOD

Mamai's reference to Apajui destroying the earth doubtless draws on the flood myth and on the belief that earthquakes are sent by Apajui. In 1928, between May and December, there was a series of earthquakes and aftershocks in this region measuring up to 7.3 on the Richter scale. I recorded numerous Aguaruna accounts of this, including eight eyewitness accounts. Aguaruna accounts describe landslides, salt springs pouring into rivers and killing fish, and crevasses splitting houses in half. Night animals called out in daytime, and day animals at night. Children were told not to "mock them." People gathered in large homes. They spoke in whispers. It was said Apajui was angry and would destroy people for being *tsuwat*—dirty. Rumors spread that women who had killed their infants would be eaten by worms. No one should have sex lest Apajui be angry. The incestuous and those who had killed unjustifiably were to be socially excluded lest everyone be destroyed. The flesh of the incestuous would dissolve into liquid. Some said a flood would destroy the world. Apajui, it was said, would send his chicken as a test. Narrators report that animals (e.g., opossum, anteater, armadillo, cat, and turkey) entered homes and acted tame. These were said to be the "animals of Apajui," which should be cared for, fed, and released, lest Apajui be angry. People danced and sang to Apajui, asking why he created them if he is now destroying them. "For what sin (*tudau*) do you now destroy us?" They asked for pity and called attention to their crying children or whimpering dogs. Later, the consensus emerged that this dancing must be done nude. Men and women undressed and danced, facing away from each other, holding up babies or puppies as they looked to the sky and asked for pity: "Apajui, you see all of me, as I was born. Have pity. Have pity on my crying baby." As they danced, the earthquake calmed. Men and women were not to look at each other, but some "bad men" did not fear and looked at women, or reached out to touch them. Each time this happened, the earthquake would start again. Adults eventually tired. The children now sang and danced, puppies held up to Apajui. In some accounts, only when the children danced, did the quakes stop. This event resulted in no lasting religious changes, but the story, frequently retold, highlights Apajui as one who brings judgment.

Fear of judgment by Apajui clearly contributes to many conversions. Anquash describes visiting a village when an earthquake occurred: "I told them, don't be afraid of the earthquake. It is Apajui you should fear. He is fearsome (*ishamainuk*). When I said this, everyone from Putjuk contracted themselves (to Apajui)." Wishu said,

> I lived in vain, killing people, getting drunk, fighting and talking in vain. Antonio announced the word of Apajui, that those not contracted to Apajui will not go to heaven (*nayaimpinmak*) but to the place of fire. And so I said, better that I contract myself to Apajui.

Chijiap provides a similar account and concludes, "Because I saw the danger, I followed Apajui." In the context of discovering herself to be a sinner, Ducitak told herself, "'Truly I am going to the place of fire.' Thinking of this I wept much." Chamik heard the word of Apajui but rejected it. Later, as he returned from participating in a homicide, he reports becoming overwhelmed with fear, "thinking what would happen to me if I did not deliver myself to Apajui." A year later, he did so. Anquash, a self-described womanizer and killer, reports having been warned, "If you don't leave your sin (*tudau*), you will suffer very much." The emergent sense of sin is, in part, an emergent fear of deserved punishment. Prior fears of retaliation by an enemy now become fear of punishment by an all-seeing and righteous God.

FORGIVENESS AND SALVATION

Dawai ends his lengthy narrative with a two-sentence summary: "Before I was a drunkard, a fighter (*manin*) and bad (*pegkegchau*). . . . Now I know what sin is, but I also know who Jesus Christ is." Esach, after months of inner turmoil over his spiritual state triggered by the death of a son, describes going to a pastor's house: "I wept when I spoke with him. He told me that it was for my sin that Jesus died. And so I confessed my life before Apajui." "Jesus is able to 'throw out' sin," Tiwi affirms. Anquash explains, "I asked Apajui to forgive me (*tsagkugtugta*), to erase (*esakatjugta*) my sin."

Conversion narratives maintain a clear focus on two alternatives, heaven (*nayainpinmak*) and hell (*jinum*). As sinners, people deserve hell. But for those who renounce sin, seek forgiveness based on the death of Jesus, and "contract themselves to" Apajui, there is forgiveness. Occasionally converts describe dreams that feature heaven. Wishu describes a dream in which he followed the "path of Apajui." Beautiful flowers, delicious fruit, and perfumed birds are encountered.

I also saw the doves of Apajui. Their breast was the color of gold, and they sang beautifully. The houses which I saw from a distance were very beautiful. A being told me, "you are going to live here. Even though you will suffer, don't be disturbed. Your suffering on earth will be in vain." Telling me all, he showed me the things of heaven. Even now I do not forget the things Apajui showed me.

In other narratives, individuals describe "dying" and being denied admittance to a large house filled with followers of Apajui. Reviving, they "contract themselves" to Apajui.

THE GOOD PATH

Aguaruna conversion narratives construct a vision of two alternative ways of life. Puanchig says, "Dati preached the word of Apajui and the good path. He preached that a follower of Apajui should not slander. From there I became a true follower of Apajui." He was also influenced by a dream in which "I saw the dove of Apajui. It signaled me saying that this is the path of Apajui. And so I contracted myself (to Apajui). Having contracted myself, I felt good." Repeatedly one hears of dreams in which two paths are faced, and the journey language of following a path or of following Apajui is frequent. Repeatedly "the good path" and "good words" and "the word of Apajui" are linked. "Truly the word of Apajui is good" (Tiwi). "Now I live following good words" (Shimpu). "I heard good words about Apajui" (Cruz). "I also want the good path" (Tiwi). Perhaps the most common phrase describing conversion is simply, "I followed (*nemagkamiajai*) Apajui."

Preconversion lives are frequently presented as lives of personal disorder. "I drank much, sometimes well, sometimes badly. Many times I fought. Village leaders put me in jail. But this didn't stop me. I drank much, killed someone, and attacked others (verbally). Those who followed Apajui I criticized. I beat my wife, and injured her, so that her brothers beat me up" (Ujukam). Drinking, retaliatory violence, slander, and marital fights and breakups are typically featured as paradigmatic elements in a way of life subsequently renounced in conversion. Testimonies and preaching construct a model of the good life characterized by peace, forgiveness, love, sobriety, and fidelity. This good life is found by following Apajui and his word. For converts, it was not simply the condemnatory aspects of the religious message that motivated them, but also the alternative vision of a good life. "With the word of Apajui, we live in peace," says Chamik, a former killer.

This is a society with a high rate of female suicide. In Brown's (1984: 197) research, 58 percent of adult female deaths were due to suicide. And in my own case material, it is clear that a majority of these are directly related to the quality of marital relationships. The stories of suffering that women tell, frequently as a result of the men in their lives, are poignant. The path of Apajui provides new ideals. As Unug describes her conversion, following that of her husband, she tells how, at his initiative, they made a promise never to leave each other. "Very beautiful it is, to follow Apajui's path," she concludes.

Many communities initially responded in mass to the new vision of peace, stability, and love. Expectations, for some at least, were utopian. The break with manioc beer was not sustained by many. Gossip, resentments, and bad feelings did not fully disappear. Conversion narratives describe great struggles, on occasion, with sexual desire, desire for manioc beer, and the wish to retaliate against some offender. Many failed to maintain the new standards and either temporarily or permanently dropped out of church life.

"The good path" was not fully instantiated in the lives of converts. But this attractive image of the good is sustained in discourse, partially exemplified in the lives of converts, and provides the context for discourses about sin. The discovery of self as sinner is in part a result of an alternative vision of the good life, against which specific actions and patterns are discovered to be sinfully problematic. As converts heard the word of Apajui—a word about the good, not just about the bad—they discovered themselves to be sinners.

APAJUI AS COMPANION AND GUIDE

Although the theme of escape from punishment is one component of these narratives, a more central theme is that of entering into a personal relationship with Apajui. Entsakua reports:

I contracted myself to Jesus. I came to know that Apajui loves us. I began to obey Apajui. Before I knew Apajui I could not travel alone. After I contracted myself to Jesus, when I traveled I felt as it there were two of us going together. Now, praying to Apajui, I travel at night to hunt, without fear.

Wishu describes a dream he had at conversion: "Apajui put fragrant medicine in my hair and bathed me. He said, I will never leave you. You are my son. Upon awakening, my body had a fragrant smell. And I prayed to Apajui with deep desire." Mamai says, "When I contracted myself, I felt very contented, light and good. I prayed all day to Apajui." Jempets describes his conversion: "I was very happy. With Apajui close by always, to talk to. And so I prayed to Apajui, asking what I should do. Every day I prayed." Again and again when narrators describe sufferings undergone, they stress the companionship of Apajui. Fifty-year-old Mamai describes her travails: "Although I suffered much, I never left Apajui. . . . Although I suffer, I am with Apajui. . . . When I get sick, no one cares for me . . . but I have Apajui. . . . I have suffered much. . . . But whatever the sorrow, it passes. In the new life there are other thoughts. We receive joy from Apajui." Again and again, Wishu intersperses accounts of his afflictions with comments like "Even if I walk alone, I am with Apajui" and "Although I suffer, I go on with Apajui. Apajui is always with me." Puanchig says,

Having converted, I felt good. It seemed the spirit (*wakani*) lived in my heart, that it taught me and strengthened me. I went into the forest to pray. In this manner I lived, happy. And because I have tried it, I say it is good to pray. . . . It seems the spirit speaks in my heart, this way I feel what I should do, in my heart.

"Don't do this, truly you cannot do this, those who work the work of Apajui do not go about doing transgressions!" And I fear. While others commit faults, and I have the thought of eating someone else's fruit—whether papaya or peanuts—Into my heart comes the thought that followers of Apajui do not eat the produce of others, and this idea enters my heart. And so it is true what they say, that when the spirit dwells in us, it teaches us.

SIN AS ONGOING REALITY

Narratives stress sins abandoned and removed at conversion: "All my sins I left with Apajui" (Shimpu). But in fact their narratives reflect ongoing struggle with sin. After mentioning his many preconversion sexual affairs, one man comments, "Because I have worked sin so much, I do not feel sure of not sinning, although I try." A traveling evangelist laments. "It is hard to preach without sinning. . . . With the strong bad desire for women I suffer. . . . Although I have bad thoughts, I do not act on them." Another says, "At that time I confronted the powerful desire in my heart pushing me to sexual (sin). But I decided to resist." Another's narrative includes this: "Then I lusted greatly for many women. When this happened I went into the mountain to pray to Apajui. (After fasting and prayer) I felt like a child, without sexual desire." The struggle with thirst for manioc beer, and ongoing struggles with anger and the desire to retaliate for offenses and insults, are likewise frequent themes.

This chapter focuses on sin in Christian conversion, not sin in postconversion life. However, it is worth noting that in these narratives "sin" is a concept continually brought to bear in all phases of the Christian's life. It is ongoing subjective experiences related to struggling with sin that add greatly to the grip that this concept has on the lives of Aguaruna converts. Many Aguaruna who initially converted and subsequently left the church did so under circumstances involving what was understood both by them and by others as the inability or unwillingness to overcome some temptation to sin. Indeed, I repeatedly encountered evidence that many such individuals believed themselves to be in a state of sin that they someday expected to repent of or that they found themselves unable to extricate themselves from. Pujupat, a former convert, describes having been slandered as a follower of Apajui, subsequently having an affair, leaving the church, adding another wife, and returning to drink. Worrying that he was "being lost for good," he decided to spend time praying to Apajui: "I wept and went into the forest alone. I said to myself, 'when I do this, I will feel good and joyful.' But I felt only empty. I noted that Apajui did not speak to me, and that I was completely abandoned. So I understood. From that time until now I have not been restored in my soul (*wakan*). Until now I am like this." In his narrative, he goes on to try and figure out what went wrong in his own life. But his reasoning continues to operate within the framework of Christian symbolism. That is, fully ten years after leaving the church, Pujupat is gripped by a set of symbols—a pivotal one being that of sin.

In conversion, people grasp and are grasped by a system of symbols that tells them about themselves and that contributes to the construction of new selves (Stromberg 1985). One such symbol in evangelical discourses is sin, a core element in what Hallowell (1976: 24) identifies as Christianity's "folk anthropology." Evangelistic narratives of sin draw on traditional vocabulary, speak to lived experiences of transgression and moral failure, construct alternative visions of the good, proclaim the existence of a morally concerned deity, reconfigure self-identity around a shared sinful condition that requires conversion, and encourage an active process of personal transformation in accord with the "word of God" and grounded in a personal relationship with God. Personal testimony is the preferred form of communication—fusing together the symbolic and the experiential. Narratives examined in this chapter fuse together personal experience and religious symbol in a way that provides personal coherence and models the route to a new self. Even when the new self remains unattained, the new symbols continue to exert influence and authority not easily ignored.

REFERENCES

Brown, Michael. 1984. *Una Paz Incierta: Historia y cultura de las Comunidades Aguarunas Frente al Impacto de la Carretera Marginal.* Lima, Peru: CAAAP.

Hallowell, A. Irving. 1976. "The History of Anthropology as an Anthropological Problem." In *Contributions to Anthropology: Selected Papers of A. Irving Hallowell,* edited by Raymond D. Fogelson and Fred Eggan, pp. 21–35. Chicago: University of Chicago Press.

Harner, Michael. 1972. *The Jívaro.* Berkeley: University of California Press.

James, William. 1902. *The Varieties of Religious Experience.* Longman, Green, and Co.

Kroeber, Alfred. 1948. *Anthropology.* New York: Harcourt, Brace and World.

Mead, Margaret. 1949. *Coming of Age in Samoa.* New York: New American Library.

Priest, Robert J. 1993. *Defilement, Moral Purity, and Transgressive Power: The Symbolism of Filth in Aguaruna Jivaro Culture.* Ph.D. diss., University of California, Berkeley.

———. 2000. "Christian Theology, Sin, and Anthropology." In *Anthropology and Theology: God, Icons, and God-talk,* edited by Walter R. Adams and Frank A. Salamone, pp. 59–75. Lanham, Md.: University Press of America.

Proudfoot, Wayne. 1985. *Religious Experience.* Berkeley: University of California Press.

Ross, Jane B. 1980. "Ecology and the Problem of Tribe." In *Beyond the Myths of Culture*, edited by Eric B. Ross, pp. 33–60. New York: Academic Press.

Sahlins, Marshall. 1996. "The Sadness of Sweetness: The Native Anthropology of Western Cosmology." *Current Anthropology* 37: 395–428.

Shweder, Richard A., Nancy C. Much, Manamohan Mahapatra, and Lawrence Park. 1997. "The 'Big Three' of Morality and the 'Big Three' Explanations of Suffering." In *Morality and Health*, edited by Allan Brandt and Paul Rozin, pp. 119–69. New York: Routledge.

Stromberg, Peter G. 1985. "The impression Point: Synthesis of Symbol and Self." *Ethos* 13: 56–74.

9

Turning the Belly: Insights on Religious Conversion from New Guinea Gut Feelings

Roger Ivar Lohmann

In this chapter,[1] I present a glimpse of a Melanesian way of experiencing one's own mind and will, in which there is not one soul but two, and one's souls are not only internal but also external. Human volition and agency are most apparent to us when in flux and transition, and one of the greatest moments of change in the will occurs when one leaves behind one set of beliefs, morals, and relationships and embraces another during religious conversion. The people I describe are the Asabano, a group of 200 living in the mountainous rainforests of Papua New Guinea.

I present an ethnographic description emphasizing how Asabano understand religious belief and conversion to occur, based on their experience of rejecting their traditional religion for Baptist Christianity. The Asabano see conversion first of all as a change in relationships with supernatural beings and only secondarily as an affiliation with new beliefs and people. Moving beyond the Asabano perspective to my own theoretical one, I argue that supernatural beings are imagined and suggest that in the case of the Asabano conversion, at least, religious conversion involves discontinuing or severing relationships with certain supernatural beings in favor of others. The old spirits have not ceased to exist for Asabano; they are merely ignored. Extending from the Asabano case, I suggest that true, voluntary religious conversion be measured in terms of this change in relationships with supernatural beings and not simply in terms of "change in religious affiliation" or even "cosmological and moral assumptions," which are consequential (cf. Barker 1993: 199).

TURNING THE BELLY

Conversion is often described as turning—away from one way of being and toward another. In fact, turning and returning are literal meanings behind the biblical Hebrew and Greek terms for conversion (Rambo 1993: 3). Nock (1933: 7) calls it

> a reorientation of the soul of an individual, his deliberate turning from indifference or from an earlier form of piety to another, a turning which implies a consciousness that a great change is involved, that the old was wrong and the new is right.

Similarly, the Asabano and other speakers of the creole language Tok Pisin describe transformations as turning, or *tanim*. "Translation" is rendered "turning speech," or *tanim tok*; a witch may "turn [into a] pig," or *tanim pik*, to stalk human prey. When referring to religious conversion, the metaphor of rotation signifies not only a transformed understanding but also a new set of desires and actions. This turning takes place in the belly, where volition in the form of two souls is understood to originate. Thus, like Nock, the Asabano describe conversion as reorienting the soul through turning.

The notion of abdominally-residing volition, common in Melanesia, is also manifested in Tok Pisin expressions. One communicates anger by saying one's belly is hot, or *belhat*, and reaching consensus is described as being of one belly, or *wanbel*. Of course, in English one might speak of having butterflies in the stomach before a performance or a gut feeling that one has an immortal soul. Desire, tension, and even supernatural revelations can be experienced and linguistically described as changes in the rumblings of human bellies around the world.

It was through abdominal goings-on that the Asabano say they converted to Christianity. Asabano personify aspects of human volition as spirits that reside in the stomach and intestines, where they direct thoughts and actions. Belief in a spirit, the Asabano say, brings it into contact with the person, and the spirit's presence in turn causes new beliefs and ideas to appear. The expression *tanim bel* means literally to turn one's belly and can figuratively mean to change one's mind, affiliation, or feelings about something—in short, to convert.

For Asabano, however, describing religious conversion as a stomach turned is not merely a metaphorical usage. They say that they accepted beliefs introduced by Baptist missionaries only when the Holy Spirit literally entered and turned their bellies—changed the orientation of their minds. For Asabano, religious conversion means taking on new directing beings and expelling others from the multipartite self located in the digestive tract. Exchanging substances with others in Melanesia is the very essence of relationships, and it indicates spiritual interpenetration as well (see Stewart et al., 2001). Therefore, the relationships with supernatural beings that make up Asabano religious commitment do not involve two independent beings. For the Asabano, religious conversion entails a blending of the person's personified volitional drives with those of the supernatural being to whom devotion is declared.

THE ASABANO

The Asabano are an ethnic group of about 200 people who speak their own language (Lohmann 2000a). They live near the mountainous center of New Guinea, in remote and rugged forest near the turbulent river Fu. They are among the last of New Guinea's peoples to be contacted by the West, having been visited by an Australian colonial patrol for the first time in 1963.

At the time of this contact, the Asabano lived in several shifting hamlets, consisting of a communal great house where women and families slept, a men's clubhouse, and a women's menstrual house. The various small groups made a living by slash-and-burn gardening, hunting, pig raising, and gathering of wild foods. Their country was sparsely populated by groups speaking Asaba and five other languages. Groups made shifting alliances and war with one another in a series of paybacks that resulted in a continual threat of violence and abduction of women and children.

According to the Asabano traditional imagination, the world always existed. Founding ancestors changed the landscape and established human groups and customs. A supernatural world suffuses and coexists with physical reality, where spirits inhabit or can transform into physical objects. Pools, trees, and stones are associated with generally belligerent spirits that attack people by making them ill. Such illnesses are still considered the physical manifestation of soul capture. In the bush also dwell *wobuno*, sprite-like people in mystical villages who can help hunters by leading them in dreams to their wild pigs.

Living people too have supernatural aspects: a big soul responsible for generous thought and behavior and a little soul responsible for selfish thought and behavior (Lohmann 2003a). Some people's generous natures and good relationships with spirits lead them to become seers, making soul journeys to supernatural haunts and healing the sick. Other people, their large intestines (called *alikamayasaw* in Asaba) inhabited by anthropophagic baby animals, are compelled to ruthlessly kill by witchcraft and consume the flesh of their own family and friends. Big souls of the dead live in their own villages in known areas of the forest and are capable of helping people in war, pig raising, and gardening, especially when their bones are preserved and honored. Meanwhile, their little souls lurk at their gravesites, ready to attack the living.

Traditional religious practices included mythological training for boys in initiation rituals, in which secret myth versions and tabooed foods were presented amidst ordeals. Initiations were conducted away from women, who were thought to have debilitating effects on men and were forbidden to know the secrets of Asabano mythology. Prayers, offerings, and magic were directed at the spiritual world to ensure success in food procurement and military actions, the two most obsessive of traditional Asabano concerns.

By the early 1970s, the Australian government had halted most raiding. Bands of Asaba speakers who had been diminished by military defeats and influenza joined together at the edge of their territory to be nearer to the Australian patrol post at Telefomin. Ethnic Telefol missionaries led by a young pastor named Diyos, themselves first-generation converts of the Australian Baptist Missionary Society, set up a Bible college and an airstrip near the Asabano village. The place is now labeled Duranmin on maps, after the Telefol name for the Asabano.

Three years after the founding of the mission, Diyos presided over a charismatic revitalization movement known locally as the revival, in which virtually all Asabano converted to Christianity amid ecstatic religious experiences. In church services punctuated with spirited preaching, people collapsed and saw visions, spoke in tongues, and publicly confessed sins. Asabano people told me that these things happened because the Holy Spirit came down and entered people's bellies. They never mentioned which specific organs were involved—perhaps because this was an unfamiliar spirit whose residential seat in the human body was unknown, or to signify that he occupied the entire belly and thus brought all aspects of volition under his control.

They said that the Holy Spirit, through Diyos, demanded that men's initiation houses and ancestral bone sacra be burned. No more initiations were to be staged; no more offerings were to be made to local spirits, who were labeled demons aligned with Satan. Prayer to God and Jesus were to take the place of all dealings with local spirits. Several people, mostly women, had visions and dreams in which the Holy Spirit informed them that some men were continuing to hide sacra and make offerings to *wobuno*, tree spirits, and ancestors. The men, many of whom really were hedging their bets by retaining contacts with local spirits, were amazed when these revelations became public. They were further convinced not only that the Christian supernaturals were real but also that they demanded an exclusive relationship.

By the time I arrived in 1994 for a year and a half of fieldwork, their revival had become a Baptist church. Most people decried their traditional religion as a set of Satan-propagated deceptions designed to hide the existence of the

Christian god. They did not doubt that the local spirits existed, but they had self-consciously turned their backs on them in order to further their relationship with the Christian god and his associates, like Jesus, the Holy Spirit, and angels. There was much to be gained from this relationship, they told me (Lohmann 2001). Since Christianization, retributive raids and executions of accused witches had been stopped. Revenge was God's business, and they were freed from the responsibility to maintain the endless chain of paybacks. With the male-centered religion abolished, the complex food taboos were abandoned. God had made everything free for all to eat, pastors told them—only Satan declared that women and children should not be allowed to share. With Christian prayer, people said, gardens grew better and hunts were more successful.

To understand the Asabano conversion, we must examine their own experience and interpretation of what happened. I turn first to the Asabano theory of volition, so that their perspective on volitional changes like religious conversion are rendered sensible to the outsider.

ASABANO EXPLANATIONS OF VOLITION AND CONVERSION

Isaguo, a middle-aged woman who always called me "grandson," described how the Asabano accepted Christianity in the revival of 1977. One of the big moments was the advent of Christian "spirit work," when the Holy Spirit entered their bellies.

> Diyos and all the pastors and missionaries from big places came and told us [that God created the world], and we ourselves got spirit work and the [Holy] Spirit Himself explained this to us. When the revival came down, all of the men and women got the spirit work, and the Spirit said to leave the old customs. So we believed it. The movement [shaking, which accompanies possession] of the Holy Spirit must be true, so we believe it. We believe strongly, when we plant food, in only one or two months the food is already ready. It will grow fast and true, so we believe it must be true. Another thing is that when the men go hunting they kill more animals, so we believe God gives them this. We see the Holy Spirit come down and go into the belly of a man in visions, so we know God is true. I myself saw the Holy Spirit come down through the head and into the stomach. The Holy Spirit is like a bird, a dove [Asaba: *madibanedu*]. We saw this first and then we saw a picture of the Holy Spirit just like this afterwards—the pastors who came to preach showed us the picture. Also in dreams we see that, so we believe it. Starting with the revival we saw this. So we believe it's true.

The Asabano say that they converted because the Holy Spirit entered and turned their bellies, but what does this really mean? How do they model the mental ability to decide and act? Virtually all peoples model volition by invoking the supernatural (Lohmann 2003b). We often envision a little person at the controls: one who perceives, reacts, and directs the body. In most ethnopsychologies, this self, will, life-spark, or witness is equated with or related to an internal spirit that is also somehow external. Many peoples believe it able to leave the body during dreams and to remain alive and mobile after the body dies. Spiritual sources of volition may also be entirely external. European Christians sometimes excuse regretted actions by saying "the Devil made me do it" or by crediting their creations to God, who used the human artist as a mere vehicle. These are versions of classic religious beliefs that are found among practically all peoples in the world, including the Asabano.

Whereas many Europeans imagine the personal volitional agent to reside in the head, the Asabano believe volitional beings are in the torso and are particularly associated with the intestines, called *alisaw* in Asaba, but also with the heart or *sosabu*, which is linked to caring for others. Witches supposedly have their hearts cut out in their nefarious initiations so that when their intestinal animal spirits demand human flesh, they will feel no compunction against killing their own family members.

For most Europeans, the individual's volition is understood by definition to be internal, with "possession" by an external spirit considered to be a fairly unusual and unnatural condition (see Goodman 1988). For Asabano, spiritual control of the individual, in the form of competing actions of both internal and external volitional agents, is considered the normal condition of life. They see plentiful evidence for this in the form of people's changing their minds, behaving generously some times and stingily other times, having awareness of certain ideas sometimes and others at other times, and wandering about in dreams while the immobile body remains alive.

As Guthrie (1993) convincingly argues, anthropomorphism is ubiquitous in religion. Virtually all peoples use anthropomorphic images to model volition, seeing whole, humanlike, more or less ethereal beings of a supernatural kind—"souls"—as responsible for human thought and action. The Asabano carry this supernatural image of the self farther than most Europeans, personifying volition very literally, seeing all beliefs and desires as spirit-manifestations. These intestinally dwelling beings direct the thoughts and actions of their human host. The person is not understood to be a completely independent being that merely reacts to them but is rather *made up of* these various spiritual influences that are also influencing others. This is at least one of the important ways that Melanesians experience themselves as much more interconnected "dividuals" than the isolated individuals of Western ethnopsychologies (cf. Strathern 1988).

Asabano traditional belief divides human volition into two basic kinds: greedy and generous. Greed, epitomized by hiding to eat alone rather than sharing, is selfish and promotes isolation. Generosity is epitomized by sharing and socializing, promoting relationships and goodwill. Asabano consider both of these volitional phases to be integral to the person—it is impossible for one to be completely good or bad, but it is common for one side to dominate under certain conditions. They model these volitional forces as two souls. As noted above, the generous side is called the "big soul" and lives in the stomach, called in Asaba *alialubu*, and the greedy side is called the "little soul" and lives in the small intestines or *alikamalanesaw*. In waking life, the big soul is with the body, promoting smooth relations with others, called in Tok Pisin *belisi* or "tranquil belly." In dreams and death, the superego-like big soul leaves the body. The id-like little soul remains closely associated with the body at all times, heating the belly by promoting selfish desires and antisocial behaviors like fighting and anger or *belhat*. Even at death, the little soul stays at the forest gravesite where it may maliciously attack the living.

Traditional Asabano religion was concerned with managing relationships with spirits. They made use of antisocial feelings by directing the little soul's taunts at outside groups in the form of payback raids, while encouraging the big soul's generosity within the group. They minimized contacts with dangerous spirits of natural objects by maintaining silence in known haunts, and they made them offerings to achieve the return of ill people's souls. Positive relations with *wobuno* were sought through offerings to ensure good hunts. *Wobuno* were supposed to sit on smokers' backs during tobacco-enhanced consultations and tell them what to say.

No one ever spoke of *wobuno* or nature spirits as actually entering the belly to direct people's thoughts and actions. Ironically, the intestinally dwelling witchcraft spirit serves as the model for conversion to Christianity because in both cases one's own will is taken over by an entering spirit. Whereas the witchcraft spirits direct a person to murder and cannibalism, the Holy Spirit allows completely positive relations with others and makes a harmonious life and afterlife possible.

Asabano explain that Christian belief, or *bilip* in Tok Pisin, means establishing a relationship with God by allowing the Holy Spirit to live in the belly. Remaining in close contact with the person, the Holy Spirit causes new feelings, thoughts, convictions, and ideas to appear, and it directs future actions. The Christian expression "God is my copilot," if taken quite literally, captures something of the sense of how Asabano experience this relationship with volitional beings in their world. When Asabano people describe their acceptance of Jesus' sacrifice and their belief in God the father or *Papa God*, as they routinely call him, they point to the Holy Spirit's presence in their bellies as having made this possible.

At the time of my fieldwork, I heard people describing their big soul as though it were somehow identical to the Holy Spirit and their little soul as though it were the same as Satan. I found myself drawing on my own cultural background to build a mental image of this equation. Recalling Saturday morning cartoons of my childhood, I pictured a cartoon devil on one shoulder encouraging naughtiness and an angel on the other urging restraint. Sometimes informants described their souls as free agents, but other comments showed that they thought of them as being closely tied or even identical to the grand external personifications of good and evil, God and Satan.

To summarize, in the Asabano view, multiple beings are responsible for human awareness and volition. Some are more idiosyncratic and internal, but others are more universal and external. They interact and even merge in the belly to result in the flow of images and thoughts that make up conscious awareness. Depending on which among these spirits are able to share residence in the belly and which are excluded or dominated by those already active there, one's belly will be turned toward this way of being or that. To behave wickedly is to nurture one's relationship with, or one's own aspect of, greedy, witch-like, or Satanic beings to the exclusion and suppression of one's generous or godly beings. To be virtuous is to maintain strong relationships with the personified sources of generous social behavior.

For Asabano, to convert from one religion to another is to reduce contact with or expel some directing spirits from one's belly and to increase contact and interactions with other directing spirits, taking them into the belly and thus making them quite literally a part of the new person. From the Asabano point of view, converting from traditional religion to Christianity involved allying one's big soul with an even bigger soul of similar disposition: the Holy Spirit.

CONVERSION AND RELATIONSHIPS WITH IMAGINARY BEINGS

Religious adherence usually has a relationship with supernatural beings at its center. A committed relationship with God is at the heart of what Asabano mean when they say "belief." Belief as a contractual, kinship, or love relationship with imagined beings provides not only intellectual satisfaction but also the enriched emotional life and sense of loyalty and obligation that come with all kinds of relationships. This accounts for the social rather than merely intellectual quality of religious experience and identity—something that is quite lacking in one-way relationships with ideas.

We have in religious relationships with imagined others what Buber (1958) calls the "I-you" relationship—a mutual dialogical relationship between two knowing beings. He contrasted this with one-way "I-it" functional relationships such as that between a person and a nonliving thing. Religious believers accept the existence of spiritual beings as "real" in the sense that they have consciousness and the ability to engage in mutual relationships with people. The I-you relationships with supernatural beings in religious belief, broken and reforged in conversion, are real in that people experience them. However, they are imaginary in that they originate in the mind as personified models of subconscious or apparently autonomous feelings and thoughts, such as those that come to us unbidden in dreams or when we are of two minds about something.

In Mead's (1930) classic study of Manus Island childrearing, she found that children only came to believe in spirits after they were introduced to them by their parents. Being told of spirits' or gods' existence as children, people can imagine that they exist in theory by exercising the intellect. The social support makes the supernatural seem so plausible that people often take its existence for granted even without having any direct religious experiences. Later, people often come to have an emotional stake in the assumed existence of spiritual beings because they begin to relate to these imaginary beings as though they were physical people. Talking to supernatural beings in prayer and interpreting natural happenings as their responses, human lives become entwined with them. This can be intensified in religious experience when the person perceives a direct encounter with the spirit, typically in dream or trance as was common in the Asabano revival. Direct religious experiences are highly convincing as evidence and as emotional assurance of one's relationship with a supernatural other. Encountering a spirit representative of a new religion provides a potent catalyst to religious conversion (Lohmann 2000b).

True conversion means taking on a relationship with new supernatural beings and possibly (but not necessarily) severing relationships with old ones. When advocates teach novices new bodies of mythology, it may at first be remembered as a list of beliefs. But novices do not truly adopt the beliefs and become true converts except as a consequence of establishing imagined relationships with the new supernatural beings who feature in the introduced myths.

When the Asabano describe the Holy Spirit turning their bellies, this shows that an experience of relation with a greater, outside, humanlike being commandeering the person's volitional controls is how Asabano perceive and model conversion. Consider this testimony by Peter, the headman of Yakob village, describing how he became a serious Christian. "I was a willful boy and used to hit my sisters. I wouldn't close my eyes when we prayed. Then I changed and I thought it must be God who had turned my belly, when I realized that these ways were no good." Only after Peter felt that God had entered into a relational, volitional exchange with him did he accept the value of Christian morality and belief.

When conceptualizing religions as a set of beliefs, it is easy to forget that converts' acceptance of beliefs and dogmas is often a secondary consequence to their choosing a social relationship with imagined beings (and their physical representatives, missionaries and other advocates). The beliefs about heavenly or cargoistic rewards that attract Christian-influenced Melanesians are but consequences of a relationship with God and his associates. A person may accept a new relationship with a recently introduced supernatural being in part because of perceived benefits, such as promises of wealth or happiness. But there is also often a sense in the convert that his or her own will has been surrendered to the supernatural being who is the focus of the new religion, and the supposed rewards are but fringe benefits.

In a survey of religious conversion, Rambo (1993: 132) writes, "The experience of surrender is, for many converts, the turning point away from the old life and the beginning of a new life, produced not by one's own controlling volition but by the power of God's grace." Conversion involves changing one's beliefs and morals, but only because of an interaction between one's own volition and that of the supernatural being into whose service one is embarking.

Depending on what characteristics particular supernatural beings have, different kinds of relationships with them are possible. Religions featuring supernaturals depicted as universally welcoming, regardless of the convert's ethnic or family background, are able to spread in a variety of social conditions, whereas those featuring ethnocentric gods and spirits allow scant possibilities for relationships with outsiders (cf. Horton 1971).

In his introduction to a collection of essays on conversion to Christianity, Hefner (1993) points out that the world religions all have their origin in early civilizations, and as such arose in response to the new problems presented by multiethnic state-level societies. What makes them so successful, he argues, is the link in their ideologies between a strong transcendentalism, with an implication that human life can be dramatically transformed for the better, and institutionalized proselytizing. This combination has produced "religions that are without parallel in human history. Political empires and economic systems have come and gone, but the world religions have survived. They are the longest lasting of civilization's primary institutions" (Hefner 1993: 34). These observations hint at how different kinds of social relationships in the human world make relevant and appealing distinctive types of imagined supernatural relationships. My point was made somewhat differently, of course, by Durkheim (1965 [1915]) when he theorized that totems and gods are emblems that allow people to worship their own societies.

Social scientists often stress the importance of relationships with religious group leaders, missionaries, and other human advocates in the religious society that the new convert joins. For example, converts may be drawn to a prophet's charisma (Burridge 1995 [1960]; Lindholm 1990; Weber 1963 [1922]). They enjoy a sense of belonging in a group that is centered on the same beliefs (Weininger 1955). And they can more easily rationalize and indulge in the attractive spiritual beliefs of the group through socially reinforced plausibility (Berger 1980). These are some of the many benefits and consequences of the new human relationships taken up in conversion (see Rambo 1993: 108–113). But there is much to learn from shifting our attention away from the relationships among members of a newly joined religious group to see those inside the convert's own imagination. Here are the relationships for which religious people themselves say they convert: mystical exchanges of volition among supernatural personas—souls and other spirits, mixing and exchanging desires and wills.

At the heart of much religion lies a sense of social relationship with imaginary supernatural beings. These beings are in fact parts of the self that appear autonomous, that appear "wholly other," to use Otto's (1958 [1923]) classic phrase. Thus, we see kinship or companionable terms being applied to supernatural beings (Rambo 1993: 160–61). For example, the Asabano call the Christian deity "Father God." This accounts for a number of emotions associated with religious conversion experiences: mystery and awe from the familiar yet strange sense of another being's presence in one's own mind, and comfort or fear as is elicited by any number of interactions with another social being. A sense of conflicting or embraced loyalty and caring are common in any emotionally salient human relationship. To convert, then, becomes an abandonment of one set of relationships with imagined beings *as well as* physical persons, and their replacement with a new set.

We can learn much about changing imaginary relationships in religious conversion by looking at how people behave in changing relationships with their rejected spirits and with physical people. Entering into relationships with a new set of supernatural beings, one carries manners of relating that were developed in the old relationships. For example, new Asabano converts to Christianity related to the Holy Spirit as though he were one of the *wobuno*, praying to incubate dreams in which he appeared with hunting information. This enables them to approach him through enacting their own relational schemas.

CONCLUSION

In this chapter, I described how Asabano themselves modeled their religious conversion to Christianity as the Holy Spirit's entering into their bellies and changing their volitional tendencies. They stressed a relationship with new supernatural beings as being at the heart of their conversion.

I have argued that by simply thinking of religions as institutionalized sets of lifeless beliefs, we miss the point that to most believers, relationships with supernatural beings are central elements of religion. These relationships are learned, of course, and exist only in the imagination, but they remain real and important to those who hold them. When religion is understood as mere cosmology and mythology, explanations for conversion can look only to the relative appeal of different theories and accounts of the supernatural. Religion appears to be nothing but a list of belief propositions. However, the personification of mental agents connects these beliefs in the idiom of group identity and loyalty. Religious conversion is, therefore, something profound—a global paradigm shift, or the transformation of relationships—rather than the mere acceptance and endorsement of a few new ideas.

NOTE

1. Versions of this chapter were presented as a Mind, Medicine, and Culture Seminar at the Department of Anthropology, University of California, Los Angeles on March 11, 2002; as a research talk at the Department of Anthropology, Central Washington University, Ellensburg, Washington, on April 2, 2002; as a colloquium at the Department of Anthropology, Bowdoin College, Brunswick, Maine, on April 5, 2002; as a part of the session "Religious Discourse and the Global Context," chaired by Phil Stevens at a meeting of the Society for the Anthropology of Religion, Cleveland, Ohio, April 6, 2002; as a guest presentation for The Sociology and Anthropology Club at The College of Wooster, Wooster, Ohio, on April 16, 2002; and as a research talk at the Department of Anthropology, Grand Valley State University, Allendale, Michigan, on January 31, 2003. I thank my listeners for their encouragement, stimulating questions, and insightful comments.

REFERENCES

Barker, John. 1993. "'We are Ekelesia': Conversion in Uiaku, Papua New Guinea." In *Conversion to Christianity: Historical and Anthropological Perspectives on a Great Transformation*, edited by R. W. Hefner, pp. 199–230. Berkeley: University of California Press.

Berger, Peter L. 1980. *The Heretical Imperative*. Garden City, N.Y.: Doubleday.

Buber, Martin. 1958. *I and Thou*. New York: Charles Scribner's Sons.

Burridge, Kenelm. 1995 [1960]. *Mambu: A Melanesian Millennium*. Princeton, N.J.: Princeton University Press.

Durkheim, Emile. 1965 [1915]. *The Elementary Forms of the Religious Life*. New York: MacMillan Publishing.

Goodman, Felicitas D. 1988. *How About Demons? Possession and Exorcism in the Modern World*. Bloomington: Indiana University Press.

Guthrie, Stewart Elliott. 1993. *Faces in the Clouds: A New Theory of Religion*. Oxford: Oxford University Press.

Hefner, Robert W. 1993. "Introduction: World Building and the Rationality of Conversion." In *Conversion to Christianity: Historical and Anthropological Perspectives on a Great Transformation*, edited by R. W. Hefner, pp. 3–44. Berkeley: University of California Press.

Horton, Robin. 1971. "African Conversion." *Africa* 41: 85–108.

Lindholm, Charles. 1990. *Charisma*. London: Basil Blackwell.

Lohmann, Roger Ivar. 2000a. *Cultural Reception in the Contact and Conversion History of the Asabano of Papua New Guinea*. Ph.D. diss., University of Wisconsin-Madison.

———. 2000b. "The Role of Dreams in Religious Enculturation among the Asabano of Papua New Guinea." *Ethos* 28, no. 1: 75–102.

———. 2001. "Introduced Writing and Christianity: Differential Access to Religious Knowledge among the Asabano." *Ethnology* 40, no. 2: 93–111.

———. 2003a. "Supernatural Encounters of the Asabano in Two Traditions and Three States of Consciousness." In *Dream Travelers: Sleep Experiences and Culture in the Western Pacific*, edited by R. I. Lohmann. New York: Palgrave Macmillan.

———. 2003b. "The Supernatural is Everywhere: Defining Qualities of Religion in Melanesia and Beyond." In "Perspectives on the Category 'Supernatural.'" *Anthropological Forum* 13, no. 2 (special issue), edited by R. I. Lohmann.

Mead, Margaret. 1930. *Growing up in New Guinea: A Comparative Study of Primitive Education*. New York: Morrow.

Nock, A. D. 1933. *Conversion: The Old and the New in Religion from Alexander the Great to Augustine of Hippo*. Oxford: Oxford University Press.

Otto, Rudolf. 1958 [1923]. *The Idea of the Holy*. Oxford: Oxford University Press.

Rambo, Lewis R. 1993. *Understanding Religious Conversion*. New Haven, Conn.: Yale University Press.

Stewart, Pamela J., and Andrew Strathern, with contributions by Ien Courtens and Dianne van Oosterhout. 2001. *Humors and Substances: Ideas of the Body in New Guinea*. Westport, Conn.: Bergin and Garvey.

Strathern, Marilyn. 1988. *The Gender of the Gift*. Berkeley: University of California Press.

Weber, Max. 1963 [1922]. *The Sociology of Religion*. Boston: Beacon.

Weininger, Benjamin. 1955. *The Interpersonal Factor in the Religious Experience*. *Psychoanalysis* 3: 27–44.

10

Constraint and Freedom in Icelandic Conversions

Robert T. Anderson

Conversion as a personal and social experience, as a cultural event, is clearly an interesting phenomenon for anthropologists to document and also to theorize by applying familiar anthropological concepts having to do with power and persuasion, agency and praxis, self and identity, and one's sense of ultimate reality in terms of the meaning of life and the inevitability of death. However, it is quite another thing to ask if conversion as a defined term, as a category of change, can be useful for cross-cultural anthropological analysis. Does it identify a widespread religious experience? Is it a worldwide sociocultural process? To explore how the concept might be useful for comparative research, in this chapter I draw on ethnographic fieldwork carried out in Iceland over a five-month period in 1998, as well as during short annual follow-up visits until 2001. Based on what I learned in those months, I compare and contrast four different conversion situations. Furthermore, I will suggest that it is helpful to interpret these conversion processes as differing along a continuum that varies from total constraint at one extreme to total freedom at the other.

CHRISTIAN CONSTRAINTS ON THE CONCEPT OF CONVERSION

If we take our definition of conversion from a Christian theologian, what do we get? Lewis Rambo observes that the word "conversion" can imply many different kinds of change, but a common thread is that a convert exchanges one orientation or belief for another that is different. In Rambo's words, conversion is a "turning from and to" (Rambo 1993: 2–3). Implicit in this is an emotional and transformative change that occurs when one becomes a Christian, although it can, of course, refer to abandoning Christianity in favor of Islam or in some other way to turn "from and to."

It is not new to conceptualize conversion as a "turning from and to." The concept was already understood in 1933 when A. D. Nock wrote of conversion as a "deliberate turning from indifference or from an earlier form of piety to another," which differs not a whit from Rambo's present-day "turning from and to" (6). David Snow and Richard Machalek discovered much the same in their survey of sociological publications on the topic. "The one theme pervading the literature on conversion," they found, "is that the experience involves radical personal change. This conception," they also note, "dates back to the Biblical use of the term" (Snow and Machalek 1984: 169). Judging from New Testament testimonials, to convert to Christianity is to turn "from and to" (I Corinthians 16:15; Romans 16:5; I Timothy 3:6).

The problem with this use of the term "conversion" as a way to frame anthropological inquiry is that it is culture bound. It is an emic term, essentially Eurocentric, deriving from the culture of Christianity. More broadly it is Abramic, taking as universal the theological doctrine of exclusivity common to Judaism, Christianity, and Islam. Defining the process as one of "turning from and to" limits inquiry because it implies a prior assumption that one must abandon one set of beliefs and practices in order to substitute another. It is rigid in that way.

The official Christian doctrine of exclusivity—"Thou shalt have no other gods before me"—authorizes a religion of constraint (Deuteronomy 5:7). You have to give up your old religion to become a Christian. For many Christians, constraints are rigorous and absolute, the iron cage of dogma (to parody Max Weber). Nonetheless, there is considerable leeway in the scriptures for interpretations that can free one, more or less, sometimes a lot and sometimes very little, for mixing and matching with supernatural beliefs from other traditions. As Robert Hefner succinctly put it, "It is misleading to assume that the formal truths embedded in religious doctrines directly reflect or inform believers' ideas or actions" (Hefner 1993: 19).

So, looking at the decisions people make (agency) and the way they live as Christians (praxis), we often find a system of constraints, but also we find that there can be considerable freedom with ample opportunities to bend the rules. Analysis in terms of constraints versus opportunities can help us better to realize that although the process of conversion always implies a change "to," it need not always require a change "from."

CONSTRAINT AND FREEDOM: EXAMPLE 1

Hefner has also pointed out that "political mechanisms . . . need to be integrated into a larger theory of conversion" (Hefner 1993: 119). A millennium ago, power and persuasion led to the conversion of Iceland. It was a time when some Vikings had already shifted allegiance from the Odin, Thor, and the other Nordic Gods to the Christian God. Nonetheless, most Icelanders at that time were still pagans and not at all persuaded to convert until raw power came into play.

King Olaf Tryggvason of Norway, himself a willing convert, forced the decision by threatening to kill some prominent Icelanders if Christianity were not made their official religion. Local chieftains and free men from all over the island gathered in the year 1000 at the annual assembly known as the Althing to decide what to do (Karlsson 2000: 33). Strong voices spoke out on both sides of the debate. At last the dispute was put to a respected arbitrator, Thorgeir, whose name reveals his family dedication to the god Thor. Thorgeir was probably a shaman, according to Jón Hnefill Adalsteinsson (1978). He recommended that Iceland should convert to Christianity, and they did.

It was a conversion as much of persuasion as of raw power, however, because the king was physically remote from this far-off island and local chieftains were free to manipulate the exclusivist constraints that normally applied on the continent. The assembly agreed that everyone must become a Christian, but they added that they would not forbid any individual who so wished to continue worshipping the old gods, as long as it was done discreetly in the privacy of one's home. Since the island-wide settlement pattern was one of isolated farmsteads, and given that the Althing only met for a couple of weeks once a year at Thingvellir, in effect anyone who wished could continue to live as a devout pagan without fear of punishment or shame, combining both Christianity and heathenism if he so chose, salted and peppered to taste.

CONSTRAINT AND FREEDOM: EXAMPLE 2

By a generation or two later, holdouts for the Nordic gods had died out and everyone had become Christian in private as well as in public. However, around the turn of the twentieth century, enthusiasts for mediumship and contact with spirits of the dead reached Iceland along with the so-called New Theology (Swatos and Gíssurarson 1997). According to young, "modernist" theologians, the Bible as a text should be evaluated the way one would evaluate any historical document—weeding out mistakes, identifying internal contradictions, and acknowledging exaggerations. Freedom rather than constraint was the enabling trope, and it permitted spiritism to become the new focus of conversion.

By then, the national church of Iceland was Lutheran, funded and authorized as an agency of the state. The Bishop of Iceland might have been

expected to invoke his considerable power to resist the New Theology. Ultimately it so happened, as we shall see. But for a generation, reigning church
officials minimized constraints against the conversion of Icelanders to beliefs
and practices centered on establishing direct contacts with the dead. Freedom
in the new conversion resembled that encountered by David Jordan in Tai-
wan, where spiritist beliefs and Christianity met as an example of "the addi-
tive character of conversion" (Jordan 1993: 286).

This new conversion was made possible not by confronting power but by
subverting it. It is an example of how fundamental beliefs can change, as Max
Heirich put it, "if respected leaders publicly abandon some part of past
grounding assumptions" (Heirich 1977: 675). It took place as a product of
persuasion within the power hierarchy of the national church.

The New Theology prepared the ground for a generation of young priests
who saw spiritism as a way to confirm basic truths in the scriptures. Spiritism
offered scientific evidence that people survived death. It was witnessed in the
contemporary successes of mediums who regularly put people in touch with
deceased loved ones. It authenticated the scriptures because it demonstrated
that so-called biblical miracles were in fact naturalistic verities. That Saul, a
living man, met and conversed with Samuel, who was dead, or that the apostles spent time with a resurrected Jesus were not miracles at all but merely the
natural activities of spirits of the dead (Luke 24:13–31; I Samuel 28:3–17).

Two men brought these iconoclastic beliefs from Copenhagen. One was a
son of the dean of the theological seminary in Reykjavík, who eventually suc-
ceeded to his father's post, and the other was a nephew of the Bishop of Iceland. Close family ties within the church hierarchy helped them override orthodoxy with their revisionist beliefs. One could be a spiritist and still be a
Christian because the scriptures were fallible, and spirit claims and predictions could be proven by checking what was said by spirits against what was
known to be fact.

CONSTRAINT AND FREEDOM: EXAMPLE 3

By the end of the twentieth century, the national church shifted from an attitude of tolerance to one of opposition, reviving old and familiar worldwide
Judeo-Christian injunctions against meeting with mediums and conversing
with ancestors. To invoke these strict constraints they turned to Leviticus, for
example, where God says, "Do not turn yourselves to the spirit mediums and
do not consult professional foretellers of events, so as to become unclean by
them," (19:31; see also Deuteronomy 17:10–11). Jesus himself compared

"those who practice spiritism" to dogs, fornicators, murderers, idolators, and liars (Revelations 22:15; see also Galatians 5:19–20). Christian constraints are, therefore, back in place today, but the hierarchy itself has little or no control over most parishioners, so it really doesn't matter to most people. The church has virtually no power at all over individuals. It is true that nearly every Icelander is baptized, confirmed, married, and buried in the Church. But very few attend church regularly or ever consult ministers about personal and family matters. People seem to feel free to ignore theological constraint and to exercise their freedom to make decisions for themselves. No longer a matter of power, conversion is now a matter of personal decisions and behaviors, of agency and praxis relating to self and identity, particularly as concerns the meaning of life and the inevitability of death.

In anthropology and sociology, two very different theoretical constructs have proven useful in the analysis of conversion as a worldwide process (Hefner 1993: 102). One embeds conversion in a universe of social relations, of power relations, in which congregations and communities have a telling effect. We encountered the need for theorizing in that way when we examined constraint and freedom examples 1 and 2.

For examples 3 and 4, however, we require a complementary kind of theory, one usually characterized as intellectualist because it links sociocultural influences with individual life histories. "Intellectualism," Hefner writes, "explains conversion as a change in religious belief, where beliefs are viewed as instruments of explanation and control of actual time-space events" (Hefner 1993: 102). For this kind of theorizing, I find it most helpful to borrow the felicitous phraseology of Heirich, who speaks of conversion as "the process of changing a sense of root reality," of revising one's "core sense of reality," or of redefining one's "grounding" (1977: 674).

In applying intellectualist theory to becoming a Christian in Iceland, we find that nearly every contemporary Icelander is automatically considered a Christian by virtue of being enrolled in the national church at birth. Icelanders tend to think of themselves as Christians, but for the most part that implies only a very superficial sense of identity or of self. They have been indoctrinated primarily by attending confirmation classes as young teenagers and by participating in "confirmation" as a culminating ritual. They give little evidence of having had a conversion experience that involves accepting the constraints, the authority, of the bishop or even of the Bible as such. For the most part, they are never "born-again" in the way charismatic Christians would define as essential to personal conversion. Charismatic conversion is an available option for Icelanders to the extent that some small evangelical congregations are well established, but very few have converted that way.

For the most part, being a Christian in Iceland is a matter of enculturation and education. It is a conversion of freedom, not a "from and to" process but a taken-for-granted state of mind that is scarcely queried by the average citizen. For anyone who does give thought to his or her core sense of reality, Lutheran eschatology is generally poorly understood, widely contested, and eminently negotiable. Repeatedly in interviews, people told me that they prayed to God. But when I asked who God was, I never got a description of the biblical Jehovah, of God as judge or master. God was always a vague and distant energy, light, goodness, love, or creativity, far more New Age than Old Testament in character.

Insofar as conversion is a process of enculturation or socialization about beliefs "viewed as instruments of explanation and control of actual time-space events," of "root reality," it has resulted for the most part in an indifference to if not an outright rejection of the biblical accounts of heaven and hell. In this highly secular society, biblical injunctions no longer have the power to constrain most people.

CONSTRAINT AND FREEDOM: EXAMPLE 4

The failure of the national church to indoctrinate or convert the populace to Christianity under exclusivist constraints leaves open the opportunity to consider oneself a Christian while remaining quite free to adopt spiritist beliefs and practices, to convert in that sense. Although very few Icelanders are churchgoers, many if not most are really quite attuned to spirits and spiritual values. They practice a religion that is scarcely noticed. It is unnamed, minimally institutionalized, and rarely articulated. Yet, although nearly invisible in the public arena, it can be of profound importance in private lives and as a nationwide inclination.

Of ninety University of Iceland students who returned a questionnaire handed out in my classes on medical and biological anthropology in 1998, 47 percent (51 percent of the women and 29 percent of the men) said yes, they had experienced contact with the spirit of someone who had died. In other words, the social life of nearly half of these young people included at least one dead person. Looked at differently, an impressive 80 percent of all student respondents, nearly all of them, also reported that if they had not themselves been in touch with a dead person, they at least knew someone who believed it had happened.

My findings reflect somewhat more spirit contact than was reported by Erlendur Haraldsson, who has done proper systematic research to investigate these beliefs. In a national survey reporting on a carefully selected random sample of 902 Icelandic adults, he recorded in 1985 that 36 percent of the women and 24 percent of the men answered yes to the question, "Have you ever experienced or felt the nearness of a deceased person?" Extrapolating from Haraldsson's scientific survey and my own opportunistic questionnaire, it is evident that meetings with the dead instantiate a nationwide "sense of root reality," a "ground of being that orients and orders experience more generally," even for young people (Heirich 1977: 674). Spirit contact and, what is more important, the ideology or philosophy of life that it endorses, the grounding that it inspires, is given no official recognition, but it is as much the religion of Icelanders as ancestor veneration is the underlying, anonymous religion of China, with or without Christianity, Buddhism, or the sayings of Mao.

And yet there is a constraint on conversion to spiritism that I have not yet discussed. It is not in the Bible or in any of the available books about spiritism. It is the pragmatic constraint of science or of logic. Apparently without exception, every spiritist at the beginning of the conversion process puts the believability of mediums to a test. Each insists on proof that a spirit is real as determined by the fact that what a spirit or medium revealed was not merely a lucky guess or an astute intuition. Every believer told me that he or she knew of a spirit who provided detailed information that only the deceased could have known.

That constraint, however, rests lightly on the process. It requires a type of proof that is never completely rigorous and indisputable. Further, spiritist theory, like a belief in God, is not falsifiable. Just as it is impossible to prove conclusively that God does not exist, one cannot disprove the reality of spirits. It is a given that wrong information is frequently provided by reputed spirits, but such errors are routinely dismissed as long as one knows of even one seemingly indisputable example of otherwise inexplicable information that was conveyed from the spirit world. Social reinforcement clearly enhances the compelling impact of this otherwise questionable kind of proof.

The people of contemporary Iceland are fully modern and globally sophisticated. They are highly educated and well informed. They are rightly characterized as essentially secular rather than as religious. Consistent with that characterization, believing in spirits is consciously thought of in Iceland as naturalism, not supernaturalism, and as scientific, not religious (Swatos and Gíssurarson 1997). Is acting on the belief that spirits of the dead really converse with the living the result of a conversion experience? Or is it merely an adaptation akin to accepting a new scientific or medical discovery? It is, in fact, both. After all, exclusivist and highly constrained Christians also insist that their beliefs are naturalistic. Based on accepting scripture as divinely inspired, God, Jesus, and the angels are believed really to exist. Miracles are offered as proof, because they demonstrate that God can do anything He wants.

CONCLUSION

As a descriptive noun, conversion has generally been understood to define a very narrow category of change in orientation or belief insofar as it refers to a process of replacement rather than of syncretism, a process of "turning from and to." So used, it is a definition of total constraint, a denial or repulsion, if you will, of the acculturative pressures likely to be present when people make major changes in beliefs about the afterlife. It is not wrong to use the term that way, but it offers very limited potential as an analytical concept for comparative analysis. It even fails to encompass much, probably most, of what we refer to in the vernacular as Christian conversion.

For anthropological purposes, it is much more useful to define conversion as a process whereby rather than inevitably substituting one belief system for another, belief systems may differentiate or syncretize depending on how the variable of constraint versus freedom is imposed or permitted. Thus, in example 1, the power of the king to impose a highly constrained Christianity was derailed by a freedom made possible by geographic isolation, a dispersed land-settlement pattern, and the influence of a respected shaman.

Similarly, conversion in which the "from" dimension is negotiable on a constraint versus freedom continuum provides a way to clarify three other examples from Iceland. In example 2, the biblical constraint against consulting mediums and contacting spirits of the dead succumbed to a freedom introduced by young members of the church elite, who achieved a power base allowing them to justify spiritism on the basis of the New Theology. In example 3, after the national church reverted to the older theology and branded spiritism as un-Christian, spiritism continued to thrive because contemporary Icelanders lived in a free and secular nation in which very few accorded final authority to the church fathers. They achieved freedom in that sense. Finally, in example 4, those who believe that the dead live on as spirits impose a constraint upon themselves based on logic and science, but they judge that constraint by lax standards that essentially free them from the far more rigorous constraints of experimental science.

As so often is the case in anthropology and sociology, we find ourselves using the language of daily life for technical and precise purposes. That practice plagues us with misunderstanding and miscommunication, but we stay with it; to that extent, at least, we are somewhat careless in our effort to be rational. Perhaps this is wise, since neologisms often impede communication in their own way. So I conclude by suggesting that when scholars use the term "conversion," we should inform our readers whether it is used as a term of complete constraint or whether it is to be understood as implying a variable mix of constraint and freedom, one that requires explication as we try to understand the process from a global perspective.

REFERENCES

Adalsteinsson, Jón Hnefill. *Under the Cloak.* Stockholm: Almquist and Wiksell, 1978.

Haraldsson, Erlendur. "Survey of Claimed Encounters with the Dead." *Omega* 19, no. 2 (1998–1999): 103–13.

Hefner, Robert W. "Of Faith and Commitment: Christian Conversion in Muslim Java." In *Conversion to Christianity: Historical and Anthropological Perspectives on a Great Transformation*, edited by R. W. Hefner, pp. 99–125. Berkeley: University of California Press, 1993.

———. "World Building and the Rationality of Conversion." In *Conversion to Christianity: Historical and Anthropological Perspectives on a Great Transformation*, edited by R. W. Hefner, pp. 3–44. Berkeley: University of California Press, 1993.

Heirich, Max. "Change of Heart: A Test of Some Widely Held Theories about Religious Conversion." *American Journal of Sociology* 83, no. 3 (1977): 653–80.

Jordan, David K. "The Glyphomancy Factor: Observations on Chinese Conversion." In *Conversion to Christianity: Historical and Anthropological Perspectives on a Great Transformation*, edited by R. W. Hefner, pp. 285–303. Berkeley: University of California Press, 1993.

Karlsson, Gunnar. *The History of Iceland.* Minneapolis: University of Minnesota Press, 2000.

Nock, A. D. *Conversion: The Old and the New in Religion from Alexander the Great to Augustine of Hippo.* Oxford: Oxford University Press, 1933.

Rambo, Lewis R. *Understanding Religious Conversion.* New Haven, Conn.: Yale University Press, 1993.

Snow, David A., and Richard Machalek. "The Sociology of Conversion." *Annual Review of Sociology* 10 (1984): 167–90.

Swatos, William H., Jr., and Loftur Reimar Gíssurarson. *Icelandic Spiritualism: Mediumship and Modernity in Iceland.* New Brunswick, N.J.: Transaction Publishers, 1997.

11

Mystical Experiences, American Culture, and Conversion to Christian Spiritualism

Thomas Kingsley Brown

The imagery of the nineteenth-century séance is well known in the contemporary West. Most Americans have seen depictions of people sitting at a table in a darkened room, summoning spirits of the dead and awaiting the appearance of ghostly visages. It is not so widely known that contemporary versions of séances are still conducted in many parts of the world by people who consider themselves Christians.

The height of popularity of the séance occurred in the mid-to-late 1800s and roughly corresponded with the emergence of a movement called Spiritualism. Although Spiritualism's popularity waned dramatically during the late 1800s, the religion did not die out completely. This chapter is based on ethnographic research conducted among two Spiritualist congregations in southern California. In the pages that follow, I will address the question of why mainstream Christians join such churches, and I will examine the meaning of "conversion" from mainstream Christianity to a particular form of Spiritualism—namely, that of Christian Spiritualism. I will address the proposal that the shifts in belief at the heart of these conversions are often sparked long before eventual converts come to Spiritualism; in particular, I will address possible roles of experiences that are termed "anomalous," mystical, and paranormal. I argue that these experiences play an important role in conversion for many Spiritualists but that pinpointing the root causes of conversion is, at best, uncertain. In addition, I will elaborate on Spiritualist conceptions of conversion by arguing that conversion has no clear point at which it can be considered complete.

First, I will outline the historical context for this study. Generically defined, spiritualism[1] is the belief in a postcorporeal afterlife and a belief in the ability of humans to communicate directly with spirits of the dead. Such beliefs are widespread. In America, Spiritualism is a religious movement that began (by most accounts) in New York State in the middle of the nineteenth century.[2] Millions (and perhaps tens of millions) participated in séances and other Spiritualist gatherings during the movement's peak in the 1850s. The movement quickly spread to Europe and eventually to other regions of the world as well.[3]

Although I have referred to Spiritualism as a "religious movement," early Spiritualists considered the movement a science aimed at proving the reality of the afterlife and of spirit communication (Moore 1977). Indeed, many early Spiritualists, particularly the so-called anti-Christian Spiritualists, explicitly rejected religious affiliation. For the most part, these Spiritualists also resisted attempts at formal organization. Another subset of the movement was explicitly Christian in its orientation. These "Christian" Spiritualists, whose aim was to "scientifically" prove biblical claims, did not object to formal organization and were more likely to establish official groups, churches, and leaders. Contrasts between these two subgroups provide a rough historical explanation as to why present-day Spiritualist groups (or at least the most prominent ones) are Christian Spiritualist groups. Some of these groups have survived since Spiritualism's peak decades in the mid-to-late 1800s.

This chapter—based on fieldwork conducted between October 1995 and September 1997—deals primarily with two Christian Spiritualist churches in San Diego, California. One church was founded in 1881, the other in 1932. There are at least a half-dozen other Spiritualist groups in the San Diego area, as well as a Spiritualist retreat center that celebrated its centennial during the time of my fieldwork.

Not all current Spiritualist churches in San Diego include the word "Christian" in their names. However, the inclusion or omission of the word "Christian" in the title is no indication of the influence of Christianity at those churches. The two churches discussed here—First Spiritualist Church of San Diego and Brotherhood Spiritualist Church—are as Christian as any Spiritualist churches in the San Diego area. Evidence of Christian influences is readily discernable at both First Spiritualist Church and Brotherhood Spiritualist Church. These churches are fairly typical of others in the area. First, it should be noted that over 90 percent of the participants in these two organizations were raised within mainstream Christians families. Interest in Christian elements varies considerably from one member to another, but almost all of the members value the Christian aspects to some extent. For many members, Christian elements are essential elements of belief and participation.

What are these Christian elements? They include aspects of belief, symbolism, and practice. A churchgoing Christian would recognize many of them after attending a weekly service. Like mainstream Christian services, Spiritualist worship services take place on Sunday mornings. Services open with a

Christian hymn, often with an accompanying pianist or organist. At First Spiritualist, a portrait of Jesus hangs on the wall. During services, the Lord's prayer and the *Gloria Patri* are recited, and a sermon—typically, but not always, mentioning God and Jesus—is delivered by a pastor.

The service also includes elements that would be unfamiliar to most Christians: for example, a ten-minute meditation accompanied by New Age music, the occasional discussion of chakras and auras, and the "spirit readings" near the end of the service. Spirit readings are divinatory "messages" delivered by specially trained members of the congregation who stand near the lectern and see, hear, or sense the presence of "spirits," "guides," or "angels" surrounding those who are seated in the hall.

Outside of worship services, there are other seemingly non-Christian practices. Prior to every service, a "healing service" is held wherein healers direct "healing energies" (through their hands) toward people sitting on stools. On some evenings and weekends, there are "psychic fairs" featuring Tarot card readings, Burmese astrology, aura photography, and the aforementioned spirit readings. Two to four times a month, there are workshops on topics such as numerology, past-life regression, and shamanic soul-travel. In addition, classes on theories and practices related to Spiritualist belief are held regularly. Moreover, there is an emotionally evocative "circle," the modern-day variant of the séance.[4] People sit in a circle, chant, sing to invite spirits, and use practiced perceptual abilities to observe and communicate with visiting spirits.

Spiritualism and Christianity are an odd blend, especially considering that of all of Spiritualism's opponents in the nineteenth century, Christians were the most vociferous. Many Christians believed that direct communication with spirits was dangerous, as it purportedly courted relations with both good spirits and evil ones. In their eyes, direct communication with spirits was not the individual's prerogative in any case. Even today, Christian Spiritualists claim that other Christians condemn Spiritualism as "devil worship."

Early in my fieldwork, I noted that most members at the First Christian Spiritualist Church had previously been members of Christian churches, and I wondered what had brought them to Spiritualism. Knowing of the antipathy that has existed historically between mainstream Christianity and Spiritualism (and already having heard stories indicating a continuation of that antipathy), I began to wonder why these people had converted to a religion that is shunned by their childhood churches and that espouses beliefs and practices often at odds with mainstream Christianity.

The question of what sparks conversions from mainstream Christianity to Spiritualism became a central focus of my research. My starting point for an examination of conversion was the definition of conversion used by many scholars of religion: *Conversion is a change in one's system of beliefs.* I initially postulated that the shift in beliefs at the heart of this conversion occurred long before the Spiritualist convert-to-be ever encountered a Spiritualist church. Specifically, I suggested that anomalous experiences (mystical experiences, the "paranormal," and so on) might have sparked conversion of many Spiritualists. The idea, in other words, was that Lofland and Skonovd's (1981) "mystical" type of conversion would fit the typical conversion motif for Christian Spiritualists. If I were correct, or so I thought, I would hear many stories concerning Christians who had undergone sudden, inexplicable, mystical experiences that motivated them to explore such experiences directly. Christians undergoing emotionally intense mystical experiences, I hypothesized, might turn to alternative religions—particularly those better attuned to experiential exploration—as a vehicle for making some sense of experiences for which their Christian backgrounds may not have prepared them.

However, I soon realized that my proposal was far too simplistic to account for emerging patterns, and I began to closely examine the nature of religious conversion. The problem was not only that there were additional influences (apart from anomalous experiences) at play in conversion. There were other influences as well, and many seemed easy enough to trace. A central problem was that in cases of conversion, it was difficult to pinpoint a set of root "causes" and equally difficult to pinpoint exactly when the supposed shift in beliefs had taken place. To make matters more complex, in many of these cases of conversion, it was unclear that the shift in beliefs had ever been complete. That is, even though the "converts" seemed to have undergone a shift in beliefs, it seemed that this change was often ephemeral, and doubt about Spiritualist beliefs could return again and again. Adherents, it appeared, were coming back to Spiritualist churches because they doubted Spiritualist beliefs.

Some questions arise: Can we meaningfully speak of conversion as a shift in beliefs? If so, at what point in the convert's "career"[5] can conversion be said to have begun? At what point can conversion be considered complete? Does it make sense to try to retrospectively determine the "causes" of religious conversion?

REVEREND THELMA'S THEORY OF CONVERSION

Early in my fieldwork, I recognized that I wasn't the only one who speculated about conversion to Spiritualism. A Spiritualist reverend shared her thoughts with me during a Friday-night psychic fair at the First Spiritualist Church of San Diego. My conversation with Reverend Thelma was less interesting for the spirit reading she provided than for the discussion that later ensued. After Thelma learned that I was studying Spiritualism from an academic standpoint, she offered her own explanation as to why people come to Spiritualist churches. She postulated that people come to Spiritualist churches because they want to find proof of the existence of spirits and the afterlife. "They want to see spirits materialize before their eyes," she told me. "They want to see hard evidence, but usually what they get are spirit readings. This satisfies them to a point, but they keep coming back because they still aren't sure."

In the course of my fieldwork, I encountered further evidence that Thelma had hit upon one reason why people return again and again to Spiritualist churches. Evidence took the form of other Spiritualists saying, in a variety of ways, that many Spiritualists never fully convert. For example, Tim (of First Spiritualist Church) told me that his belief "waxes and wanes" and that he comes back in hopes of having "mind-blowing" experiences that bolster his beliefs. Reverend Ida, of Brotherhood Spiritualist Church, openly discussed the fact that most Spiritualists are uncertain about Spiritualist beliefs and that they seek proof that will spark their shift from merely "believing" in the spirit world to "knowing" for certain that it exists.

Clearly, the quest for certainty cannot be the sole attraction of Spiritualist churches. Such proof isn't a major draw for people such as Reverends Thelma and Ida (as well as numerous other members of the congregation) who are already certain of the reality of the spirit world. Even if the desire for such proof is a draw (and I believe that it is), there have to be other attractions as well. In addition, reasons why people *return* to Spiritualist churches may be quite different from reasons people visit them for the first time. Spiritualists, I found, do seek proof of the afterlife. But what makes them curious about Spiritualism in the first place?

Reverend Thelma's case provides a possible answer to this question. Her father was a Spiritualist reverend in England (where, interestingly enough, his houseguests included famous Spiritualists such as Aleister Crowley and Arthur Conan Doyle). Thelma's father passed his interests and beliefs in Spiritualism on to his daughter. But Thelma is unusual among Spiritualists in having been raised as a Spiritualist. Explanations as to why the other 95 percent chose Spiritualism are harder to come by.

An overview of all cases from my interview material reveals a general four-stage pattern. Each stage occurs for nearly everyone, regardless of what caused their initial shifts in belief. In the first stage, the eventual convert develops a sense of discontent toward the mainstream worldviews of Christianity and scientism. In this stage, uncertainties about the nature of God and reality become prominent. In the next stage, in order to make some sort of sense of it all, the person embarks on a "religious quest," becoming a "religious seeker" (many people used these very words to describe themselves and their lives). At some later point, the third stage, he or she discovers a Spiritualist church, which becomes a spiritual "home." It is among the Spiritualist "family" where these people feel comfortable exploring questions about spirits, the paranormal, and the afterlife, and where they find satisfying answers in a community of like-minded seekers. The fourth stage is characterized by a fluctuating belief in Spiritualism in which convincing experiences are sought in order to solidify beliefs.

In many cases, the initial discontent with Christianity derived from an anomalous experience. Such experiences have been categorized as belonging to two similar types. The first type is the sudden, profound, religious experience often referred to as a "mystical experience," and the second involves so-called paranormal experiences that appear to defy scientific explanation. William James examined the capacity of mystical experiences to cause significant shifts in beliefs (1961 [1902]). But he did not examine the impact of paranormal experiences as thoroughly. Paranormal experiences, like mystical experiences, have the potential to impart apparent "knowledge" about the nature of reality—knowledge that often conflicts with previously held beliefs and that could lead one to question those beliefs. In James's terms, this subjectively apparent reception of knowledge is the "noetic" quality of mystical experiences.

William James portrayed mystical experiences as brief, overwhelming phenomena that impart new, indescribable understandings. A classic example is that of a person sitting and quietly reading at home one night, and then suddenly sensing the seemingly undeniable presence of a deceased friend or relative. Paranormal experiences, according to James McClenon, are those that seem (at least to those who experience them) to defy explanation according to scientific understandings as construed by the general public (McClenon 1994). There is significant overlap between the categories of mystical and paranormal experience. Often, experiences that are called "mystical" are those that are labeled religious, whereas paranormal experiences are not.

My interviews with Spiritualists elicited examples of both types of experience. Reverend Paul (of First Spiritualist) recalled an experience that occurred when he was only 7 or 8 years old. One night while lying in bed, he observed a "very bright light in the corner of the room." He "knew" it was the spirit of Jesus, even though, as he points out, he did not then understand the concept of "spirit" as he does now.

Cynthia, a member of First Christian Spiritualist Church, experienced what she refers to as a "premonition" that occurred years before she knew what

Spiritualism was. She was at home, standing in front of the bathroom sink and brushing her teeth, when, as she relates:

> This thought intruded into my mind. I thought about how I hadn't heard of an airplane crash for a while—then I caught myself, saying "no, I hear about *small* plane crashes a lot; I just haven't heard of any big commercial planes crashing."

Before she walked away from the sink, Cynthia felt the house shaken by a loud explosion. Nearby, a commercial airliner had been torn apart by its violent impact with the ground. "Stunned" by these events, she called her mother to tell her about the "premonition." This experience occurred more than ten years before she went to a medium for a reading, and longer still before she visited a Spiritualist church. However, Cynthia points to *this* event as one of those that led her to question her former views of reality and that eventually made more sense from the perspective of Spiritualist understandings.

Carla, of Brotherhood Spiritualist Church, offered an experience she later interpreted as a vision of herself in a past life. When Carla was about 15 years old, she and a friend, Mark, were riding Mark's motorcycle to a party. In relating the story, Carla noted that neither of them had been drinking nor were either of them under the influence of any drugs. As they rode, they passed by a large mansion and estate with an arched entry to the walkway, where they noticed two figures who looked, Carla recalls, "as physically real as ordinary people":

> Me and this guy Mark . . . looked over to our left, and there were these two people standing in this archway. And they were dressed up like—well, I kind of thought she looked like Scarlet O'Hara, you know, with the little bitty waist and the poofy skirt out to the floor, you know what I mean? And she was wearing white, and the man was wearing a black tuxedo and a top hat. And I looked over, and I looked at the woman's face, and it was almost like a zoom lens on a camera, [my vision] zoomed into the face, and it was *my* face! And it was really shocking! And we said to each other, "did you see that?" "Oh, yeah!" And we looked back and they were gone.

Mark had seen much the same thing, although he had "zoomed" into the man's face, and, like Carla, saw an image of himself there.

When the two arrived at the party, their tale had little impact on others present, who accused Carla and Mark of fabrication. By contrast, the experience affected Carla profoundly:

> It was from that moment on—and I *knew* that there was more than what the Catholic church was telling me. I think I knew that anyway, you know. I never really—I loved the spirituality in the Catholic church, but there were many

things I didn't agree with, even when I was a child. So I knew that there was something more out there for me. . . . [The experience] proved to me that something like that existed—I saw it with my own eyes.

Whether the experiences of Paul, Cynthia, and Carla should be classified as mystical experiences or as paranormal phenomena is debatable. The main point, however, is that such experiences are viewed by the converts as events that shaped their religious careers.

Both "mystical" and "paranormal" experiences have the capacity to spark a shift in beliefs. People who claim to have had such experiences believe that these experiences provide evidence of phenomena that defy or overturn scientific or Christian understandings about the nature of reality. Cynthia, for example, said of her experience that these are "things that can't be explained scientifically." Another Spiritualist told me that such experiences prove that "the Christians got it all wrong" when they told him that "miracles no longer happen."

Whether or not Spiritualists are correct in asserting that such experiences overturn scientific or Christian understandings is irrelevant. The fact is that they *believe* that the experiences provide such proof. Some informants told me that anomalous experiences were important turning points in their religious careers. In a number of cases, the experiences prompted them to question Christian or "scientific" understandings, whereas in other cases the experiences seemed to strengthen doubts they already had. For some, anomalous experiences had affected their beliefs prior to their becoming Spiritualists and had entered into their conversions to Spiritualism.

Anomalous experiences are not, however, the only route to Spiritualist conversion. Indeed, people who had such experiences comprise less than half of those I interviewed. Another quarter of the cases could be considered "intellectual" conversions (Lofland and Skonovd 1981), that is, people who studied spiritualist literature and came to be interested in Spiritualist ideas. For example, Tim read books on sorcery and magic (by Carlos Castaneda and Hans Holzer) and claims that his study of this literature prompted him to question Christian and scientific understandings of God and of reality. One reverend at First Spiritualist stated that the movie *The Trouble with Angels* profoundly affected her at the age of 12. Together, the combination of "mystical" and "intellectual" conversions accounts for almost three-quarters of the cases in my study.

Why did the remaining people in my study become Spiritualists? Answers varied, and in many cases there were no specific events, whether "mystical" or "intellectual," that prompted their conversions. Answers may come from the general American culture of the post–World War II period in which my informants grew to adulthood. Particularly in the "baby boomer" years of 1946 to 1964 and following, Americans witnessed dramatic changes that threatened the stability of mainstream views (at least for some people). These included (1) an increasing availability of occult literature (and materials on Eastern mysticism), (2) an increasing acceptance of the exploration of altered states of consciousness, (3) the rise of television, and (4) an increasing cultural pluralism and rising neolocality.[6] It would be erroneous to suggest that these influences affected everyone the same or that they caused *everyone* to question mainstream values. The mainstream is still the mainstream. However, I agree with Robert Wuthnow, who notes that such cultural changes contributed to an increasing acceptance of social experimentation: political activism, explorations of alternative sexual practices, and (most importantly for the topic at hand) participation in alternative religions (Wuthnow 1976). The changing social milieu did not result in everyone becoming a religious seeker, but the "occult revival" of the 1960s (and its descendents, the "new religious movements" and the New Age movement) reflected a growing *proportion* of religious seekers.

In summary, there are many possible influences on the shifts in belief that take place during the process of conversion to Spiritualism. Anomalous experiences are important events in the religious careers of many, but there are other experiences that can similarly lead a person to question his or her beliefs. Indeed, it may be that even the role of anomalous experiences is more ambiguous than converts tend to believe. It is generally not possible to determine which influences are the most important for any convert, nor is it easy to determine a point in time at which conversion can be said to have taken place. For example, unlike the dramatic conversion of the apostle Paul, Paul the Spiritualist experienced a number of mystical events over a long period of time. Can it be said that one of these events was the overriding influence in his conversion? If not, when did the major shift in belief occur? Another complication is that Paul's interpretation of the bright light in his bedroom may (or may not) indicate an unusual predisposition toward such views. How can we ascertain the point at which a shift in belief occurs or starts to occur?

Similar problems arise for other converts. Cynthia, for example, says that events such as her "premonition" had a profound impact upon her beliefs. However, she first encountered Spiritualism thirteen years later in a meeting with a medium she'd visited on the basis of a friend's recommendation. She says that the interactions with the medium "helped explain things to me in ways consistent with my gut feelings" in ways that the "Christian spiel" never had. She was so impressed with the medium that the following year she decided to attend a Spiritualist church where the medium was a reverend. Can we determine when conversion actually occurred for Cynthia? She cites both the "premonition" and her relationship with the medium as prominent influences in her religious career. Had she never met the medium, would she be Spiritualist? Had she never experienced seemingly "paranormal" events, would she have met the medium? (Of course, in any conversion, there must be some initial motivation for the convert to interact with the religious group.)

Carla's case is not so simple either. Long before her mind-altering motorcycle ride, Carla had already developed misgivings about the Catholic Church, largely because of her impression that it "teaches too much fear and guilt." Indeed, most other Spiritualists I interviewed exhibited an early interest in spiritual matters, as well as a precocious readiness to question religious doctrine.

If the starting point of conversion is hard to pin down, so too is the ending point. It is very difficult to determine exactly when conversion to Spiritualism is complete. People come to Spiritualist churches to witness and observe proof of an afterlife. Interestingly, this stance implies that many members are not entirely convinced that the spirit realm does exist—or, at least, that once they become certain, they may not remain so indefinitely. Reverend Ida points out that dramatic experiences (referred to as "miracles" or "God-stories" by those at Brotherhood Spiritualist) are often critical in the shift from "believing" in the "spirit realm" to "knowing" that it exists. Spiritualists acknowledge that the desire for certainty is one reason they seek such experiences. The fact that belief waxes and wanes, even for longtime members, throws doubt on the completeness of the shift in beliefs that is assumed by Heirich (1977), among others, to underlie conversion. The exchange of "one ordered view of the world for another" (Heirich 1977) may not be as neat as the definition suggests. If members had already converted, then why were these experiences necessary to solidify their beliefs?

CONVERSION TO SPIRITUALISM: TRUE CONVERSION?

It could be stated that if we cannot determine *when* a shift in belief occurred, then perhaps there never *was* a shift in belief. Travisano's distinction between conversion and "alternation" provides an avenue along which to pursue this issue (1970). Travisano's distinction hinges on the extent to which an individual's identity and life are rearranged: "Complete disruption signals conversion while anything less signals alternation" (1970: 598). His own data from his fieldwork with Hebrew Christians and Jewish Unitarians provide the illustrative example of this difference (1970). Jews who become Christians, he explains, must be considered converts because they have abandoned their Jewish identity and have developed entirely new lifestyles as a part of their change. Jewish Unitarians, on the other hand, still (as the name implies) consider themselves Jewish and have not reorganized their lives in becoming involved with the Unitarian Church.

If we accept Travisano's stipulation that "conversion rests upon the adoption of a pervasive identity" (1970: 600), then the vast majority of established Spiritualist churchgoers should be considered converts. The pivotal points here are that they consider themselves Spiritualists and that this fact is a major influence in the ways in which they organize their lives. In addition, this new identity is antithetical to their former religious identities, as the belief in (and practice of) spirit channeling is considered heretical in some branches of mainstream Christianity. Travisano notes that "the ideal typical conversion can be thought of as the embracing of a negative identity. The person becomes something which was specifically prohibited" (1970: 601). Aside from the Spiritualists who were raised as Spiritualists, the vast majority of Spiritualists have "embraced a negative identity" and therefore can be considered converts.

The concept of conversion as a "shift in one's system of beliefs" is problematic. In closing, I will suggest ways to address this issue. One strategy is to consider conversion a shift in behavior as well as a shift in beliefs.[7] One can imagine that the determination of causes and timing of these shifts would run into complications such as those discussed above. Perhaps the best way to avoid such difficulties may be to relinquish the quest for definite causes and timing. Conversion to Spiritualism can be seen as a series of stages. I have come to appreciate Richardson's (1985) perspective, in which conversion is viewed as a complex, long-term process that involves behavioral changes as well as cognitive ones.[8] The quest for a strict definition of conversion is thereby abandoned, but the payoff in terms of realism is well worth the sacrifice.

NOTES

1. Lowercase lettering will be herein used for the generic meaning of spiritualism, whereas references to the movement of Spiritualism (including present-day manifestations) will be capitalized.
2. See Moore (1977) and Carroll (1997) for excellent historical treatments of American Spiritualism. Nelson (1969) provides a perspective on the British Spiritualist movement that followed on its heels.
3. In addition to the continents of North America and Europe, Spiritualism has also found its way to Australia and New Zealand and probably elsewhere as well.
4. I have heard of no explanation for the switch in terminology from "séance" to "circle," but I strongly suspect that Spiritualists of the twentieth century gradually diminished the use of the word séance in order to distance themselves and their prac-

tices from the scandals and derision with which Spiritualism had become associated. Séances were targets of skeptics from the beginning, and many cases of outright fraud were discovered by investigators or admitted by insiders. One consequence, I believe, is that modern-day participants in circles do not claim to witness (nor attempt to generate) the physically palpable spirit incarnations sought in the nineteenth century. Instead, participants learn to hone their senses in order to see, smell, hear, or feel the presence of spirits purportedly unnoticeable to untrained senses (T. K. Brown 2000).

5. Here I borrow Richardson's (1985) wording in referring to the "career" of the religious convert.

6. For further discussion of these trends, see especially Wuthnow (1976), S. L. Brown (1992), Roof (1993), and T. K. Brown (2000).

7. This strategy is implied in Lofland and Skonovd's (1981) discussion of the timing of the shift in beliefs versus the change in behavior.

8. Richardson (1985) also emphasizes the active (as opposed to passive) role of the convert in his or her own conversion. This is an important point that we will not explore further here; I have discussed this point at greater length elsewhere (T. K. Brown 2000).

REFERENCES

Brown, Susan Love. "Baby Boomers, American Character, and the New Age: A Synthesis." In *Perspectives on the New Age,* edited by James R. Lewis and R. Gordon Melton, 87–96. Albany: State University of New York Press, 1994.

Brown, Thomas K. *Religious Seekers and "Finding a Spiritual Home": An Ethnographic Study of Conversion to Christian Spiritualist Churches in Southern California.* Ph.D. diss., University of California, San Diego, 2000.

Carroll, Bret E. *Spiritualism in Antebellum America.* Bloomington: Indiana University Press, 1997.

Heirich, Max. "Change of Heart: A Test of Some Widely Held Theories about Religious Conversion." *American Journal of Sociology* 83, no. 3 (1977): 653–80.

James, William. *The Varieties of Religious Experience: A Study in Human Nature.* Reprint ed. New York: Collier Books, 1961 [1902].

Lofland, John, and Norman Skonovd. "Conversion Motifs." *Journal for the Scientific Study of Religion* 20, no. 4 (1981): 373–85.

McClenon, James. *Wondrous Events: Foundations of Religious Belief.* Philadelphia: University of Pennsylvania Press, 1994.

Moore, R. Laurence. *In Search of White Crows: Spiritualism, Parapsychology, and American Culture.* New York: Oxford University Press, 1977.

Nelson, Geoffrey K. *Spiritualism and Society.* New York: Schocken Books, 1969.

Richardson, James T. "The Active vs. Passive Convert: Paradigm Conflict in Conversion/Recruitment Research." *Journal for the Scientific Study of Religion* 24, no. 2 (1985): 163–79.

Roof, Wade Clark. *A Generation of Seekers: The Spiritual Journeys of the Baby Boom Generation.* San Francisco: Harper San Francisco, 1993.

Travisano, Richard V. "Alternation and Conversion as Qualitatively Different Transformations." In *Social Psychology through Symbolic Interaction*, edited by G. P. Stone and H. A. Faberman, 594–606. Waltham, Mass.: Xerox College Publishing, 1970.

Wuthnow, Robert. *The Consciousness Reformation.* Berkeley: University of California Press, 1976.

III

CONVERSION AND INDIVIDUAL EXPERIENCE

12

"Limin' wid Jah": Spiritual Baptists Who Become Rastafarians and Then Become Spiritual Baptists Again[1]

Stephen D. Glazier

Every person has two parts: the body and the spirit. You cannot escape the spiritual side. Truly, all men and women of Trinidad are Spiritual Baptists already. Our goal is to make them aware of their convictions.

— Archbishop Muhrain addressing the Spiritual Baptist Council of
Elders, Maraval, Trinidad, July 1999

The Rastaman speaks to the world of the Righteous who have suffered at the hands of the Unrighteousness. The Rastaman cries out for Justice because He knows that all have suffered. You may not know it in your head, but in his heart every man is a Rasta.

— Derek "Ziggy" Manville, Port of Spain, Trinidad, July 1999

As contributors to this volume have pointed out, typical notions of "conversion" are derived from Hebrew, Greek, and Latin terms meaning to turn, to return, and to turn again (as well as turning, returning, and turning about) (see Paloutzian et al. 1999: 1051). Within the Western tradition, conversion is often understood as a dramatic and solitary process like St. Paul's experience on the road to Damascus. Some Rastafarians and Spiritual Baptists also accept this ideal of conversion, and there is even a Baptist church near Pt. Fortin named Damascus Road Spiritual Baptist Church. On two separate occasions, I encountered Rastafarians who described their conversion as "leaps of faith."

For other Spiritual Baptists and Rastafarians, conversion is seen not so much as a leap of faith as a series of baby steps (see Austin-Broos, chapter 1; Rambo 1993). Their accounts of conversion are considerably less dramatic and more social than the conversion of St. Paul and could be described as gradual, incremental, and, oftentimes, more linear than circular. As is apparent from the above quotations by Archbishop Muhrain and Derek Manville, many Spiritual Baptists and Rastafarians understand conversion not so much as a dramatic shift or turning than as a "reawakening" of preexisting religious beliefs and sentiments.

I should qualify at the outset that conversion from the Spiritual Baptist faith to Rastafarianism and vice versa is not a common occurrence. Members of both faiths—like believers throughout the world—tend to remain loyal to their respective religions. Given the vast number of religious alternatives and the rapid social, economic, and political change that characterizes Trinidadian life, memberships within both groups are astonishingly stable.

Moreover, the religious lives of Caribbean peoples—like the religious lives of people throughout the world—are punctuated by periods of intense religious involvement followed by stretches of relative inactivity sometimes interpreted as a "falling away" from faith. Spiritual Baptists and Rastafarians who are inactive still identify themselves as Spiritual Baptists or Rastafarians, respectively. Adherents do not feel that they must break all ties with former religions prior to becoming involved with a new religious group. For many, it is possible to belong simultaneously to multiple religious organizations. As Austin's (1981) aptly titled essay "Born Again and Again and Again . . ." indicates, Caribbean peoples "try on" various religious identities, and participants in Caribbean religious groups do not feel that affiliation necessarily implies a total acceptance of that organization's belief system. For many, conversion is understood primarily as a behavioral process. Persons who find themselves spending large amounts of time with adherents of a particular religious group are seen as converts (at least temporarily) to that group. Thus, Caribbean notions of conversion do not assume the same degree of exclusivity that is common in parts of Europe and North America. Of course, religious organizations in Europe and North America are also becoming more pluralistic (see Buckser 1995).

Spiritual Baptists and Rastafarians represent two competing religions battling for potential converts on the Caribbean island of Trinidad. As Protestant fundamentalists, the Spiritual Baptists devote a great deal of time, energy, and money to proselytizing and to extensive missionary activity (Glazier 1983). On the other hand, Rastafarians seemingly expend little effort trying to attract new converts and occasionally chase away prospective members from their compounds. Despite their lack of effort, Rastafarians have been spectacularly successful in attracting new adherents, whereas Spiritual Baptists have been considerably less successful. In some cases, Baptists have barely managed to hold their own.

This is a matter of great concern for the Baptists. Being converted and converting others is a central focus of their religion (see Glazier, 2001; Zane

1999). Baptists expend a lot of time and money proselytizing, and even more energy trying to keep recent converts committed. Nevertheless, in terms of membership, the most spectacular Spiritual Baptist growth has been outside the Caribbean—notably in the United States, Canada, South Africa, and Europe. In some respects, the most rapid growth for Rastafarianism has been outside the Caribbean as well.

This paper discusses processes of conversion, disengagement, and reconversion to the Rastafarian and Spiritual Baptist faiths in Trinidad with respect to their differing worldviews, differing notions of the self, differing notions of what constitutes "conversion," and differing treatment of new converts. My initial impression was that conversion from the Spiritual Baptist faith to Rastafarianism and back again would be highly unlikely because the religions differ so much from one another and because the Baptists are considerably less successful in winning converts than are the Rastafarians. But on closer examination, it is apparent that Rastafarians and Spiritual Baptists share common values, beliefs, and aspirations. Organizationally, both groups are on their way to becoming world religions. Both groups were born out of oppressive conditions in the Caribbean in the early years of the twentieth century; both groups are religions that emphasize "the Word," are essentially Protestant in outlook (see Pulis 1999), and are what Max Weber (1963) would have classified as "this-worldly" in orientation. Both groups have had their greatest appeal among lower classes but are making inroads among the middle classes, and both groups have experienced considerable economic and political success over the past twenty-five years.

With respect to cosmology, neither group focuses on the afterlife. "Heaven," "hell," and "salvation" do not play central roles in Spiritual Baptist or Rastafarian theology. Some Baptist leaders insist that only those who affirm the basic tenets of Christianity (e.g., belief in salvation through Jesus Christ) should participate in major church rituals like baptism and mourning, but Baptist leaders seldom exclude participants on the basis of belief. Like the Spiritual Baptists, Rastafarians also tend to be inclusive rather than exclusive. They debate whether or not theirs is truly a religion at all, claiming that Rastafarianism is first and foremost a way of life. There are few fixed beliefs, and all beliefs are in the process of being worked out. Rastafarians acknowledge that other Rastas may have different ideas—but different ideas do not usually result in exclusion from the group. They take great care to distinguish between beliefs and the believer, and they contend that adherents who hold other viewpoints are accepted even when their ideas are not. Nevertheless, individuals frequently leave Rasta compounds when they feel others are not receptive to their ideas. Baptists seldom change churches on theological grounds.

ANTHROPOLOGICAL STUDIES OF CONVERSION

As noted, studies of religious conversion reflect strong Western biases and are often predicated on an assumed Euro-Christian monopoly on Truth. For example, the most cited studies of religious conversion in the twentieth century are those of William James (1929) and A. D. Nock (1933). According to James (1929: 89), conversion is "the process by which a self, hitherto divided, and consciously wrong, inferior and unhappy, becomes unified and consciously right, superior, and happy, in consequence of its firmer hold upon religious realities." James's focus—like St. Paul's on the road to Damascus—is on the conversion of a solitary individual. In many respects, Rastafarians subscribe to James's ideas about conversion. They, too, profess that their faith offers those who are divided and consciously wrong in their beliefs an opportunity to become "unified and consciously right, superior, and happy" as a result of a firmer hold on religious realities.

Robert W. Hefner (1993) aptly noted that in the nineteenth century, conversion to a world religion (especially Christianity) was seen as part of a natural, inevitable progression, what scholars of the day referred to as "the civilizing process" (see also Tippet 1992; Van der Veer 1999). The usual direction of conversion was thought to be expansive from local traditions to more universal, worldwide religions—from little traditions to the Great Traditions. It was assumed that these world religions are generally supportive of the state systems that gave birth to them, although there is some evidence to the contrary (e.g., Kee 1982). Less attention has been paid to conversion from universal religions back to local beliefs and practices or to conversions from one local tradition to another local tradition. In "African Conversion," Robin Horton (1971) successfully challenged this point of view by asserting that African tribal religions should be seen as every bit as sophisticated and/or "rational" as their Western counterparts. Tribal religions, Horton contended, differ from world religions only because they are narrower in focus (see Landau 1999). Tribal religions deal primarily with local events and personalities.

As A. D. Nock (1933: 5) astutely observed, "There is a middle country—that of the changes in belief and worship due to political development or cultural interplay." Nineteenth-century scholars paid little attention to these religions of the middle range, what Richard P. Werbner (1977) has identified as "regional cults." Religions like the Spiritual Baptists and Rastafarianism—which are somewhere on the road between local religions and full-blown world religions—serve as prime examples of regional cults.

Hefner (1993: 4) also correctly emphasized that "only a very few religions have shown great success in propagating themselves over time and space." Both the Spiritual Baptists and Rastafarians are among those rare religions that have successfully propagated themselves. Since these are young religions, their temporal success has yet to be proven, but their spatial success is indisputable. Spiritual Baptist churches can be found throughout Europe and the Americas, and Rastafarianism has spread from the Caribbean to all continents. It is even known among tribal peoples like the Maori, the Hopi, and Australian aborigines, and it has become a religious movement of immense importance and influence in North America, South America, Europe, Asia, and Africa.

There is a need to look at the Spiritual Baptists and Rastafarian as products of individual, social, and historical processes (see Berkhofer 1963). As James W. Fernandez (1982: 283) suggested, one of the greatest problems faced by European missionaries in Africa was their "tendency to concentrate religious experience on [the] individual rather than the group." This contrasts with the nineteenth-century view that religious conversion is primarily a group phenomenon (e.g., The Great Awakening in the United States). Revivalist conversions entail intense social pressures and are of fairly short duration. Nevertheless, Tom Robbins (1988: 69) insists that "scholarly rationalism must not be allowed to obscure the fact that crowds *can be* brought to ecstatic arousals that have a critically transforming effect on people."

Contemporary Rastafarians and Spiritual Baptists understand conversion in mainly individualistic terms. This is ironic because—like many Caribbean religions—both groups trace their origins to great Protestant revivals of the nineteenth century. The Spiritual Baptists, for example, claim to be an outgrowth of a great revival on St. Vincent, where, they claim, evangelist Charles Wesley preached (Henney 1974: 18). As is evident from other essays in this volume, the relationships between colonialism and revivalist movements are both varied and complex. A central question becomes "Is conversion simply the colonization of consciousness?"

Studies of conversion focus not only on engagement but on disengagement as well. Both the Spiritual Baptists and Rastafarians have developed strong commitment mechanisms. Their rituals serve to promote loyalty and attachment, and entrances and exits take place over years rather than months or weeks. Since neither the Spiritual Baptists nor the Rastafarians trace their religion to a single founder, both groups display very different patterns of defection than has been predicted by social scientists. Janet Jacobs (1987: 294–308), for example, concluded that leaving religious groups is a two-stage process: (1) first defectors loosen bonds with other group members, and (2) then they become disengaged from group leaders. Jacobs's model—developed to account for disaffection in New Religious Movements—is not applicable to either the Spiritual Baptist or Rastafarian situation. Leadership is not as central to either group as it is in new religions like the Unification

Church or Hare Krishna, and members of both religions move freely from congregation to congregation. Spiritual Baptists, for example, seldom attend services in their own neighborhoods. Moreover, they rarely attend the same Spiritual Baptist church twice in a row. Becoming disengaged from other group members seems to be more pivotal than disenchantment with a particular leader. I have observed that individuals continue to attend a particular congregation even when they do not get along with that church's leader.

DEFINITIONS OF SELF

Conversion to the Spiritual Baptist faith or to Rastafarianism is best seen as a process of identity development, reference group formation, and/or social drift. Although psychological studies stress a supposed unitary nature of self-identification, Trinidadians' reference group orientations may also be pluralistic or contradictory. As Tom Robbins (1988: 75) suggests, "People become converts gradually through the influence of social relationships; especially during times of personal strain. Conversion is viewed as precarious and open to change in response to shifting patterns of association" (see also Long and Hadden 1983: 1).

In their survey of sociological studies of conversion, Snow and Machalek (1984) concluded that conversion entails changes in the values, beliefs, identities, and, most important, universes of discourse of individuals. Although Snow and Machalek tend to focus on internal change, they also give special attention to changes in speech and changes in reasoning styles as major components of religious conversion. Conversion to Rastafarianism underscores the importance of looking at conversion as changes in speech and changes in reasoning since a major focus of the religion is on word play. Adherents are expected to contribute to an ever-expanding discourse on justice and the nature of the universe. Snow and Machalek have argued convincingly that individuals who actively participate in rituals but do not change their worldviews cannot truly be considered converts.

A. D. Nock (1933) made a similar observation in distinguishing between "adhesion" and "conversion." Nock contended that in the Roman Empire, Christianity and Judaism were the only "exclusive" religions, which meant that converts to these religions were cut off from past lifestyles and identities as well as from other religious groups. By contrast, devotees to the competing cults of Isis, Orpheus, and Mythra were merely "adherents" to these groups. A major difficulty with Nock's argument, however, is that belief and practice are difficult to separate, and practice can be a major influence during the early stages of the conversion process. Ritual behavior is learned behavior, and one must first be an observer of ritual before becoming a participant. Both Rastafarians and Spiritual Baptists report exposure to their religions at a very early age. Robbins (1988: 66) offers a partial resolution to this problem by suggesting that no single definition of conversion is either desirable or possible. Robbins asserts that religious conversion is a complex process and must allow for at least two perspectives: (1) the perspective of the convert and (2) the perspectives of existing adherents.

RELIGIOUS ORGANIZATION AND RELIGIOUS CONVERSION

Rastafarianism is a social, political, and religious movement that began on the Caribbean island of Jamaica in the late 1920s. Followers of the movement, sometimes called Rastas or Dreads, are best known as the originators of the popular musical style *reggae*, for their extensive ritual use of ganja (marijuana), and for wearing their hair in long, rope-like braids called dreadlocks.

The name "Rastafarianism" is borrowed from Ras Tafari, a name given to former Emperor Haile Selassie I of Ethiopia, who reigned from 1916 to 1974. Although a number of the founders of Rastafarianism (notably Leonard Howell and Archibald Dunckley) preached that Haile Selassie was the Living God, Emperor Selassie himself remained a devout leader within the Ethiopian Orthodox Christian Church. When Selassie visited Jamaica in 1966, he was greatly puzzled by Rastafarians who seemed to be worshipping him.

Although there are many variations within Rastafarianism, and few Rastafarians would agree with all that follows, a 1983 Rastafari Theocratic Assembly passed a resolution declaring a single variant—that associated with the House of Nyahbinghi—as the only orthodox faith. The House of Nyahbinghi Creed proclaimed that Haile Selassie was the Living God, that all African peoples are one, and that the descendants of those who were taken from Africa to be slaves in Babylon will be repatriated. It stated that all African people are descendants of the ancient Hebrews and that the reason Africans now live outside Africa is because their descendants disobeyed "Jah" (short for Jehovah, the god of the Hebrews), who punished them by making them slaves to whites. Haile Selassie I was expected to arrange for the return of all people of African descent to Africa, but following the death of Selassie in 1974, there has been less emphasis on a physical return to Africa and greater emphasis on a "spiritual" return.

The Spiritual Baptists are a rapidly expanding international religious movement with congregations in St. Vincent, Trinidad and Tobago, Grenada, Guyana, Venezuela, London, Amsterdam, Toronto, Los Angeles, and New York City. Like other religions of Caribbean origin, the Spiritual Baptists seem to have started out as a "religion of the oppressed." In recent years, how-ever, congregations in Trinidad have attracted membership among wealthy East Indians, Chinese, and Europeans. Nevertheless, the religion is still over-whelmingly black, with Asians and whites comprising less than 5 percent of the total membership. A central Spiritual Baptist ritual is called "mourning." Spiritual Baptists participate in mourning ceremonies for a variety of reasons: to cure cancer, to see the future, or to communicate with the deceased. For most participants, however, the major reason for participating in the rite is to discover one's "true" rank within an elaborate twenty-three-step church hier-archy. Every Baptist is expected to mourn as often as possible, and it is ex-pected that all Baptists seek to advance within the church hierarchy.

The 1990s ushered in a period of increasing respectability and visibility for the faith. In 1996, a general conference of Spiritual Baptist bishops was held at the Central Bank Auditorium in Port of Spain, Trinidad. Archbishop Muh-rain's address to the conference called for: (1) building a new cathedral, which would include a library for researchers who want to "make a history" of the Spiritual Baptist faith; (2) the establishment of a trade school; and (3) the con-struction of a "Spiritual Baptist Park" that will serve as a pilgrimage site for Spiritual Baptists from the Caribbean and throughout the world. A seminary— the Southland School of Theology—was established, and a comprehensive *Spiritual Baptist Minister's Manual* was published in 1993. In addition, the day of the repeal of the Shouter Prohibition Ordinance in 1951 is now cele-brated as a national holiday in Trinidad and Tobago. Between 1917 and 1951, Spiritual Baptists were forbidden to practice certain rituals, including bind-ing the head with a white cloth, holding a lighted candle in the hands, ringing bells, violent shaking of the body and limbs, shouting and grunting, holding flowers, and making chalk marks on the floor (Herskovits and Herskovits 1964: 344–45). The Prohibition Ordinance was not uniformly enforced.

It is difficult to gauge the impact of these changes on rank-and-file believ-ers. Thus far, the impact has been minuscule. Southland School of Theology has no full-time students, the *Spiritual Baptist Ministers' Manual* is rarely consulted, and construction has yet to begin on the park, the trade school, and the cathedral. The majority of Spiritual Baptist churches in the Caribbean re-main small and lack a solid financial base. For the average Caribbean church member, things continue "pretty much as before." There has, however, been tremendous church growth outside the Caribbean. Again, I emphasize that the largest and most prosperous Spiritual Baptist churches are located in Great Britain, Canada, and the United States.

Spiritual Baptists are pluralists. They acknowledge that some of their mem-bers might simultaneously consider themselves part of another, competing faith. This point of view is reflected in basic principles of Spiritual Baptist organization. Their church buildings serve as a nexus for Orisha and Kabala work (Glazier 1991; Houk 1997; Lum 1999), and many of their longer ceremonies formally begin as Catholic and/or Protestant services. Baptists also admit that some of their members drift away only to return years later. This is not seen as desirable, but it is considered normal.

Rastafarians, to the contrary, are not as pluralistic. They expect the brethren and sistren to maintain a degree of exclusivity. They are not concerned with orthodoxy per se, but they are concerned that religious discourse be carried out within the parameters of Rastafarianism. Every "i'teration" gets a Rasta slant. Switching from one Rastafarian compound to another is not viewed as a problem, but switching from Rastafarianism to another religion is seen as "most vexing." That some Spiritual Baptists should become Rastafarians is OK, but that some Rastafarians should become Baptists is considered highly unlikely by the Baptists and unthinkable by Rastafarians. It is a disconcerting event that gives rise to intense speculation and heated debate.

There is considerable internal movement among Trinidad Rastafarians. Rastas who find that they are not in accord with other Rastas in their compound often move to another, distant compound (e.g., from Maraval to Curepe or from Tacarigua to Sangre Grande). Rastafarians do not interpret such movements as "backsliding." It should be emphasized that although a large number of Rastafarians in Trinidad live in communities with other Rastafarians, Rastafarianism is by no means a communal movement. There are perhaps as many hermit Rastafarians as there are Rastafarians who reside in compounds. A majority of Rastafarians in Trinidad live in religiously mixed neighborhoods. As long as one continues to support the basic tenets of Rastafarianism (in the words of Nazma Muller, "Eat no meat, smoke plenty 'erb, and try to live Righteously"), one sees oneself and will be seen by others as a Rastafarian.

At times, Rastafarians seem more concerned than the Spiritual Baptists about the comings and goings of members. This may be because Rasta compounds are believed to be centers for marijuana trafficking and receive constant attention from law enforcement. Ganja is illegal in Trinidad, Jamaica, and elsewhere in the Caribbean, but it is central to Rastafarian belief and practice. Contrary to outsiders' expectations, ganja use is not universal among Rastas. I am struck by the number of Trinidadian Rastas who claim not to use ganja at all. Nevertheless, both users and abstainers profess that ganja should be legal and made available to those who want it.

Organizationally and ideologically, Spiritual Baptists and Rastafarians bring a great deal to each another. To Rastafarians, Spiritual Baptists bring (1) Kabala (which entails a reading and interpretation of scripture similar to that utilized by Rastafarians—see Lum 1999) and (2) a source of African pride contained within the myths and worldviews of the Orisha and Rada traditions (Glazier 1991; Houk 1997). Although many Rastafarians do not accept Orisha or subscribe to theories of spirit possession, they respect the high civilization (the Kingdom of Dahomey) that the Orisha represent. To Spiritual Baptists, Rasta brings (1) a heightened political consciousness—a new perspective on the place of Africa and Africans in world history, (2) an entrepreneurial spirit that complements and supplements Spiritual Baptist business ventures, and (3) an organizational nexus. Just as they have served Orisha and Kabala devotees in the past (Lum 1999), some Spiritual Baptist churches are fast becoming gathering places for former Rastafarians who now utilize Spiritual Baptist buildings as meeting places.

CASE STUDIES: INCREMENTAL (SYNCRETIC) VERSUS RADICAL (DISJUNCTIVE) CONVERSIONS

Social psychologists (Gallagher 1990; Lamb and Bryant 1999; Loewenthal 2000; Paloutzian et al. 1999) emphasize that there are degrees of personal transformation and religious change. The five cases presented here represent incremental rather than radical transformations. The issue is complex: How different are new meaning systems from former ones? This is often difficult to ascertain because although the conversion process itself may be gradual, it appears sudden and dramatic because of the way it is symbolized. Moreover, conversion is not an all-or-nothing proposition. Elements of the old are preserved alongside the new. As James W. Fernandez (1982: 568) noted in his study of religious conversion among the Fang, "One cannot argue that something entirely new has been created, but it is not just something old either." A. D. Nock (1933: 7) expresses it thusly: "The bottles are old but the wine is new."

The sample in this study is limited both by my experiences with members of these religions and by the comparatively small number of individuals who actually convert from one religion to the other and back again. Like all field workers, I can only report on those cases that have come to my attention. Neither Spiritual Baptists nor Rastafarians publicly proclaim their past religious affiliations. But since I have been conducting fieldwork on Trinidadian religions for over twenty years, I have dealt with a number of the same informants in various religious incarnations. My sample consists of four males and one female. All names and places have been changed to disguise identities, but informants insist that fellow religionists will recognize them instantly— "before they read the second line." Two informants requested that I use their real names in this paper, but I was unable to comply because to honor their requests would violate the Code of Ethics adopted by the American Anthropological Association.

I am struck by both the similarities and differences in my sample. Because Spiritual Baptists and Rastafarians differ in so many ways, it is significant whenever any convert reports similar experiences of conversion, defection, and reconversion. Although my sample is by no means representative, I was surprised that so many Spiritual Baptists who later convert to Rastafarianism are over forty and that there is a considerable lag between initial exposure to Rastafarianism and affiliating and identifying with the religion.

Paloutzian et al. (1999) attempted to relate psychological research on personality change and research on conversion. Does religious conversion foster fundamental changes in personality? What is meant by personality? Research suggests that joining a religious group is largely a matter of self-selection and that basic personality structure remains very much the same over time. People with certain personality traits seek those groups that attract and reinforce those basic traits. The question is "Do core traits change at all?" Paloutzian et al. argue that much evidence supports William James's (1929) assessment that by the age of thirty, the human character is "set like plaster." Why, then, do Spiritual Baptists and Rasta conversions and reconversions happen relatively late in life?

Younger converts report that they were initially attracted to Rastafarianism primarily by the music, but they did not act on this attraction immediately. One of the largest Rastafarian sects in Trinidad, Twelve Tribes, operates a highly successful nightclub in Curepe (near the University of the West Indies). The club features ska and reggae and offers a venue for local talent and musicians from other Caribbean islands. Of course, only a very small number of those who frequent the club ultimately identify with Rastafarianism. Bobo Walton is one such individual.

Bobo "Destiny" Walton

Bobo "Destiny" Walton is now a regular performer at the Curepe club. He admits that his Rastafarian connections have helped his professional career. Walton, who was raised a Spiritual Baptist but converted to Rastafarianism at the age of forty-one, sees himself as following in the footsteps of other prominent Trinidad performers turned reggae masters like Karega Mandela, Black Stalin, and Roy Cape. He points out that prior to adopting reggae, Black Stalin was a legendary calypsonian and Roy Cape was the leader of Trinidad's most respected brass band.

Walton states

> There was always a spiritual and musical culture in my house. I come from a line of Spiritual Baptists. My mother did a lot of singing and my father taught dancing. I was baptized and my mother and I went to church and did confirmation

and read the Bible from a very early age. . . . I came from a rural background and supported the rights of the poor whenever I could. I wanted to join the marches at the time of the Black Power Movement in Trinidad, but my mother wouldn't let me because I was a "little guy." I began reading books on Rastafari and His Majesty Haile Selassie I, listening to Bob Marley and what he was saying, and I learned to play the guitar. Later, when Bob was sick, I remember sleeping with a book on my bed, and a pen, writing, writing, always writing. Rastafari brought me to understand myself a little more. To know my direction. To know exactly where I was going. Now I know where I come from, it changed me and changed people around me in some way, too. Rastafari is not just the hairstyle (he grins shaking his dreads for effect). It's the way a man thinks. People are taught to judge by appearances, but it's what's inside the clothes that counts. Rasta is in the heart. If I reject you, I restrict myself. If you come to me with love, then I will have to deal with you with love. No one wants to be hassled. A man's culture should be respected. Who is man to come criticize us? Jah made the herbs on this planet. Who is man to come and eliminate it? I build higher heights of *"I-Iration,"*[2] and I smoke Jah-herb for higher dedication. This is the reason. I would like to say that I give thanks and praise unto the Most High God. Jah Rastafari Selassie I the First. I want to see the people accepting Rastafari. I want to know people are listening to my music. Yes, I would love to go to Africa. Any day. Any time. Right now!

Bertie Johns

There is no typical Spiritual Baptist or Rastafarian conversion narrative, and a great deal of personal style goes into each performance. Bertie Johns's story of his conversion differs from most because he delivers it in an understated monotone:

I was born a Spiritual Baptist, but I found that Rastafari is the religion for the Black Man. Orisha is not for me. My mother was a follower of the Orisha. It was hard for me and my brother. I liked the Baptist music. I went to Baptist service with my mother; I baptized; mourned; mourned three times. It's good for some. Not the way for me and my brother who became a Pentecostal. Rastafari people understand the world. They don't hold back. Any Rasta can say what he feel. Better for me than the Baptists cause I always say what I feels.

Bertie Johns is forty-seven years old. He was born in Grenada and baptized in the Church of England. His family moved to Trinidad when he was six, and his mother became a Spiritual Baptist. Johns grew up in the Baptist church. He was baptized at the age of twelve and mourned three times.

Eventually, he found himself "spending more time with the Rastas." He lived briefly in a Curepe compound (next to the Twelve Tribes nightclub) but found that he liked "his own space." Later, he moved to a deserted plot of land along the road to Maracas Beach, where he sold sweet drinks and snacks to beachgoers. When he was forty-two, the Orisha Ogun began calling him. Much to his surprise, he found that many Rastafarians were not supportive of Orisha work. Bertie says he had to go back to the Baptist church because Baptists are "more supporting of those who serve the Orisha." He emphasizes that he himself would like to have remained a Rasta, but many Rastafarians are intolerant of African spirits. They mocked him publicly. "I could live with it," he states, "but Ogun could not. Ogun is too proud."

Fitzroy Gibbons

Fitzroy Gibbons was born in Trinidad. He says that he has always been a Rastaman at heart. He moved to London when he was sixteen. There, he "limed" with Jamaican-born Rastas and "smoked plenty weed." He never identified himself as a convert to the Rasta faith but admits that he had little contact with non-Rastafarians. After a brief stay in Brooklyn, he returned to Trinidad at the age of twenty-five. At that point, his biological mother—who had converted to the Baptist faith while Fitzroy had been abroad—encouraged him to go to a Spiritual Baptist mourning chamber to "take an inventory" of his life. He ended up going to the mourning room three times and advancing to the rank of captain (a rank that is near the middle of the Spiritual Baptist leadership hierarchy for males). At that time, he also became involved in Kabala work and hosted several banquets each year.[3] He continued to use ganja recreationally but not for religious purposes. His suppliers, however, were committed Rastafarians who were friends of friends he had met in London. They were wary of providing ganja to a non-Rastafarian and threatened to cut him off. He began to spend more time with Rasta friends and suppliers in Daberdie. His local Spiritual Baptist leader denounced him from the pulpit for using drugs. He was repentant and decided to recommit himself exclusively to the Baptist faith. He again mourned and was given the rank of Pointer (the second highest rank a Spiritual Baptist male can attain). After becoming a Baptist Pointer, Gibbons found that he was no longer welcome at the Daberdie compound. At the age of fifty-one, he is one of the better-known Spiritual Baptist leaders in Eastern Trinidad. Frequently, he preaches against Rastafarians and condemns their use of drugs. He also continues to use ganja, which he now obtains from non-Rastafarian sources.

   Fitzroy Gibbons's movement between faiths is not typical. It is rapid, and—unlike other informants—he does not attempt to account for his conversions in exclusively religious terms. This raises issues of durability and reversibility. Why do some conversions last whereas others do not? In their "elaborated likelihood model" (ELM), Hill and Bassett (1992) predicted that a "well thought out" conversion is more likely to be durable. In Trinidad, the majority of conversion narratives are exceptionally "well thought out." When religious switching occurs later in life and within a cultural tradition that values verbal performance, conversion accounts tend to be highly elaborated and detailed, and they attempt to provide a religious and/or philosophical rationale for changing faiths. Baptists and Rastafarians speak of conversions that have taken place over many years, and converts usually indicate what they perceive as multiple benefits from their current religious affiliation as well as shortcomings of their former religion. To the contrary, Fitzroy Gibbons offers little justification. His narrative is not as practiced, coherent, or elaborate as those given by other informants.

Ganja is a factor in all five of these conversion accounts, but not in the way I had anticipated (see Hamid 2002). For most Spiritual Baptists, ganja use is seen as a push rather than a pull factor. It makes the religion appear less attractive to some. Spiritual Baptists tend to be socially and politically conservative. An overwhelming majority strives for middle-class respectability (Glazier 1991). They seek to avoid contact with the law and scrupulously avoid any appearance of impropriety. Ganja use is perceived as a source of potential trouble. For Baptists who become Rastafarians, Rasta teachings concerning ganja are almost always the basis for an ongoing and vexing struggle. Gibbons, of course, is an exception to this pattern.

Julia De Gibbs

The only female convert in my sample, Julia De Gibbs, began her religious career in Grenada as a Spiritual Baptist. Julia mourned seven times and by the age of thirty-two had advanced to the rank of Spiritual Baptist mother. She separated from her husband (who was not a Spiritual Baptist) and moved with her children to Maraval, Trinidad, in the 1980s. She was attracted to Rastafari and especially to Rastaman Desmond K. She became his Queen (consort) for four years, after which they separated. During her first years at the compound, she did not feel accepted. She complains that "it usually takes two or three years to be accepted." Even after Desmond K. moved to another compound, Gibbs remained in Maraval for several more years. Julia was outspoken about what she saw as unfair treatment of women in the Maraval compound, especially sexual taboos and restrictions on clothing (see Collins 2000).

When Julia reached the age of forty-seven, Oshun (the female consort of Ogun) began to call her. She was restless, she experienced difficulty sleeping, and things in her life "did not seem right." Her patience was exhausted. She lacked discipline and found herself becoming agitated at the least thing.

Eventually, she went to Grenada and consulted with her former Spiritual Baptist leader, who recommended that she visit the mourning room. Her trip to the mourning room was a limited success. Initially, she felt better and experienced less trouble sleeping, but within six months reverted to her former restlessness. She continued to dream of Oshun. The following spring, she went to a feast for Oshun sponsored by a member of a Spiritual Baptist church in Maraval. She was possessed by Oshun and began preparations to sponsor her own feast. The opening prayers for her feast were held at the Maraval Spiritual Baptist Church, where she had earlier become an active member. The Rasta compound and the Spiritual Baptist church are less than half a mile from each other. Julia still sees friends at the compound but now sees her major religious affiliation as being Spiritual Baptist.

Treatment of women in Rastafarianism is a complex and controversial issue (see Collins 2000; Murrell, Spencer, and McFarlane 1998). Some Rastas claim that there is total equality between brethren and sistren: "Jah say we treats all the same." Other Rastas complain that although sexual equality is an ideal, it is seldom practiced. Treatment of women is also complex and controversial among Spiritual Baptists. Although females constitute the majority of Spiritual Baptists, there is no assumption of sexual equality. A number of congregations still practice separate seating for males and females (men on the right, women on the left), and women are never permitted to preach from the front of the church. They must speak either from the back or while kneeling at the center pole. But in Trinidad, many women actually own and operate churches. Male leaders are invited guests who are paid to conduct services, and males who do not act in accordance with the desires of church owners are not invited back. Thus, women exercise considerable authority over daily church affairs. Although sexual inequality is central to the Baptist belief system, it is not always practiced.

Rawley Coombs

Rawley Coombs is one of the best-known Orisha leaders in Trinidad. Coombs lectures at the University of the West Indies, was a principle organizer for the 1999 World Orisha Conference held in Port of Spain, has written several books on Orisha (one a self-published guidebook for conducting Orisha ceremonies), and regularly conducts Orisha ceremonies in Africa and in the United States. He emphasizes that he has remained steadfast to the Orisha throughout his life and has been a follower of Ogun since he was eighteen years old.

In *Africa's Ogun: Old and New*, Sandra T. Barnes (1997) points out that on the African continent Ogun is often associated with potentially dangerous technology (e.g., weapons, motor vehicles, trains, and electricity) and with dangerous male professions (e.g., iron-making, hunting, warfare, construction, and engineering). An ambiguous figure, Ogun exhibits distinctive personality traits. He is known to be fierce, angry, vengeful, and linked to destructive forces. But at the same time, Ogun is closely associated with innovation and acts of discovery. Ogun is pragmatic. He is "this worldly" and measures success in military and economic terms. In both Africa and the Caribbean, women may not serve as priestesses in the Ogun cult.

In Trinidad, by contrast, many of Ogun's associations with technology and innovation have been minimized and his role as a military leader is stressed. Followers of Ogun, Coombs asserts, must live lives of strict military discipline. Devotees rise early, make offerings, follow a strict dietary code (no pork, no salt, few spices—a considerable sacrifice on an island where most food is highly spiced), consume no recreational alcohol (although Ogun likes rum and his devotees are encouraged to drink rum at feasts), and use no drugs. A major complaint is that Ogun's devotees are required to maintain the same strict discipline even when they are on holiday or out of work. Ogun is said to deal harshly with those who do not follow his strict codes of conduct, and, according to Coombs, "Once Ogun chooses you, you must follow his way or he will make your life very hard." Rawley Coombs and Bertie Johns cite multiple cases in which Ogun has killed followers for disobedience.

Although Coombs's loyalty to Ogun remains constant, his major religious affiliations fluctuate. During his early years, he considered himself a Spiritual Baptist. Unlike most Baptists, he claims to have attended the same church (in Belmont) for most of his adult life. From the age of forty-three to forty-eight, he became inactive at the Belmont church and affiliated mostly with Rastafarians. Coombs lived for six months on a Rastafarian compound near Sangre Grande but says he didn't like it very much. He was attracted to Rasta because Rasta, like Orisha, is "a black man's religion." He speaks positively about Rastafarian concerns for social justice and their focus on taking care of one another and bettering themselves economically. Coombs believes that blacks would be better off if "we all could return to Africa." He does not smoke ganja. Still, he agrees with Rasta theology and admires Rastafarians for their ability to put their beliefs into practice: "Rastas take care of each other. Baptists are selfish. They mainly take care of themselves first." At the Sangre Grande compound, Rawley began to realize that Rastafarians did not respect the Orisha. Some members criticized him for holding a feast to Ogun, calling Orisha work "obeah," "mumbo jumbo," and "magic" that doesn't really help anyone.

There is—as Coombs contends—a major difference between the way in which followers of the Orisha see the world and the way in which Rastafarians see the world. Orisha devotees recognize three separate levels of reality: the material, the mental (the inner self), and the Orisha (the spirits). Orisha, he points out, are not merely in your head nor are they wholly material. Rastafarians, by contrast, posit only two levels of reality: (1) the material world and (2) the inner, mental world. According to Coombs, Rastas do not use ganja to escape to another level of reality. Coombs believes that ganja is "Jah-given. It puts you in touch with your inner self (the 'I-and-I') so you see the material world more clearly. For a true Rastaman, there can be no spirits."

Rawley has lived with the spirits all of his life. He has never doubted their existence. His mother was a follower of Oshun, and he was raised by the Orisha as much as by his own mother. Orisha were always present in his household. As a young child they talked to him, they played with him, they praised him, they punished him, he attended their ceremonies, and he sponsored his first Orisha feast at the age of eighteen. As noted, Ogun is a demanding Orisha (see Barnes 1997) and compels his followers to live a life of exacting military precision. As Rawley emphasizes, "There are no 'part time' followers of Ogun. Ogun never lets go." Spiritual Baptists may condemn the Orisha by claiming that only God the Father should be worshipped, but at least they recognize their existence.

Rastas interpret their dealings with Coombs differently. They point out that there are other followers of Orisha who live on the compound and that it is Coombs who was being intolerant. Rawley, they complain, was unwilling to allow his beliefs in Ogun to be scrutinized by others. All members of a Rasta compound should expect to be criticized by other Rastas. In the words of one leader, "Rastas should never vex over scrutiny."

CONVERSION AND COMPORTMENT

Psychologists of religion have been criticized for failing to address the full context of religious conversion. Rambo (1993: 164) contends that psychologists' emphasis on the individual caused them to focus on issues that ignored or downplayed significant cultural and social variables. Rambo cites Pierre Bourdieu (1992), who suggested that the actual body is molded to carry within its very tissues and muscles the story of a given ideology.

In many cultures, religion is not seen as just a specific practice, but—as Jacob Belzen (1999: 246) argues—it is transmitted through practice (see Norris, chapter 13). Religion, Belzen contends, is best understood as an all-pervading style—a life form in which "the believers' body reveals his or her religious experiences" (246). As Meredith McGuire (1990: 283–96) correctly notes, the human body is central to religious experience: (1) in self-experience and the experience of others, (2) in the production and reflection of social meanings, and (3) as the subject and object of power relations.

Both Rastafarians and Spiritual Baptists transmit their religions through practice. These are embodied faiths. Rastafarians would wholeheartedly concur with the observations of Rambo, Bourdieu, Belzen, and McGuire. Spiritual Baptists would also agree, but reluctantly. Rastafarianism is more than a belief system. To be a Rasta is to participate in a way of life that is encapsulated in the body. The Rastafarian focus on the body goes beyond a concern with exits and entrances (Douglas 1970). What goes into and out of the body is a concern (e.g., observing a strict diet that proscribes meat, salt, alcohol, coffee, and other items commonly consumed in the Caribbean), but Rastafarian concerns are not just about dietary prohibitions. The holy act of smoking ganja is in itself both an exit and an entrance. It is a bodily sensation, calling into play all of the senses: watching the smoke as it is exhaled (sight), taste, smell, and hearing yourself breathe. But it is more. Clothing (yellow, green, and black) and hairstyle (dreadlocks) make a strong bodily statement. But it is even more than that. More than any outward manifestation, it is a concern with how one carries his or her body. Rastas stand erect and proud. They do not stoop; they do not curtsey. Rastas bow to no one. All Rastafarians are considered equal. They acknowledge none as their betters, nor do they expect obeisance from others.

This is in marked contrast to Spiritual Baptists, especially those Baptists who are followers of the Orisha. Like Rastafarians, many Spiritual Baptists observe dietary restrictions. Many do not smoke, eat no pork, and seldom consume alcohol (except when possessed by the Orisha). High-ranking Baptist leaders are easily identified by their dark-colored (navy blue or black), immaculately pressed suits, black umbrellas, and briefcases. Their clothing is the embodiment of a nineteenth-century British colonial officer. But more important, Baptist bodily comportment is that of obeisance. They stoop, they curtsey, and they bow. In their Christian services, they bow to the Holy Spirit. In their African services, they bow to Orisha. Their bodies transmit a very different message about the subject and object of power relations than does the Rastaman's.

How, then, can a Spiritual Baptist become a Rasta and a Rasta become a Spiritual Baptist? There is only one member of the Orisha pantheon whose comportment is similar to that of a Rastaman: Ogun, the god of iron. As noted. Ogun is a military leader, and those who follow Ogun must be disciplined. Ogun stands proud and erect. He never stoops; he never curtseys. Ogun bows to no one. Because Ogun is so demanding, he attracts few followers. But among Rastas who become Baptists and Baptists who become Rastas, Ogun is disproportionately represented. In addition, the female member of my sample is a follower of Oshun (the consort of Ogun). Like Ogun, Oshun stands erect: she never bows; she, too, never curtseys.

CONCLUSION

In my limited sample, Spiritual Baptists who became Rastas did so in their late thirties and early forties. Music seems to have been a major attraction. Ganja is sometimes a negative one. Some Baptists retain loyalty to Rastafarianism for ten or more years. By contrast, I have also interviewed Rastafarians who converted to the Spiritual Baptist faith in their late forties and mid-fifties. Usually, they are "called" by the Orisha. An inducement is that Orisha spirits are rejected by Rastafarians but are tolerated by Spiritual Baptists. As noted, the Baptists provide a meeting ground for followers of Orisha, Kabbala, and many other faiths (Glazier 1991, 2001; Houk 1997; Lum 1999).

All conversion narratives in my sample emphasized travel. References to physical travel are also metaphors for spiritual journeys. Informants reported that their religious conversions were often accompanied by physical movement from one congregation to another or from one place to another. Contrary to expectations, their conversion narratives are never circular. Both Spiritual Baptists and Rastafarians understand spiritual journeys as lineal.

All cases support a social interactionist view of conversion. If one spends more time with one group than another, one is seen as a "convert" to that faith. Following Robert Wuthnow's (1998) typology of religions, both Rastafarianism and the Spiritual Baptists would not be classified as mass religions but as "boutique religions." Both faiths are designed to attract a limited number of converts. Neither religion sees mass conversion as either possible or desirable. Both religions seek converts gradually—one at a time. A major difference is that Baptists see religious drifting as inevitable, while Rastas interpret defection as a moral, social, and ethical problem. But as Belzen (1999) has pointed out, "Religion is not always, everywhere, and for everyone, the same thing. Every religion produces experiences and behavioral dispositions of its own" (237).

NOTES

1. To "lim" is to hang out, laugh, talk, and drink with a group of friends in a public place. Trinidadians differentiate between "limin'," which is essentially aimless behavior, and productive behavior, which is characterized as "work." One of the best descriptions of Trinidadian limin' behaviors is provided by Michael Lieber (1981).

2. "I-Iration" is an example of Rasta wordplay. In this case, it literally means an oration about the inner self (the "I-and I").

3. Banquets are literally feasts to honor and consult with spirits associated with the Kabala; see Lum (2000), 279–80. Banquets are sometimes referred to as "suit and

waistcoat" ceremonies because sponsors are required to wear formal attire. Unlike feasts sponsored for the Orishas, spirits consulted at banquets are predominantly of European origin.

REFERENCES

Austin, Diane J. 1981. "Born Again and Again and Again. . . : Communitas and So-cial Change among Jamaican Pentecostalists." *Journal of Anthropological Re-search* 37: 226–46.

Austin-Broos, Diane. 1997. *Jamaica Genesis: Religion and the Politics of Moral Or-der.* Chicago: University of Chicago Press.

Barnes, Sandra T., ed. 1997. *Africa's Ogun: Old and New.* Bloomington: Indiana Uni-versity Press.

Belzen, Jacob A. 1999. "Religion as Embodiment: Cultural-Psychological Concepts and Methods in the Study of Conversion among 'Bevindelijken.'" *Journal for the Scientific Study of Religion* 38, no. 2: 236–54.

Berkhofer, Robert F. 1963. "Protestants, Pagans, Conversion and Sequences among the North American Indians, 1760–1860" *Ethnohistory* 10, no. 3: 201–32.

Bourdieu, Pierre, and L. J. D. Wacquant. 1992. *An Introduction to Reflexive Sociol-ogy.* Chicago: University of Chicago Press.

Buckser, Andrew S. 1995. *Communities of Faith: Sectarianism, Identity and Social Change on a Danish Island.* Oxford: Berghahn Books.

Collins, Loretta. 2000. "Daughters of Jah: The Impact of Rastafarian Womanhood in the Caribbean, the United States, Britain, and Canada." In *Religion, Culture and Tradition in the Caribbean*, edited by Hemchand Gossai and Nathaniel Samuel Murrell, pp. 227–55. New York: St Martin's Press.

Douglas, Mary. 1970. *Natural Symbols*. New York: Routledge.

Fernandez, James W. 1962. *Bwiti: An Ethnography of the Religious Imagination in Africa.* Princeton, N.J.: Princeton University Press.

Gallagher, Eugene V. 1990. *Expectations and Experience: Explaining Religious Con-version.* Atlanta, Ga.: Scholar's Press.

———. 1994. "A Religion without Converts? Becoming a Neo-Pagan." *Journal of the American Academy of Religion* 62, no. 3: 851–96.

Glazier, Stephen D. 1983. "Spiritual Baptist Outreach from Trinidad." *Cultural Sur-vival Quarterly* 7: 69–73.

———. 1991. *Marchin' the Pilgrims Home.* Salem, Wisc.: Sheffield.

———. 2001. "Adumbrations of Dread: Spiritual Baptists at the Dawn of the Millen-nium." *Journal of Ritual Studies* 15, no. 1: 17–26.

Hamid, Ansley. 2002. *The Ganja Complex: Rastafari and Marijuana.* Lanham, Md.: Lexington Books.

Hefner, Robert W., ed. 1993. *Conversion to Christianity: Historical and Anthropo-logical Perspectives on a Great Transformation.* Berkeley: University of California Press.

Henney, Jeannette H. 1974. "Spirit Possession Beliefs and Trance Behavior in Two Fundamentalist Groups in St. Vincent." In *Trance, Healing and Hallucination*, edited by Felicitas D. Goodman, J. H. Henney, and Esther Pressel, pp. 6–111. New York: John Wiley.

Herskovits, Melville J., and Frances S. Herskovits. 1964 [1947]. *Trinidad Village.* Reprint. New York: Octagon Books.

Hill, P. C., and R. L. Bassett. 1992. "Getting to the Heart of the Matter: What the Social-Psychological Study of Attitudes Has to Offer Psychology of Religion." In *Research in the Social Scientific Study of Religion*, edited by M. Lynn and D. Moberg, pp. 159–82. Greenwich, Conn.: JAI Press.

Horton, Robin. 1971. "African Conversion." *Africa* 41: 85–108.

Houk, James T. 1992. *The Orisha Religion in Trinidad.* Philadelphia: Temple University Press.

James, William. 1929. *The Varieties of Religious Experience: A Study in Human Nature.* New York: Penguin Books.

Jacobs, Janet. 1987. "Deconversion from Religious Movements: An Analysis of Charismatic Bonding and Spiritual Commitment." *Journal for the Scientific Study of Religion*, 26: 294–308.

Kee, Alistair. 1982. *Constantine versus Christ.* London: SCM Press.

Lamb, Christopher, and M. Darrel Bryant, eds. 1999. *Religious Conversion: Contemporary Practice and Controversies.* New York: Cassell.

Landau, Paul. 1999. "Religion" and Christian Conversion in African History: A New Model." *The Journal of Religious History* 23, no. 1 (February): 8–30.

Lieber, Michael. 1981. *Street Scenes: Afro-American Culture in Urban Trinidad.* Cambridge, Mass.: Schenkman.

Long, Theodore E., and Jeffrey K. Hadden. 1983. "Religious Conversion and the Concept of Socialization." *Journal for the Scientific Study of Religion* 22, no. 1: 1–14.

Loewenthal, Kate M. 2000. *The Psychology of Religion: A Short Introduction.* New York: Oneworld.

Lum, Kenneth A. 2000. *Praising His Name in the Dance: Spirit Possession in the Spiritual Baptist Faith and Orisha Work in Trinidad, West Indies.* Amsterdam: Harwood.

McGuire, Meredith. 1990. "Religion and the Body: Rematerializing the Human Body in the Social Sciences of Religion." *Journal for the Scientific Study of Religion* 29: 283–96.

Murrell, Nathaniel S., William D. Spencer, and Adrian McFarlane, eds. 1998. *Chanting down Babylon: The Rastafari Reader.* Philadelphia: Temple University Press.

Nock, Arthur Darby. 1933. *Conversion: The Old and the New in Religion from Alexander the Great to Augustine of Hippo.* Oxford: Oxford University Press.

Paloutzian, Raymond F., James T. Richardson, and Lewis R. Rambo. 1999. "Religious Conversion and Personal Change." *Journal of Personality* 67, no. 6: 1047–79.

Pulis, John W., ed. 1999. *Religion, Diaspora, and Cultural Identity.* New York: Gordon and Breach.

Rambo, Lewis R. 1993. *Understanding Religious Conversion.* New Haven, Conn.: Yale University Press.

Robbins, Tom, ed. 1988. *Cults, Converts, and Charisma.* Newbury Park, Calif.: Sage.

Snow, David A., and Richard Machalek. 1984. "The Sociology of Conversion." *Annual Review of Sociology* 10: 167–90.

Tippett, Alan R. 1992. "The Cultural Anthropology of Conversion." In *The Handbook of Religious Conversion*, edited by H. Newton Maloney and Samuel Southard, pp. 192–205. Birmingham, Ala.: Religious Education Press.

Troeltsch, Ernst. 1960 [1890]. *The Social Teachings of the Christian Churches.* New York: Harper.

Van der Veer, Peter. 1996. *Conversion to Modernities: The Globalization of Christianity.* New York: Routledge.

Weber, Max. 1963. *The Sociology of Religion.* Boston: Beacon Press.

Werbner, Richard P. ed. 1977. *Regional Cults.* New York: Academic Press.

Wuthnow, Robert. 1998. *After Heaven: Spirituality in America since the 1950s.* Berkeley: University of California Press.

Zane, Wallace W. 1999. *Journeys to the Spiritual Lands: The Natural History of a West Indian Religion.* New York: Oxford University Press.

13

Converting to What? Embodied Culture and the Adoption of New Beliefs

Rebecca Sachs Norris

Conversion involves not just adopting a set of ideas but also converting to and from an embodied worldview and identity. Since the symbols and practices of any religion have developed historically within a specific context, they cannot convey the same meaning to both native practitioners and converts. Given that cultural beliefs and practices shape experience, and that the meaning of religious language and ritual is grounded in embodied experience, converts initially understand the symbolism and language of their adopted religion through the filter of their original language and worldview. This applies not only to ideas but also to gesture, posture, and ritual, which involve deeply ingrained associations and learned relationships between bodily practice and inner states of consciousness. This chapter discusses three consequences of this embodiment for the nature of voluntary spiritual conversion. First, although a convert experiences conversion as a reorientation to a new religious belief system, the conversion occurs primarily because it corresponds with the convert's preexisting ideas or feelings about truth or meaning. Second, unless they are converting to a different branch of their old tradition, converts usually exhibit one of two ways of relating to the laws and rituals of their adopted religion: zealous adherence or selective performance. Third, since the worldview of the convert exists not only as abstract ideas but also as embodied reality, practicing the adopted religion requires not only the gradual assimilation of the meaning of terms and concepts based in the language and symbols of another culture, but also the performance of ritual postures and gestures requiring retraining of deep-seated somatic responses.

Interviews used in this chapter were taken in 1994 in the greater Boston area for a study of conversion, with the exception of F. D., with whom I spoke in 2000. The interviewees are all middle-class, though not necessarily upper middle class. All came from Jewish or Christian backgrounds, and all were in their forties at the time of the interviews. Fieldwork with the Threshold Order in Vermont took place in 1993 and 1994. By the term "conversion," I refer to the voluntary adoption, for personal spiritual reasons, of a religion or set of beliefs other than the one with which the convert was brought up. What the French call "reversion," an experience of a new depth of belief in one's own religion, which is also referred to in English as conversion, is not discussed in this chapter.

HOW NEW IS NEW?
CONVERSION AND THE ROLE OF PREEXISTING BELIEFS

Voluntary converts choose a new religious affiliation based on preexisting deep-seated beliefs. According to Rolf Homann (1990),

> Theories of recognition or understanding plainly show that our mind always leans first towards recognizing what we already know. Transferring this to cultures, it can be said that we recognize in another culture whatever is a component of our own culture. (65)

How, then, is it possible to convert to a religion that is based in another culture? Understanding of the language and symbols of an alien tradition can only develop gradually, and, in fact, a voluntary convert is adopting beliefs interpreted through an already existing meaning system. A few examples from my fieldwork illustrate this pattern.

A. F., an artisan who builds and repairs harps in the Boston area, told me that he had no church background, but it was clear that his family was strongly attached to "normal" American Judeo-Christian culture. They would not use the Islamic name he took but insisted on using the name given him at birth. In spite of having no church background, he stated that at one time he "thought he was a Christian," but he "had no teacher to show him the inner strength [of Christianity]." An identity crisis—"I had no identity"—was followed by a period of being a Sikh, a follower of Yogi Bhajan. He said in retrospect that he had needed that particular path at that time because it provided strict controls. When he no longer needed those controls, he left. He later became a member of the Sufi Order—an Americanized Sufi order founded by Anayat Khan—and after that he found the Mevlevi order of which he is now a member. A. F. found the Sufi Order after being involved with various meditation practices—he was looking for something that worked better, something "more like home." He attended introductory Sufi classes, but it was an intense experience at his first *dhikr* (a religious ceremony consisting of recitation from the Quran, music, and movement intended to lead to a sacred state of remembrance of Allah) that led him to his strong connection with Sufism. He also stated that the language of Sufism called him, conveyed something that the language of Buddhism, for example, did not. He knew "my path is Sufism but it might not be this school," and in looking for a group with which to perform *dhikr* he found the Threshold Circle, the Mevlevi order in Vermont, and felt it corresponded to his needs. He stated that Sufism was "inside me, waiting to be uncovered or released . . . it's just there." A. F. thinks of himself as a Muslim, although he doesn't follow all the laws and he admits that some Muslims might not think of him as one.

F. D., another man I interviewed, decided with his brother not to go ahead with their intended conversion to Judaism, because the Rabbi's ideas of what Judaism was did not conform to theirs. F. D. stated that he had had a lot of contact with Jewish culture due to "strange thoughts" he and his younger brother had when they were in high school. He and his brother decided to convert to Judaism after reading the Bible together. They felt there was a break between Judaism and Christianity that was not correct. They went and spoke with the Orthodox rabbi in the town where they lived, who sent them away, saying that even people who were born into Orthodox Judaism worked all their lives to learn and understand the traditions. They later found out that this is part of the conversion "ritual"—that one is turned away three times but must come back. In any case, they decided to take classes in Judaism and to move to Israel. The conversion did not work out because the rabbi who was instructing them took the main tenets of Judaism (the temple, the laws, etc.) and deconstructed them one by one. These being the basic principles that F. D. and his brother felt were so important, they could not tolerate the Rabbi's treatment of what they valued so highly, and the conversion fell through. (F. D. now belongs to a sect whose members consider themselves Messianic Christian Jews.)

The third example is from a written account of conversion to Islam (Moore 1985):

For the three days following our meeting, two other Americans and I listened in awe as this magnificent story teller unfolded the picture of Islam, of the perfection of the Prophet Muhammad, peace be upon him, of the Sufis of Morocco, and of the 100-year-old plus Shaykh, sitting under a great fig tree in a garden with his disciples singing praises of Allah. It was everything I ever dreamed of. (16)

These same sentiments can be found in interviews with converts conducted by others and in conversions to a wide variety of traditions; they are not rare but are a common element in conversions. In an interview with the *Boston*

Globe, a convert to Islam who had been actively seeking a new tradition reports, "I didn't stop believing in God, but I started looking for the right way
to worship God" ("Americans" 2000: A16). In contrast, a convert to Hinduism who was not actively seeking for something (she was a "totally content human being" before her trip to India) states: "When I arrived at the
Ganges in 1996 for a holiday, I knew that I had come home. I was in pure ecstasy" ("American" 2000: A6). Such sentiments also occur when the conversion is only from one type of Christianity to another: "I feel comfortable, as
though this is where I should have been" ("Catholicism" 2000: A19)

These statements suggest that conversion is a matter of matching a tradition to an ideal or experience that already exists. Converts in my interviews
recognized something that was previously a part of their inner life: "Sufism
was inside me," "It was everything I ever dreamed of," "I started looking for
the right way to worship God," "I knew that I had come home." Similarly,
R. A., A. F.'s girlfriend, felt that her experiences with birth and death as a
nurse were in a way her initiation, so that when she met the Sufi teaching it
was a matter of recognizing a quality, an authenticity, that she already knew.
(Her affiliation is with the Sufi Order.)

FORMS OF PRACTICE

Having acknowledged something in a religion that answers an inner need, the
convert then, only after discovering that this is the "right" tradition precisely
because it corresponds to something already existing, begins the process of
assimilating the beliefs and practices of the adopted religion. Usually this
takes either of two forms. One is the zealous convert's devoted adherence to
laws and rituals. Simon Lichman, referring to Orthodox Jewish converts he
has encountered in Israel, suggests that they are attempting to be "Jewish by
performance," since they are forever denied the possibility of being Jewish by
birthright.[1] This may be a particularly strong impulse for converts to Judaism,
given its concern with birthright and Jewish bloodlines (see Buckser, chapter
6), but it also occurs with converts to other traditions. Converts to Sufism, for
example, often take new names (as with A. F., whose family refused to use
his Muslim name) in order to complete the change of identity. This insistence
on a total immersion may relate to a feeling of inauthenticity. The fact that the
convert comes to the newly adopted religion through the lens of an already
existing culture creates an experience of not quite feeling like a member of
the new tradition, a feeling that the convert may try to overcome through rigorous adherence to laws and practices. Having converted to a new tradition,
it may also be too difficult at first to face any contradictions between the old

and new worldviews, in which case rigid obedience prevents these contradictions from surfacing.[2]

The other form in the case of middle-class Americans converting to a distinctly different tradition is a partial and ongoing process that continues to be based on already established identities and ideas. Some Sufi converts, for example, adopt only those practices and beliefs that concur with preestablished cultural viewpoints. This tendency is informed by American cultural ideals involving independence and freedom of choice. I observed an example of selective performance, as we might call it, at a meeting of the Threshold Society, the Mevlevi order in Vermont. At that time, the society was composed entirely of American converts of varying degrees of experience. It was announced at a weekly meeting that a sheikh from the Helveti order in Turkey had been invited as a guest, but that he would be leading the evening prayer, the *salat.* A number of women asked if they would really have to cover their heads for the *salat*—a ritual requirement that was being taken quite casually there. They were American, they wanted a choice in the matter, and they wanted to discuss the whys and wherefores. Covering their heads made them uncomfortable, and the fact that it was required was not sufficient reason for them to relinquish their autonomy.[3] Moreover, evidently even performance of the *salat* was not regular, as a practice session followed this announcement and discussion.

Just as Americans understand religion to be a matter of "spirituality" whereby we can choose to adopt any tradition we want, so too we will adopt only those practices that make sense to us or with which we feel comfortable. In the Middle East, Sufism is highly formal in practice. In America, it can be taken up as an inchoate spirituality, perhaps aided by Sufism's orientation toward inner meaning rather than outer form. A. F.'s objection to the word "conversion" exemplifies this attitude: "With the word conversion I think of religious practice." I asked him whether Sufism is religion. He replied that his understanding is that religious practice is related to written law; Sufism is spiritual practice.[4]

Americans believe deeply that it is our right to have a choice of religion and that we can pick any religion that resonates with our individual experience. Furthermore, we can take a piece of one tradition and combine it with a piece from another if we so please. We can practice yoga and Zen Buddhism and read Rumi, and at the same time consider ourselves Jews or Christians, because the inclusion of each element is based on personal meaning. This individualized modular spirituality, disassociated from any one specific religious practice, is not universal but reflects American ideals and values regarding freedom and individualism.[5] Adopting the whole of a tradition from another culture goes against the grain, especially since for us adherence to ritual requirements must come from personal meaning, not authority—a point of view with a distinctly Protestant flavor.[6]

R. L. was formerly a maternity nurse, but at the time of the interview she was not able to work because of rheumatoid arthritis. She converted to Orthodox Christianity yet still considered herself a Jew, partly due to the fact that she sees Orthodox Christianity as an "extension of Judaism, not a change." Orthodoxy is rigorous in its ritual requirements—how did a Jew who considered herself "almost an atheist" in her early twenties experience this? R. L. did not see the rigor as a matter of absolutes. Part of her understanding of the rigor and commitment required by her adopted religion is that the monks who were the sources of the ritual and practices lived very different lives than hers. Thus, it was acceptable for her relationship to those requirements to be different than theirs. She stated that she did not perform rituals out of "obedience," although she felt that others sometimes do. She said that she doesn't "do things unless they feel real," even if they have been explained to her. She gradually takes on more as "it becomes more real to me, more important." Adherence to ritual requirements, for her, is a choice based on a preexisting sense of what is real.

Americans are very concerned with things being real, and ritual is often suspect because it is seen as insincere or empty. Every convert with whom I have spoken, without exception, has referred at some point to the adopted tradition being more real, to searching for something more real, and so on. This more real "reality" is understood to be beyond language. R. A stated: "There's a lot in us that's essential. I can be in tears from Hindu *puja* too. It's beautiful. There's something underneath language, otherwise how could we do these things, there's something in hearing those words. . . ."[7] R. A., along with A. F., also spoke about communication taking place even when one doesn't understand the language. In fact, according to A. F., "Coming from the appropriate culture might be a block, [because one] might not see the mystical practice within the ritual."

CULTURAL TRANSLATION AND PERFORMANCE

Though many converts refer to the spiritual reality behind the words and phrases used in a given religious tradition, nonetheless they must be able to derive meaning and direction from the written and spoken instructions of teachers and texts. One factor that was influential in bringing a couple I interviewed to their particular teacher of Tibetan Buddhism was that the first lectures they attended were given by Rimpoche Trungpa, who was "Americanized," meaning that he had grown his hair and married. (I have also been told that he eats meat.) More importantly, he spoke English fluently and understood Americans well enough to bring a Tibetan Buddhism that L. T., one of the converts, referred to as "freshly baked for Americans." He rendered this particular form of Buddhism more accessible by using concepts that were relevant to contemporary culture and by speaking English instead of using a translator and leaving many Tibetan terms in their native form. Similarly, according to an American convert to Buddhism who now teaches Buddhism, "I'm trying to make Buddhism more accessible to Westerners. So I'm less monastic, emphasizing seclusion less and integration in daily life more, and include other things that people need like exercise and good eating and healthy relationships and therapy" ("A Voice" 2000: B2).

Ritual practices are subject to selection because of embodied and established attitudes and concepts. These ways of knowing the world are so deeply ingrained that we do not normally even recognize the ways in which they shape our experience:

> We say that our first culture, inherited by birth, becomes "second nature" to us in such a profound way that at times we no longer can distinguish what is genuinely of our human nature as such biologically and philosophically, and what is acquired and learned. (Ranly 1991: 65)

Religious concepts of inner states such as emotions are even more difficult to relate to coming from outside a tradition, as they can be experienced only through preexisting cultural conditioning (see Asad 1993).[8] For example, when the Turkish sheikh did attend the evening meeting of the Threshold Society, there was a conversation and a number of the converts expressed their gratitude to have found Sufism. One woman spoke, with tears flowing, of the love she felt through her connection to Sufism, her language and gestures clearly expressing a sentimental love. Rumi, known as Mevlana, the founder of the Mevlevi order, spoke, however, not of sentimental love but of mystical love, a love through which he was not only "cooked" but "burned."[9] Converts bring preexisting ideas and experiences to terms and concepts of the adopted tradition, affecting their understanding of those ideas. Even more difficult to comprehend than emotions are references to states of prayer or of transcendence—abstract and mysterious even to those with a background in the given tradition.

Like our everyday experience, religious emotions and worship experiences are learned through association and enculturation. Children initially take gestures or postures, like the kneeling position of prayer, in imitation of others or because they are told or taught. But gradually the physical and emotional dimensions of worship become embodied, personal experience, and each time a gesture is repeated, the kinesthetic, proprioceptive, and emotional memory of that gesture is evoked, layering, compounding, and shaping present experience. Images, ideas, and emotional and physical associations are all active and present in the experience of a ritual gesture or posture. These gestures and postures express inner attitudes or states, and they correspond to a particular concept of deity or the transcendent (Csordas 1994: 3). For example, full prostration during Islamic prayer expresses submission to God. In contrast, the position of sitting meditation in Zen Buddhism communicates that awakening comes from within, not from obedience or surrender. For charismatic Christians, the concept of surrender to the will of God (Csordas 1994: 19) corresponds to their experience of "resting in the spirit," which Thomas Csordas describes as "the sacred swoon in which one is overwhelmed by divine power and falls in a state of motor dissociation" (1994: 32). These practices are acquired, embodied experience, and there is a correspondence between the outer form and the inner state.[10]

Ritual takes advantage of two truths about the body: it is capable of learning certain states, and it has its own manner of knowing. Through the physical, perceptive experience of worship, as David Levin says in *The Body's Recollection of Being* (1985), "The sacred language is woven, is insinuated, into the very fibers and bones of the body" (215); ritual gestures encompass religious ideals as well as emotional experiences. Just as the process of coming to understand the ideas of an adopted tradition is a gradual process, so too the performance of ritual gestures and postures will have different inner associations and feelings for a convert than for a native practitioner. The body and feelings as well as the mind are influenced by a preexisting worldview and must learn the new tradition. For example, the Orthodox sign of the cross is a specific set of symbols[11] that can gradually become meaningful experience. This was the experience of a former student of mine who had converted to Russian Orthodoxy before leaving her native Russia. She said that at first she just performed the gestures and thought about the meaning (each time the hand touches the body to make a part of the cross, it has a specific inner significance), and gradually she came to experience the inner meaning in her feelings and body. For R. L., who converted from Judaism to Orthodox Christianity, this was a complex process. She said that having grown up as a Jew, "Jesus Christ is like a swear word." She also spoke of how difficult it was even to cross herself when she first started.

The convert's relation to worship practice can change over time. Malleability, multidimensional memory, and the direct perception of impressions of the world are some of the qualities of the human organism that enable learning of new inner states and transformation of old ones. These capacities enable converts to gradually understand the meaning of terms, symbols, and rituals of their adopted traditions. (This is not to claim that there is only one real meaning of any word, gesture, or belief system. Not only are embodied symbols polysemic even for one given individual, but also it is clear that each culture puts its own imprint on any given religious tradition.)

CONCLUSION

A convert does not take on merely a new set of beliefs but rather a new set of beliefs as understood through the old. From within a preexisting worldview and identity, a convert chooses his or her adopted religion because it corresponds with ideas or wishes that have arisen within an existing psychological context. Thus, though the converts with whom I have met speak of a reality beyond language, one is attracted to (or through) the language of Buddhism, another to that of Sufism.

Having found a tradition that satisfies specific needs, the concepts and practices of the adopted religion are filtered through the convert's language and associations. This affects not only the meanings of ideas and symbols but also the attitude of the convert toward ritual requirements. Some converts take on their adopted tradition with rigorous adherence; others perform selectively, accepting only what corresponds to preexisting attitudes. Selective performance can be vindicated in the eyes of converts since they have converted for spiritual reasons, and the spirituality of the tradition is not understood to be synonymous with ritual performance. This view is at odds with much of Islam, Eastern Orthodoxy, and certain forms of Hinduism, where the religion exists through performance of ritual.

The experiences of those gestures and postures that are performed, like emotional and spiritual states, are filtered through embodied associations. Any term used in the adopted tradition, such as "love" or "prayer," can only be understood by the convert through already existing internal definitions. In a related fashion, experiences of bodily practices such as performing full prostration in the *salat* or making the sign of the cross are affected by preexisting kinesthetic, proprioceptive, and emotional memories automatically evoked when taking a posture or moving in a certain way.

These three aspects—correspondence with preexisting ideals and wishes, performance choices based on preexisting cultural conditioning, and understanding and experience colored by embodied association—lead to a natural question: to what the convert has actually converted? Do new members of Islam, Christianity, or Judaism join the same religion as native members, or do they enter something fundamentally different, a distinctive world known only to the convert? I leave that question hanging for the present; more research is clearly needed. As we pursue an answer, however, we should remember that the features of human experience that produce these three patterns—those same qualities that enable culture to become embodied, meaningful experience in the first place—make it possible for converts, through verbal and physical practices, over time to profoundly transform their understanding and experience of adopted traditions based in another culture.

NOTES

1. Personal conversation at AFS meeting, Columbus, Ohio, October 26, 2000.
2. In contrast, those born into a tradition, even an Orthodox one, may not practice strict obedience but still consider themselves full members of that religion.
3. Numerous other questions were brought out in the discussion: for example, as the sheikh was their guest, should they behave according to the traditions of the guest or should the guest accommodate himself to the traditions of the host? Does this change when the host represents not only himself and his order but also the historical Turkish tradition? What does covering the head signify? Why should women be required to create a sacred space by covering their heads but not men?
4. In contrast, two practitioners of Tibetan Buddhism that I interviewed objected to the use of the word conversion on the grounds that "Buddhism is so all-encompassing that you can be anything else and still be a Buddhist."
5. To the extent that this model of spirituality is found in Europe as well as the United States, it could be referred to as Western rather than American.
6. The exceptions to this are those who welcome the freedom *from* choice that comes from submission to the rituals and laws of a tradition. This is also a strong force in conversion, as it eliminates confusion and uncertainty, and provides definite answers.
7. She also stated that Sufism is trying to take the wrappers off: "You take all the wrappers off, when nothing is there then you've got it."
8. Talal Asad, in *Genealogies of Religion* (Baltimore: The Johns Hopkins University Press, 1993), writes

> The formation/transformation of moral dispositions (Christian virtues) depended on more than the capacity to imagine, to perceive, to imitate—which, after all, are abilities everyone possesses in varying degree. It required a particular program of disciplinary practices. The rites that were described by that program did not simply evoke or release universal emotions, they aimed to construct and reorganize distinctive emotions—desire (*cupiditas/ caritas*), humility (*humilitas*), remorse (*contritio*)—on which the central Christian virtue of obedience to God depended. This point must be stressed, because the emotions mentioned here are not universal human feelings. . . . They are historically specific emotions that are structured internally and related to each other in historically determined ways. (134)

9. This is expressed in Rumi's writings by such passages as "Go and die, go and die, For this love go and die. . . ." (Rumi 84, Divan-e-Shams) and "O love, O tumul-

tuous love, O restless bleeding dove, This fire from above, Makes love in your heart reign, With His love I am raw, I am confused and in awe, Sometimes my flames withdraw, Sometimes consumed and slain" (Rumi 65, Divan-e-Shams).

10. Likewise, the changes in communion ritual brought about by Vatican II express a shift in theological orientation and *experience* from transcendence to immanence. Whereas formerly the parishioners were not allowed to touch the communion wafer and sometimes didn't even bare their hands before it, they now take it in their own hands and give themselves communion. Formerly, they knelt before the mystery of Christ; now they stand.

11. The thumb and first two fingers touching each other represent the trinity; the ring and little fingers touching the palm represent Christ in two natures. The fingers are held in these positions to make the Orthodox sign of the cross. Crossing oneself is done in the opposite direction than that of the Catholics, and each time a part of the body is touched it is meant as a specific reminder of an inner state.

REFERENCES

"Americans Speak of the Joys of the Hajj." 2000a. *Boston Globe.* March 16, 2000, sec. A16.

"American Woman at Home as a Hindu." 2000b. *Boston Globe.* January 22, 2001, sec. A6.

Asad, Talal. *Genealogies of Religion.* Baltimore: The Johns Hopkins University Press, 1993.

"Catholicism Sees Surge in Adult Conversions." 2000c. *Boston Globe.* April 23, 2000, sec. A1, A19.

Csordas, Thomas. *Embodiment and Experience: The Existential Ground of Culture and Self.* Cambridge: Cambridge University Press, 1994.

———. *The Sacred Self: A Cultural Phenomenology of Charismatic Healing.* Berkeley: University of California Press, 1994.

Homann, Rolf. "Cross-Cultural Dialog or Attempting the Impossible." *World Futures: The Journal of General Evolution* 28 (1990): 65–71.

Levin, David. *The Body's Recollection of Being.* London: Routledge & Kegan Paul, 1985.

Moore, Abd al-Hayy. "Choosing Islam: One Man's Tale." *Whole Earth Review* 49 (Winter 1985): 16.

Ranly, Ernest. "Cross-Cultural Philosophizing." *Philosophy Today* 35, no. 1 (Spring 1991): 63–72.

Rumi. *Divan-e-Shams.* www.rumionfire.com.

"A Voice for American Buddhism." 2000d. *Boston Globe.* February 3, 2001, sec. B2.

14

From Jehovah's Witness to Benedictine Nun: The Roles of Experience and Context in a Double Conversion

Mary Ann Reidhead and Van A. Reidhead

CONVERSION NARRATIVES ARE MULTIDIMENSIONAL

In this chapter, we examine the narrative conversion account of Sylvia,[1] a young woman who has twice converted, first from Jehovah's Witness to Roman Catholicism and later to Benedictine monasticism. Each of her conversions was announced by a personal world-changing religious experience. Her first conversion represented a radical discontinuity and precipitated a total reorganization of her life. Her second conversion was dependent on the first but—like other conversion accounts contained in this volume—documents how life-changing conversion events play out as a continuity rather than as discontinuity. This second conversion opened Sylvia to a culturally distinct monastic understanding of what it means to be converted, and, over time, caused her to redefine her life's work in terms of "constant conversion."

The juxtaposition of before and after contexts, especially when mediated by revelatory religious experience, is our focus. Our aim is to understand the determinative, probable, or random elements in choices made by individuals who have had conversion experiences. Sylvia's narrative illustrates how long-term consequences of conversion experiences can be directed and shaped by the ideological mission and cultural structures of earlier and subsequent religions. We will address a number of related questions: How did the context of Sylvia's Jehovah's Witness upbringing prime her for a religious experience? How did Sylvia's original Jehovah's Witness upbringing co-impact her actions after her religious experience? How did her conversion to Catholicism shape her subsequent choices? How did conversion to Benedictine monasticism vary with respect to the cultural matrices that preceded and followed it, as relates to her original conversion experience? How has

Sylvia's sacred narrative discourse been altered by the distinctive Benedictine approach to conversion? Would Sylvia's outcomes have varied if the contexts of her conversion experiences had been different?

Sylvia's conversion narrative was recorded between 1997 and 2000. It is presented in the order of telling. We approach Sylvia's narrative at two levels. First, what happened to Sylvia in the sequence of her conversions, and what she says about how this sequence affected her (see Mattingly 1998: 7–11)? Second, how is this narrative a source of phenomenological facts about her understanding and adaptation? Neither Sylvia's narrative nor the facts of her life justify positioning our own analysis outside the authority of Sylvia's personal history.[2]

GOD EVENTS AND CONVERSION TO CATHOLICISM

Mary Ann Reidhead first met Sylvia at St. Hildegard Monastery in May 1997. Sylvia had come for the weekend as a vocation guest, and Reidhead was collecting data for a paper on vocations in religious life (Reidhead 1998). Sylvia was delighted to tell her story and recounted her sudden movement from Jehovah's Witness to Roman Catholicism. Within a week, she had left her family and entire social network, moved in with people she hardly knew, and begun life in a new religion among strangers.

In her initial narrative, Sylvia provided information that helped us understand the context that set the stage for discontinuity. Sylvia was born into Jehovah's Witness culture and enculturated within its cosmology and narrative traditions. In Sylvia's own words:

> When I became a Roman Catholic I had been a full time minister for the Jehovah's Witnesses. I could not understand why I could not feel God. I thought I was serving him. Literally, I'd be on my knees, "Why can't I feel you? Where are you? Why aren't you in my life?" I was afraid and lonely, because I couldn't figure out what my sin was, what I was doing wrong.

Sylvia began her narrative by providing a historical anchor that divides time before and after her first conversion and established her knowledge about the context of preconversion. As a door-to-door Jehovah's Witness minister, she yearned to be rewarded with an experience of God that would proclaim her worthiness and reward her fidelity. Sylvia was on a quest. She sought an experience that would make her feel successful. But rather than rising to glory, elected by God, she felt that God was absent from her life. This caused her much suffering. A Catholic coworker invited Sylvia to her daughter's baptism, and she accepted the invitation. Sylvia states:

I walked into a Catholic Church, which was taboo for me. I had no idea what Eucharistic presence was or meant. I did not know who was behind the tabernacle doors, but all of a sudden I could feel God. To this day I describe myself as one of those stainless steel milkshake containers, cold and empty, and then being filled up with warm, fuzzy hot chocolate with marshmallows, because I felt like I was being filled.

Her description of the sacred event is that she felt like a "cold and empty" "steel milkshake container," suddenly filled with "warm, fuzzy hot chocolate with marshmallows"—a religiously unadorned representation straight out of Dairy Queen culture that stands in marked contrast to her explanation of its source—"Eucharistic presence [God mystically] . . . behind the tabernacle doors." Her explanation comes from a later narrative construction because this imagery could only have been incorporated after some Catholic instruction. In 1997, when this later part of the narrative was collected, Sylvia had enough knowledge to construct a Catholic representation of the pivotal event in her life. The absence of such language poignantly illustrates how she tried to depict her ineffable, revelatory event using familiar words and images, ones with evocative power and meaning in her own experience. She chose images and narrative style from the comforting experiences of the life of a young person with little world experience. The persistence of this "every American," "soda fountain" imagery, contrasted with the sanctified Catholic imagery that is paired with it, suggests that the pivotal segment, the representation of the religious experience, has its real time origin very close to the event itself.

Sylvia felt that she had experienced God, but what does a Jehovah's Witness do when she feels God for the first and only time, and it occurs in a Catholic church? Everything, including the event, because of the context in which it occurred, fell outside the sacred categories that Sylvia needed to maintain her identity as a Jehovah's Witness. The desired confirmation came within a context not easily incorporated, and there would be consequences, by dint of a sacred encounter happening outside the sanctified categories of Jehovah's Witness cosmogony, where (according to what Sylvia had been taught) it was not possible for such an encounter to take place (see Douglas 1982a). How would Sylvia deal with her conundrum? Hypothetically, she might have done the cynical thing and taken the experience back to the Witnesses, and reconfigured it to fit within their cosmogony and sanctifying discourse. Alternatively, she could have used her experience to complete her quest within a Jehovah's Witness context. But she did neither and states:

Within a week I moved out of my home. I left my family, friends, job; all were Jehovah's Witnesses, the only world I knew, and they practice shunning. I knew

I would become the living dead. I called the person who had invited me to the baptism and said, "I need a place to stay." I could still feel God inside, so I had to follow this.

By choosing not to deny her experience of God, and, most significantly, where her experience of God had occurred, Sylvia understood that she had exhausted her options among family and friends. From a Jehovah's Witness context, she had crossed from the sanctified categories of the living into the polluted, noncategory of the "living dead" who must be shunned to protect those who are alive in the faith. Religious groups with strongly guarded categories defining who belongs and what behaviors are permitted expect people to take action to protect against the special destructive agency of insiders who are in communion with people in polluted categories (Douglas 1982a, 1982b, 1982c; see also Buckser, chapter 6). From our data, it is not possible to identify all the considerations that influenced Sylvia's assessment that she had no choice except to abandon her social world. Was it a preemptive move to avoid the inevitable? Did she do it as an act of conscience to protect her family? Was it a proactive immigration into the sacred landscape where she now felt God's presence resided? Perhaps it was a combination of all of the above. Her plea, "I need a place to stay," made to an unnamed "person" who had invited her to a baptism, illustrates the desperate nature of her situation. She told us that the God event continued for some time; "I could still feel God inside, so I had to follow." And she followed her feelings into the arms of people whose classification in her universe had changed by virtue of their association with the God event.

We know Sylvia's experience had been a world-shattering event for her that paradoxically also held generative capacity through the experience of warmth, goodness, acceptance, worthiness, and love. It brought her into a new world with new categories. Victor Turner's concept of the ritual processes attempts to explain how such events unfold when people within a tradition are deconstructed of their childhood categories and reconstituted in a world of adult understanding (see Turner 1969: 61). Sylvia's experience is also consonant with Eric Gans's (1990) concept of "generative anthropology" as configured through analysis of the world-changing experiences of Moses and Saul of Tarsus.

Sylvia chose to manage the generative discontinuity in her life by converting to an existing religion with ready-made categories for her and her experiences. She attended classes to become a Catholic. She reported,

I felt like I'd been duped. Someone had told me what they thought Catholics believed—that's how they had been taught, and the person before them, and none of them had it right. I felt myself in the middle of this rich, deep, heritage-type faith, and I loved it.

In the above passage, Sylvia expresses her disillusionment with Jehovah's Witness enculturation. She says that she "felt duped." For her, disillusionment with Jehovah's Witness knowledge about Catholicism facilitated her reconstruction into a Catholic cosmology by authenticating Catholicism in the same movement that it dismantled the knowledge she had learned as a Jehovah's Witness. This unlearning and learning is part of the process identified by Lewis Rambo (1993: 82–86), especially through the work of the "advocate," the authoritative guide who, like Sylvia's instructors, worked to reposition her in a new world. This learning and unlearning evoked feelings that were expressed in terms familiar to her description of the original religious experience—"rich," "deep," and warm "hot chocolate." She felt herself becoming immersed in a "deep, heritage-type faith" with a succession of people and events. She began to feel at home in this new heritage because God had "spoken" to her in it and had put her there Himself, and her senses confirmed that she belonged. As her story progressed to the commitment stage (see Rambo 1993: 132–37), she accumulated experiences, relationships, and knowledge that reinforced the reality of her God experience and her decision to order her life around it.

In April 1994, Sylvia was baptized. Right away, she joined the parish choir and took on other church duties. Having traversed the usual stages of conversion, Sylvia might have concluded her narrative there and settled down to live an ordinary Catholic life, but for Sylvia, that was not enough.

"WANTING TO DO MORE": ONGOING EFFECTS OF JEHOVAH'S WITNESS ENCULTURATION

Sylvia spoke about a vague restlessness, a need to continue, an indication that something more was required to complete the plot that only appeared to have reached its end. She states, "Having been a fulltime minister as a Jehovah's Witness, I desperately wanted to do more, but I had no idea where God was pulling me."

Despite all that had happened, she felt the need to do more. But she was unsure as to what it was and attributed her disposition to her Jehovah's Witness upbringing that now informed her Catholic self. It was not herself, however, but God who was "pulling" on this cultural predisposition, telling her that the quest was not finished and that there was something special that she still needed to do. In articulating this quest, she exhibits a capacity to position the personal and sacred in flexible categories. She did feel a need to renounce everything about her Witness self in order to follow God in a Catholic context. That Sylvia told us this story inside a Benedictine monastery where she intended to become a nun demonstrates her comfort with ambiguous categories. It is clear that conscious elements of a Jehovah's Witness "self" resided inside Sylvia the Catholic.

Sylvia saw great irony when she contrasted her actual life as a Catholic and what should have become of her according to Witness beliefs. She delighted in her new knowledge of God and the freedom it afforded her. Sylvia believed her material success validated her conversion experience and actions, providing proof to her former Jehovah's Witness friends that God had shown her the truth.³ She states,

> Meanwhile, I became the success story the Jehovah's Witnesses never wanted to hear. I had a car, my own apartment, and a good job. When you leave Jehovah, you turn your back on God. Organized religion, crowned by Roman Catholicism, is the Whore of Babylon, so I literally walked into the arms of Satan. I would have no joy in my life, no friends. I would be on welfare. I was damned. Well, all of a sudden I wasn't!

The "Whore of Babylon" is a highly charged reference among Jehovah's Witnesses, and it was a super category for Sylvia because it predicated what was possible in all aspects of life once she became a Catholic. But her early experiences undermined Jehovah's Witness categories and helped her to define herself in a new materially successful way that she had never enjoyed before. Moreover, these newfound qualities endowed her life with unexpected delights. And it all started, she noted, with her encounter with God:

> But I was blessed with more. I had people that enriched my life—people in my own age bracket. As a Jehovah's Witness I was locked into an older age bracket. For the first time I had a life, and I could see it was a gift from God.

Sylvia acquired an enriched social life that was sanctified within the sacred geography that it opened for her. She felt "blessed" because it was all "a gift from God," stemming from her first experience of Him and her response to Him. Without that event, she knew that she would have none of this. It was quite literally a gift.

She put herself under a spiritual director, Father Timothy, who knew Mother Kathleen, prioress at St. Hildegard monastery (a fact that Sylvia later understood as prefiguring her call to Benedictinism). She was directed by Father Timothy to read classics of women's spirituality. After reading St. Teresa of Avila's *Interior Castle*, Sylvia declared: "I'm going to become a Carmelite nun, in a full cloister, somewhere in the middle of nowhere." But her life was full, and she was comfortable.

A year later, Father Timothy suggested a visit with Mother Kathleen. This visit was Sylvia's first encounter with living nuns, and in this and earlier events, she saw signs that God had been leading her to the Benedictines. Until the day of her visit, she had not known that Mother Kathleen's monastery was Benedictine, and that gave certain prior events even greater meaning. She states,

> I had no idea that the Jubilee medal of St. Benedict[4] that my Godmother gave me before baptism would have so much influence in my life. All of these little pieces of this puzzle God was putting in place in my life, but I couldn't see it at the time.

Here, Sylvia prepares us for something dramatic by telling the story backwards, foretelling the meanings of things that had already happened but that she had not yet revealed in her narrative. Something big was coming, and she emphasizes that everything that had happened and was yet to come was put there by God to prepare her for what He was about to reveal. According to her logic, God was putting her life puzzle together, but she couldn't discern how the pieces fit when He first put it in place. Only in the case of a few dramatic events does her narrative show signs of an alternative logic, the option to take things as signs immediately and act accordingly.

SECOND CONVERSION EXPERIENCE: THE BENEDICTINE SISTERS OF ST. HILDEGARD

From the moment Sylvia arrived at the monastery, everything was transfigured. She states,

> Here was this woman, welcoming me, and all I could think about was how beautiful she was. To me she was glowing inside. Here was this community where they were all smiling, happy, glowing, and full of God. "This," I said, "is the way it's supposed to be." I was allowed to pray with them, but I couldn't, because I was crying.

God again touched Sylvia, this time through the embodied symbols of His love in the fully habited, traditional Benedictine nuns of St. Hildegard. She recognized in these nuns people who—like herself—felt that God had given them everything freely, and who, in response, were compelled to give it all back to Him freely by giving up all their treasures—not as a sacrifice, but as an act of love, as a gift. Her recognition did not come in the form of an intellectual realization, an "Aha!" event, or an inspiration, but as yet another revelatory event, something mentally and bodily bigger, with the power to encompass and integrate all smaller mental and bodily ways of knowing.

Her second religious experience, although revelatory as a distinct event, does not stand alone. Its significance is dependent on her original conversion experience. It was a spontaneous rehappening of the original event in which she was freely created and thus liberated to life by God (see Gans 1990). The revelatory power of such events was identified in Victor Turner's recognition of spontaneous *communitas*, in which individuals experience all things and events as a unity (Turner 1974: 231–71). Taking this further, Edith Turner (1996) has shown how similar sacred encounters or revelations function in the context of a community that is, through experience and knowledge, prepared to receive them. Due to its context and how Sylvia had responded to events and opportunities in it, she was prepared for her conversion experience. It occupied a place in Catholic practical and sacred categories, and experienced specialists were there to help her. Sylvia felt that she personally understood what the experience meant and what she should do. Mother Kathleen and Father Timothy took her experience seriously but cautioned against her immediate interpretation of its practical meaning. It would be two years before she was positioned to enter St. Hildegard as a postulant, a would-be nun.[5]

Four months later, Sylvia attended her first retreat at St. Hildegard. The retreat reinforced her experience, and she asked if she might join. "I had all of these questions, like, 'So, do you wear slips?'" She had a "gut instinct that God was tugging" her, and she "had grown accustomed" to following.

She visited the monastery regularly after that, and a tentative date was set for her to enter, but much had to be done. Mother Kathleen insisted, "You need to look at other places too." Sylvia visited other religious orders, but none felt "like community" to her. Eventually she was able to say,

> Now I have answered those questions. Everything I have is a gift from God. I could see where the pieces were being maneuvered. You could tell God was fitting them together, and that's one thing, but *knowing* that your life is from him comes in at a totally different level. The one thing that is mine to do with what I want is my life and my freewill. It is like God says, "This is your freewill. You decide what you want to do with your life." My choice is to give it back. That's why St. Hildegard's is right for me.

In this segment, recorded shortly before she entered St. Hildegard, Sylvia felt that everything was ready. But the singular power of this segment comes from its being the clearest statement of her now-conscious understanding of what had happened to her in the original God event and how it had reshaped her thinking. Nothing in her narrative so clearly evidences her evolving interpretation of the meaning of the original event. God revealed that her life is a free gift from Him. This revelation liberated her to develop a full life of her own, and now, out of gratitude experienced in her second conversion event and subsequent preparation, the only fitting response was to reciprocate with the gift of her own life to God. According to Gans (1990), encompassing gratitude is the predicted natural response of a "religious spirit" to such an event as Sylvia experienced (21, 120).

The discursive structure of this section of Sylvia's narrative is monastic and shows how Sylvia had come to incorporate Benedictine ways of thinking as she explains the more inchoate experiences of the first event and the yearnings that it triggered. She now taps the discourse of a 1,500-year-old reflexive tradition to supply her with the words and logical structures to verbalize what she originally felt.

When Mary Ann Reidhead first interviewed Sylvia in 1997, Sylvia said she knew what to expect when she crossed the threshold and became a Benedictine nun. "I have seen the whole life cycle," she said: new nuns becoming novices, an old one's sixtieth jubilee, even a funeral. She had worked side-by-side with the sisters, witnessed their "huge smiles" in the grunt work of changing bed sheets in the guesthouse, "Because," she said, "they're changing that bed for Christ. He's in whoever comes on retreat, whoever is going to stay in that bed." But Sylvia was still in the early romantic stage of becoming a nun. When she was actually at St. Hildegard, she felt that she could enter and stay from that moment. But it took a dramatic event in the material world to move Sylvia, a young woman with "a life," into the monastery.

At St. Hildegard, shortly after entering in August 1997, she exclaimed,

> The last two weeks before I entered were nothing but a snowball of miracles. I got laid off on Monday. Tuesday I was asked to house sit for three months. Wednesday our cantor said her uncle could sell my car. All of a sudden, God took me to the wire and then answered everything. It's a leap of faith.

The materiality of Sylvia's life was not separate from the call to Benedictinism. She had been holding back from the decisive step, though she had long pronounced herself ready. Then, unexpectedly, she lost her job, and in this act God took her "to the wire," and she let it happen.

Becoming unemployed, her first concern was how to make ends meet, but within a day events began to confirm what she was thinking: it was time to make the monastic commitment. Her circle of friends could have found her a new job, but through a combination of her own agency and events facilitated by others, she understood the meaning of what had happened. She found a rent-free place to live for three months, which is about the time it takes to wrap things up and move to a monastery. The sale of her car would save money, helping her be debt-free, a typical precondition for entrance to a monastery. In her experience, she took the "leap of faith" beginning with the event of being laid off. God took care of the rest. Within a few months, she was in the monastery.

TRANSFORMATION: ENCULTURATING
TO A LIFE OF PERMANENT CONVERSION

When Mary Ann Reidhead next interviewed Sylvia in 1998, Sylvia was approaching age thirty and had completed six months of her postulancy.[6] The role that Sylvia's Catholic friends played in her entering St. Hildegard was initially one of resistance, a common response in Catholic culture; then acquiescence; and finally participation. After she had divested herself of possessions, her friends threw a bridal party—a "mystical wedding," they called it. Then, "They brought me home," she said.

What Sylvia most appreciated about St. Hildegard was the nonjudgmental way the nuns treated one another. Having been brought up in a severe home, during the first few months she jumped every time Mother Kathleen spoke her name. Mother Kathleen quipped that she was going to bring in a pack of cigarettes and say, "At ease, soldier! Here have a smoke."[7] But after six months, she felt that the monastery was becoming her emotional home. She felt accepted.

She had seen that everyone has "bad veil days." But mostly she was aware of love, acceptance, and equality. These experiences, which were shared with the other sisters, were further reenactments of her experiences in the original and second revelatory events, and they progressively confirmed the appropriateness of her response to God's love for her. And in the sisters' interactions with each other, she began to see a human relationship prototype for herself. "Like an old married couple," she said, "these nuns are joined at the hip." She wanted that for herself.

At the last interview in August 2000, Sylvia had been a nun for three years. She had completed a nine-month postulancy and a two-year novitiate. She had made her first vows and taken a new name, Sister Margaret. The blush of first romance was long gone, and Sylvia had gotten down to the daily grind of life in a Benedictine monastery. She had been a nun of St. Hildegard long enough to position her story within the Benedictine discourse of ideals and practices.

Sylvia is an excitable extrovert, and her religious passages were presented dramatically. By contrast, the Benedictine lifeway is steady, obedient, and disciplined. Conversion, known as *conversatio morum* (conversion of life), is a canonical vow. In Benedictine culture, *conversatio morum* results in docile abandonment to a life defined by continuous conversion, through little non-events, until death. The *conversatio* process is reflexive, textual, historical, and experiential (Reidhead and Wolford 1998). The storytelling opportunities are few because narrative performances are discouraged. This is illustrated by a Florida study in which a group of monks was encouraged by their abbot to tell their life stories. Many monks chose not to participate, partly for reasons of nonnarrative ideology and partly from the effects of life in an environment where oral histories are seldom told (Angrosino 1991).

The classical narrative form in cloistered Benedictine culture is the "lived life," unspoken and unseen. The *conversatio* quest is embodied, not spoken. In terms of narrative style, a nun's life is unfinished, unplotted as it were, until she dies and the gift of her life is handed over completely in a final union with God. A cross in a Benedictine cemetery is the only narrative that most nuns and monks leave. In another sense, however, it is believed that "this life" is a beginning, and perseverance in the *conversatio* process successfully ends a nun's story because it is a point at which she submits herself completely to the loving work of God. God's grace will continue beyond the grave until He brings her to perfect union with Himself. This has been her quest and desire since her awakening to monastic life. A nun's story is concluded when she reaches union with God, after death, but she enacts this final union daily by submitting her fate to God. Each time she enacts this, the plot of her story is brought to its end. But at each stage, the plot is union with God, and its successful end is foretold by the acts of mutual self-giving that define the relationship between the nun and God. Sylvia's most important public enactment is yet to come when she makes her solemn vows in the summer of 2003.

Will Sylvia make it through solemn vows and become a professed nun? In August 2000, Sylvia faced new challenges and tests of her Benedictine conversion. She spoke of personal conflicts with the prioress, whom she had idolized, but rather than harbor grudges, she learned to complain directly to the prioress. A greater challenge, however, is that the liturgy has become the object of a community-wide struggle. A protracted contest of wills is likely, and Sylvia's superiors have asked her to observe community discussions on the issue. This dispute pits the monastery's most sacred domain—the community prayer life—against its most profane one—the power of competing personalities. This was Sylvia's first look at a community-wide dispute that may go on for years. This test of her *conversatio* raises a pivotal question: When the dust settles, will Sylvia be able to reintegrate her original experience in a mature, sophisticated understanding of what it means to be a nun in a community of prayer? Will her faith that St. Hildegard is a vessel worthy of nurturing her gift of her own self to God survive? Despite her initiation into the monastery's troubles, in August 2000 Sylvia said,

> For three years I've been on this roller coaster ride with the Holy Spirit. When I came here I had no idea what to expect. I don't know what tomorrow will bring, but I'm OK. I'm enjoying it.

This concluding statement from Sylvia's evolving narrative is more nuanced than earlier statements. She has been on a "roller coaster ride" with peaks and valleys, slow ascents and rapid drops, but it has been a ride with the Holy Spirit. Whenever the Holy Spirit is reported as an active God presence, it indicates that more subtle experiences have replaced the more dramatic ones of early conversion. Three years earlier, Sylvia was sure she knew what to expect at St. Hildegard. Now she doesn't "know what tomorrow will bring," a confession that would bring nods of approval from superiors, because candidates who persist in knowing what to expect have a tendency to try to make it happen, and this augers badly among people questing for abandonment to the will of God. The time when Sylvia was certain that God would bless her with smiles and happiness among the sisters of St. Hildegard forever has given way to days and years of not knowing how or when God will speak again, except through the daily routine of ordinary life.

CONCLUSION

This chapter examined a conversion experience in relation to the before and after contexts of conversion and its relation to a later conversion experience that focused the direction, understanding, and actions of the convert following the first experience. Sylvia's Jehovah's Witness upbringing primed her for religious experience that would confirm her as someone chosen by God. But when this did not occur, cognitive dissonance and suffering followed. The longed-for religious experience occurred, however, in a Catholic Church, instantly changing Sylvia's understanding of the world, albeit at an inchoate level, and precipitating a sudden discontinuity in her life. Unwilling to deny her God event and shunned by the Jehovah's Witnesses for claiming it in a Catholic context, Sylvia left her mother's home and moved in with a Catholic family. The place where the event occurred and the Jehovah's Witness practice of shunning strongly predisposed Sylvia to see Catholicism as her personal link to God. Nevertheless, this was a personal choice, and by making it Sylvia's religious experience became a conversion experience in the sense of converting to a new religion. The institutional structure—ancient ritual traditions, well-formulated theology, and local faith community of Catholicism—

provided a stable environment with tools and support for Sylvia to use in re- constructing her world and her identity. Over time, Sylvia acquired skill in Catholic discourse and logic of spiritual experiences, which she was able to apply to her own life.

Catholicism opened new horizons and choices for Sylvia to express her gratitude to God, and her Jehovah's Witness upbringing scripted that she should do more than just become Catholic. Catholic culture provided her with the option of identifying a spiritual director to guide her in the synthesizing, interpretive, meaning-making process after baptism. Her spiritual director took her to a Benedictine monastery to show her an alternative way to serve God. Her yearning to "do more" perhaps primed her for another religious ex- perience that would clear up the uncertainty about what she should do. This happened on her first visit to the monastery. She experienced this event as a call to Benedictinism and a conversion, because it set in motion her transfor- mation from lay Catholic to Benedictine nun, a movement that required change in all outward aspects of her life and encouraged new perspectives for understanding her psychological/experiential/spiritual life. Unlike the discon- tinuity caused by her first conversion experience, however, Catholic cos- mogony provided Sylvia with options for integrating this conversion event, and despite its sudden announcement, her transformation from lay person to nun was gradual and continuous (Austin-Broos, chapter 1).

Guided by the monastic context of her second conversion and by Benedic- tine religious adepts with responsibility for her formation, Sylvia developed a sophisticated, adaptive theological understanding of her original conversion event: what has happened since, what it means, and what this requires of her. She now understands the event as prefiguring her call to a life of freedom, de- fined by acts of giving and receiving in mutuality with God, her sister nuns, and the outside world to which she gives her life in prayer. Her conversion story has grown more subdued as she has adopted a narrative stance in which her life per se has become her narrative. She now defines herself in terms of her commitment to lifelong conversion and lives a life of embodied enact- ments of God's free creative act of self-giving in her original conversion event and her free self-giving response to him.

The narrative categories of Jehovah's Witness sacred discourse were in- flexible and could not incorporate Sylvia's God event. The narrative cate- gories of Catholicism, however, were flexible enough to allow for her second conversion, providing an alternative way for her to position herself in rela- tion to God and society without having to leave the church. Sylvia's narra- tive brings into focus the power of context in predisposing people who have conversion experiences to alternative courses of action. Sylvia's narrative leaves little doubt about the world-changing nature of her first and second conversion experiences. But circumstance played a strong role in determining the specific kinds of post-event actions and beliefs that evolved. The context of events strongly prepositioned how Sylvia would proceed toward post-event interpretation and action.

Conversion events can happen in any context—an institutional church, tent revival, charismatic meeting, Lakota sweat lodge, or grove of trees. But for Sylvia, the before, during, and post-event contextual categories for expression and interpretation, strongly influenced by who was present to help reassemble her altered world, played critical roles in determining her life direction. Lewis Rambo's (1993) work has established the general importance of these factors in shaping the lives and decisions of converts. In a world of intensive religious experience and conflict, it is important for researchers to develop more sophisticated processual knowledge about conversion and its creative and destructive capacities.

NOTES

1. Sylvia is a fictitious name, as are all others, including the name of the monastery.
2. See Mattingly's (1998: 23–47) comprehensive critique of narrative theory and support for approaches that can find the real, experiential, and historical in narrative data.
3. Eventually Sylvia's mother did reconcile with her. In Sylvia's understanding, this happened when her mother was forced to see that her daughter was living a good, sincere religious life, the demonstration of which was seeing for herself that her daughter prayed for her daily.
4. The sixth-century founder of Benedictine monasticism.
5. Today people who feel themselves called to monastic life are never, based on our observations, encouraged to act immediately but to continue investigating, letting things unfold while staying in touch with the monastery vocation director. Thus, the movement to the monastery is gradual.
6. Postulancy is the first of three continuous periods of preparation (formation), usually spanning five to six years, before a Benedictine makes solemn vows.
7. Smoking is forbidden among the sisters at St. Hildegard's.

REFERENCES

Angrosino, Michael V. "Conversations in a Monastery." *Oral History Review* 19, nos. 1–2 (1991): 55–73.
Douglas, Mary. "Cultural Bias." In *In the Active Voice*, edited by Mary Douglas, pp. 183–254. London: Routledge & Kegan Paul, 1982a.

———. *Natural Symbols: Explorations in Cosmology.* New York: Pantheon Books, 1982b.

———. "Introduction to Group Grid Analysis." In *Essays in the Sociology of Perception*, edited by Mary Douglas, 1–8. London: Routledge & Kegan Paul, in cooperation with the Russell Sage Foundation, 1982c.

Gans, Eric. *Science and Faith: The Anthropology of Revelation.* Savage, Md.: Rowman & Littlefield, 1990.

Mattingly, Cheryl. *Healing Dramas and Clinical Plots: The Narrative Structure of Experience.* Cambridge: Cambridge University Press, 1998.

Rambo, Lewis R. *Understanding Religious Conversion.* New Haven, Conn.: Yale University Press, 1993.

Reidhead, Mary Ann. "Meaning, Context, and Consensus in Becoming and Remaining a Benedictine." *Magistra* 4, no. 1 (1998): 44–56.

Reidhead, Van A., and John B. Wolford. "Context, Conditioning, and Meaning of Time-Consciousness in a Trappist Monastery." In *Toward a Science of Consciousness II: The Second Tucson Discussions and Debates*, edited by S. R. Hameroff and A. C. Alwyn, 657–65. Cambridge, Mass.: The MIT Press, 1998.

Turner, Edith. *The Hands Feel It: Healing and Spirit Presence among a Northern Alaskan People.* DeKalb: Northern Illinois University Press, 1996.

Turner, Victor. *The Ritual Process: Structure and Anti-Structure.* Chicago: Aldine, 1969.

———. *Dramas, Fields, and Metaphors.* Ithaca, N.Y.: Cornell University Press, 1974.

15

Converted Christians, Shamans, and the House of God: The Reasons for Conversion Given by the Western Toba of the Argentine Chaco

Marcela Mendoza

"One of the most fascinating topics in the study of conversion and commitment," says Rambo (1993), "is the nature of people's motivation for conversion. This is a concern for scholars of conversion as well as for those who are advocates" (137). People's motivation reaches a peak of relevance during the initial commitment, and it may change as the converts acquire a new mystic language and reconstruct their personal life stories. Some anthropologists have studied the distinctive religious structures and shamanic practices that make it more difficult for members of egalitarian band societies to convert to a Christian creed (Yengoyan 1993). Other anthropologists—following the analysis of the Comaroffs (1991)—have studied the imposition of hegemonic political and economic powers over hunter-gatherer groups that experienced missionization (Blaser 1999; Gordillo 1999). Instead of discussing the structure of the native religion or the broader sociopolitical context in which the people are immersed, this study is focused on the religious explanation given by former hunter-gatherers who have already converted to Christianity. The explanation that I analyze below is an after-the-fact validation provided by Western Toba adults converted to Anglicanism, initially preached to their parents by missionaries from Great Britain in the 1930s.[1]

HUNTER-GATHERERS AND MISSIONARIES

The distinctive encounter and eventual conversion of hunter-gatherer peoples by Christian missionaries around the world presents an interesting case of missionization. In the Americas, from Alaska to Tierra del Fuego, Jesuits,

Franciscans, Salesians, and Oblates Roman Catholic missionaries (Caraman 1976; Fritz 1997; Helm and Leacock 1988; Martinic 1997; Saeger 1989; Teruel 1998) and Russian Orthodox ones as well (Kan 1985) have established missions among hunter-gatherers since the beginnings of the European colonization. Presbyterian, Anglican, Mennonite, and other Protestant Christian missionaries have also opened numerous missions among foraging peoples of the Americas and Australia (Broock 2000; Miller 1974; Swain and Bird Rose 1988).

In North America, conversion of the native peoples was stimulated by the belief that they were descendants of the ten lost tribes of Israel. Many times the missionaries initiated the contact, but at other times the hunter-gatherer bands approached the missionaries. The bands that sought out a relation with missionaries were experiencing encroachment of their land or an increased level of aggression by neighboring ethnic groups. The missionaries were successful only in those areas where early contacts had undermined the aboriginal lifeways. Once the relationship between a hunter-gatherer group and Christian missionaries was established, both participants in the cultural dialogue made efforts to adapt to each other's different approaches to society and religion. For example, Franciscan Father Rafael Gobelli, head of Nueva Pompeya Mission among the Wichí of the Bermejo River in the Argentine Chaco, wrote on February 8, 1913:

> I don't know what to do with these Indians. It is extremely difficult to make them work, even for their own benefit. They only want to have free meals, rest all day long, and leave for the bushes. (Cited by Teruel 1998: 114; my translation from Spanish)

The organization of small, mobile, and highly cooperative foraging groups around the world has been described as nonterritorial, oriented to direct consumption, and egalitarian. To adapt to the bands' mobility, Protestant missionaries have attempted to follow the families' seasonal trekking. These unsuccessful attempts ended with the construction of permanent mission stations—a strategy that fostered the sedentarization of the bands (Grubb 1925; Russo 1980). The stations were built as a base to proselytize. Missionaries could not dissociate Christianity from their own cultural context, which included a church community, wage labor, and a settled nuclear family. Besides their role in evangelization, the missions offered various services—such as food, schooling, and healthcare—that effectively attracted the bands. The stations also offered to the indigenous people a safe heaven from the violence generated by colonizers and soldiers. The foragers were initially more enticed by the practical advantages of a mission than by the Christian theology preached to them.

To many hunter-gatherer societies, their contact with missionaries was followed by the traumatic impact of epidemics and diseases. Shamans and healers were often unable to counteract the devastating effects of these epidemics, a failure that, in turn, emphasized the people's sense of social and cultural crisis. Anglican missionary Alfred Leake—who in 1927 started Mission San Andrés among the Wichí of Upper Pilcomayo River—wrote:

> Measles and flu epidemics had been raging among the Indians and also among many of the Argentines, and on every side we saw sick people lying on the ground in filthy rags, utterly miserable. Their only hope is that a witch-doctor may, by singing chants, rattling gourds and making other unearthly noises, be able to drive away evil spirits that are afflicting them. (Cited by Makower 1989: 64)

Shamans and elders generally opposed Christian evangelism, although there were also examples of individuals in such roles offering themselves for baptism into the new creed. Among hunter-gatherers, individuals rather than communities were the ones who withdrew their support by leaving the village near a mission and moving to another place. Many missions among hunter-gatherers of southwest Australia and the South American Gran Chaco experienced seasonal fluctuations in their populations. Indigenous people who lived around the stations often left the area in search for employment, to visit relatives, and to forage in their traditional ranges. Although some missionaries were able to introduce new ideas and practices to hunting-gathering communities, it proved to be more difficult to induce the people into religious conversion.

THE WESTERN TOBA

The Western Toba hunter-gatherers inhabited the land north of Pilcomayo River, between the parallels 23° 20' and 23° 30' latitude south, at least since the 1600s, when the first colonial documents reported on their existence. Today, the Western Toba of Formosa Province, Argentina, constitute a population of some 1,200 individuals. They live in three main villages and several small settlements located at the intersection of Pilcomayo River and the Tropic of Capricorn (Mendoza 1999). In the late 1800s, Bolivian settlers and soldiers established cattle posts and forts north of Upper Pilcomayo River. In 1903, Argentine colonists began pasturing cattle in Indian land south of the river. They initiated a process of encroachment that ended in 1989, when the Argentine state granted to the Western Toba legal property over 35,000 hectares of their traditional ranges south of the Pilcomayo River (De la Cruz and Mendoza 1989).

Initially, the Western Toba reacted to the presence of the cattle breeders with contention. Between 1915 and 1917, a native prophet preached the need to expel the settlers from Indian land. He had a vision from *Cadetá* (Our Father) announcing that the indigenous people would become rich again and the world would be as it was before the intrusion of the Europeans. Warriors from different Toba bands actually raided cattle posts and drove the families of settlers out of the area. From the point of view of the colonists, it was a rebellion that deserved swift punishment. From the point of view of the Western Toba, it was a nativistic movement that ended with their most significant defeat at the hands of the Argentine military. The doctrine of the indigenous movement is comparable to the doctrine of the Ghost Dance studied by Mooney (1886). In fact, both movements present surprising similarities regarding their hostility toward Europeans and the return to idealized aboriginal times. My point here is that until the late 1910s, the Western Toba believed in the power of their shamans and their warriors to overcome the intrusion of colonists. Several years after the defeat of Toba warriors by the Argentine Army, some bands consensually decided to request a mission from Anglican missionaries, who had already opened a station among the neighboring Wichí, upstream the Pilcomayo River.

In 1930, the South American Missionary Society established El Toba Mission at the core of the area inhabited by the Western Toba. Not one of the missionaries spoke Toba language, but one Toba man spoke Wichí—a language the missionaries could understand—and another Toba spoke some Spanish. They were able to help in the early days of the mission. From the start, the missionaries offered schooling, healthcare, and food in exchange for indigenous labor and local products, such as animal skins, feathers, and crafts. They met the resistance of some Toba shamans and elders. The missionaries regarded shamans as "Satan's chief weapon" (*SAMS Magazine* 1935a: 121). However, the missionaries also received the support of several other individuals who became preachers for the new creed.

Shortly after the establishment of the mission, the missionaries created a Toba alphabet—which closely follows the Spanish alphabet—and began to teach the people how to read and write their language. This newly acquired ability was widely used to send messages back and forth to distant indigenous communities. Beginning in 1934, the names of the Toba inquirers appear frequently in the reports of the missionaries (see Leake 1970; Makower 1989; Mann 1968; Sinclair 1980). The first Toba baptism took place in 1936. The next year, a booklet of parts of the Old Testament and the Gospel of Mark was published in Toba language. These were the first texts that the Toba were able to read in their own language. In 1937, a missionary at El Toba Mission reported: "In three of the villages actually on the station, and on one about two leagues away, prayer huts have been built entirely on the initiative of the people themselves" (*SAMS Magazine* 1937: 59).

However, the missionaries still doubted the extent of the people's conversion. For example, Alfred Leake reported in 1943:

> Uraiqui, one of our best Christian evangelists, is an ex-witch-doctor, and although we are convinced that he has given up all evil practices connected with his old craft, the Tobas are not so sure. Every now and then we are told that such and such a sickness has been sent by him, or that he has bewitched such and such man . . . twelve and a half years after being welcomed amongst the Tobas by Chief Choliqui, the Gospel has hardly scratched below the surface in very many hearts. This knowledge makes us all the more thankful for those eighty-odd faithful ones who have really broken with the old life. (*SAMS Magazine* 1943: 11)

In the 1990s, Western Toba adults who had converted to Christianity explained to me the reasons why they believe in the God of the scriptures, about whom the missionaries and native pastors have been preaching for the past sixty years. The experiential knowledge of the converted adults comes not only from listening to the missionaries' preaching but also from listening to the shamans' experiences. The scriptural God, they say, is a real spiritual presence that lives up in the skies. Ultimately, they believe in this God's existence because the shamans have confirmed and validated such a conclusion.

THE SHAMANIC ENCOUNTER

During their mystical flights to the upper sky, powerful shamans have been able to reach the entrance of a very bright and large place guarded by the owner's helpers. The Toba used the word *piguem'lec* (translated as "angels") to name these helpers. The shamans said that this bright place was the "House of God." However, they were not allowed to enter there.

Toba religion is based on personal relationships between an individual and spirits that are the "owners" of the animals and plants found in their habitat. The Toba also establish relationships with other spirits that "embody" natural forces and elements such as the thunder, the northern wind, the morning star, and so forth. Each individual seeks to incorporate as many spiritual companions as possible because these companions would help the person to succeed in daily hunting and foraging trips, and to overcome life-threatening situations. Every person—man or woman—can establish a relationship with a spiritual companion. However, the individuals who are ritually initiated as shamans count with the assistance of the most powerful of all spirits, who teach and guide them. Empowered by a personal spiritual relation with their helpers, Toba shamans devote themselves to heal the sick and make predictions of future events.

None of the shamans' spiritual companions—not even the most powerful ones, they say—has ever been granted entrance to the House of God. It is a place reserved for the owner's servants, fiercely guarded by his helpers.

THE AFTERLIFE

The Anglican missionaries preached that all Christian believers would go to heaven after death and that they would live forever in the "house" of the God of the Bible. Nevertheless, they emphasized that only the faithful ones would be welcomed there. Toba believers describe the House of God as a place where food and water are abundant and the animals are tame and friendly to humans (the animals would voluntarily become a hunter's prey, they say). Several Toba adults explained to me that this image of a peaceful and pleasant afterlife was an important consideration in their conversion to Christianity.

The extent to which Anglican missionaries have overemphasized a rewarding afterlife for all the believers is unsure. What really matters is that Toba converts became interested in the idea and elaborated over it. Traditional Toba religion does not pay much attention to the afterlife. In oral narratives, the dead carry on a peculiar existence on an opposite plane below the surface of the earth. When the sun shines on Earth, it is night in the land of the dead. The food eaten by the dead is considered inedible for those who are alive. The souls of the recently dead often feel lonely and miss the company of their loved ones. The recently dead would try to return to their village, the Toba say, with the purpose of taking their loved ones back with them to the underworld (see Wilbert and Simoneau 1982, 1989). The souls of sorcerers and shamans who have betrayed their spiritual companions (for example, by using their power to kill people) and the souls of those who were defeated by another shaman during a shamanic duel are kept in confinement below the surface of earth. They are condemned to a solitary life with scarce food and water at hand.

To Christian converts who have been enculturated in the native religion and believe in the power of Toba shamans to heal and to cause harm as well, the oral story validating the existence of a House of God "up in heaven" represents a very important piece of information. The Toba converts talk about it as if the story would have happened a long time ago. They say that the oldest shamans had already been denied entrance to the celestial house before the arrival of the Europeans.

It's impossible to determine when the Toba shamans have created their explanation about the "reality" of "God" and the "House of God"(before or after the spread of the Christian teachings). From a native point of view, the explanation gives credit to the native cosmology and supports the shamanic authority. From the converts' point of view, the shamans' mystical experiences confirm the existence of a mighty "God" who owns a place up in the sky and whose helpers would deny entrance to individuals unrelated to the owner.

Today, Toba adults converted to Christianity affirm that they will enter the House of God after death and live in there. It is described as a place where they will be happy forever in the company of their loved ones. To enter the House of God, believers need to fulfill two conditions: they have to participate frequently in prayer meetings and they need to be in peace with their kindred. Participation in prayer meetings creates bonding among believers and, equally important, it propitiates the participants' physical health and good fortune through collective prayer. Future happiness is also anticipated (and confirmed) in the people's dreams. Those who are not believers—who practice witchcraft, cause harm to their neighbors, refrain from sharing food, lie, and steal—would not enter the House of God and would not enjoy the pleasures reserved to the faithful.

CONCLUSION

Conversion to Christianity is a complex, multifaceted process involving personal, cultural, social, and religious dimensions. "While conversion can be triggered by particular events," says Rambo (1993), "for the most part it takes place over a period of time" (165). To be successful, a process of conversion needs to be rooted in the indigenous religious traditions of the people. Also, as various Christian denominations would emphasize different aspects of their creed and would carry on distinct missionary styles, the missionaries' preaching could possibly elicit diverse responses from hunter-gatherers that share similar religious conceptions. For example, the preaching of Mennonite missionaries among the Eastern Toba of the Argentine Chaco (Miller 1967, 1995) nourished a Pentecostal-type movement. Eastern Toba religious services emphasize healing and intimate communication with the spirits (trance or spirit possession) that are reached in the course of dancing, singing, and praying. "Pentecostal emphasis upon healing, Holy Spirit infilling, and apocalyptic eschatology," says Miller (1967: 186), has provided Eastern Toba hunter-gatherers with a central theme around which the new beliefs could be organized and disseminated.

Instead of personal communication with the Holy Spirit, the Western Toba chose to highlight from the Anglican preaching the notions about a heavenly God and a promised afterlife. They could have done it differently, however, because the native Toba religion provides the conditions to understand and incorporate the Christian notion of "possession" by the Holy Spirit. After several decades of missionization, Western Toba Christians have come to separate themselves from nonbelievers. They manifest a change of beliefs and behavior that could potentially endanger the survival of the native religion. The recourse to the old shaman's explanation to legitimate the existence of the House of God made by the converted could be interpreted as a intent to restore some of the authority (and integrity) of the traditional native religion without seriously compromising the basis for the people's conversion.

NOTE

1. I carried out fieldwork among the Western Toba in 1984, 1985, 1987, 1988, and 1993–1995. The research has been supported by the Argentine Council for Scientific and Technological Research (CONICET) and by the Graduate College of the University of Iowa.

REFERENCES

Blaser, M. 1999. "Blessed Words: Missionaries, Chamacoco Leaders and the Politics of Hegemonic Coincidence." Paper presented at the Indigenous Peoples of the Gran Chaco, Missionaries, and Nation-States conference, St. Andrews University, Scotland, March 22–25.

Broock, P. 2000. "Mission Encounter in the Colonial World: British Columbia and South-West Australia." *Journal of Religious History* 24, no. 2: 159–79.

Caraman, P. 1976. *The Lost Paradise: The Jesuit Republic in South America.* New York: The Seabury Press.

Comaroff, Jean, and John Comaroff. 1991. *Of Revelation and Revolution: Christianity, Colonialism and Consciousness in South Africa.* Chicago: University of Chicago Press.

De la Cruz, L., and M. Mendoza. 1989. "Les Tobas de l'Óuest de Formosa et le processus de reconnaissance légale de la propriété des terres." *Recherches Amérindiennes au Quebec* 19: 43–51.

Fritz, M. 1997. *"Nos han salvado." Misión: Destrucción o salvación?* Quito, Ecuador: Ediciones Abya-Yala.

Gordillo, G. 1999. *The Bush, the Plantations, and the "Devils": Culture and Historical Experience in the Argentinean Chaco.* Ph.D. diss., University of Toronto.

Helm, J., and E. B. Leacock. 1988. "The Hunting Tribes of Subarctic Canada." In *North American Indians in Historical Perspective*, edited by E. B. Leacock and N. O. Lurie, 2nd ed., 343–74. Prospect Heights, Ill.: Waveland Press.

Grubb, W. B. 1925. *An Unknown People in an Unknown Land.* London: Seely, Service and Co.

Kan, S. 1985. "Russian Orthodox Brotherhoods among the Tlingit: Missionary Goals and Native Responses." *Ethnohistory* 32: 196–223.

Makower, K. 1989. *Don't Cry for Me. Poor Yet Rich: The Inspiring Story of Indian Christians in Argentina.* London: Hodder and Stoughton.

Martinic B. M. 1997. "The Meeting of Two Cultures. Indians and Colonists in the Magellan Region." In *Patagonia. Natural History, Prehistory and Ethnography at the Uttermost End of the Earth*, edited by C. McEwan, L. Borrero, and A. Prieto, pp. 110–26. Princeton, N.J.: Princeton University Press.

Mendoza, M. 1999. "The Western Toba: Family Life and Subsistence of a Former Hunter-Gatherer Society." In *Peoples of the Gran Chaco*, edited by E. S. Miller, pp. 81–108. Westport, Conn.: Bergin and Garvey.

Miller, E. S. 1967. *Pentecostalism among the Argentine Toba.* Ph.D. diss., University of Pittsburgh.

———. 1974. "The Christian Missionary: Agent of Secularization." In *Native South Americans*, edited by P. Lyon, pp. 391–97. Prospect Heights, Ill.: Waveland Press.

———. 1995. *Nurturing Doubt. From Mennonite Missionary to Anthropologist in the Argentine Chaco.* Urbana: University of Illinois Press.

Mooney, J. 1886. *The Ghost-Dance Religion and the Sioux Outbreak of 1890*, vol. 14, part 2. Washington, D.C.: Smithsonian Institution.

Rambo, L. 1993. *Understanding Religious Conversion.* New Haven, Conn.: Yale University Press.

Russo, G. 1980. *Lord Abbot of the Wilderness: The Life and Times of Bishop Salvado.* Melbourne: Polding Press.

Saeger, J. S. 1988. "Eighteenth-Century Guaycuruan Missions in Paraguay." In *Indian-Religious Relations in Colonial Spanish America*, Latin American Series, edited by S. E. Ramírez, vol. 9, pp. 55–86. Syracuse, N.Y.: Maxwell School.

South American Missionary Society *(SAMS) Magazine*. 1935a. "The Toba Mission." *South American Missionary Society (SAMS) Magazine* 69: 128–29.

———. 1935b. "On the Banks of the Pilcomayo River." *South American Missionary Society (SAMS) Magazine* 71: 54–59.

———. 1943. "A Chief Dies." *South American Missionary Society (SAMS) Magazine* 77: 11–12.

Swain, T., and D. Bird Rose, eds. 1988. *Aboriginal Australians and Christian Missions.* Bedford Park, Australia: The Australian Association for the Study of Religions.

Teruel, A. 1998. "Misioneros e indígenas en el Chaco Salteño en el siglo XIX." In *Pasado y presente de un mundo postergado*, edited by A. Teruel and O. Jerez, 103–31. Jujuy, Argentina: Universidad Nacional de Jujuy.

Wilbert, J., and K. Simoneau, eds. 1982. *Folk Literature of the Toba Indians*, vol. 1. Los Angeles: University of California Press.

————. 1988. *Folk Literature of the Toba Indians*, vol. 2. Los Angeles: University of California Press.

Yengoyan, A. 1991. "Religion, Morality, and Prophetic Traditions: Conversion among the Pitjantjatjara of Central Australia." In *Conversion to Christianity. Historical and Anthropological Perspectives on a Great Transformation*, edited by R. W. Hefner, pp. 233–57. Berkeley: University of California Press.

AFTERWORD

16

Anthropology and the Study of Conversion

Lewis R. Rambo

The study of conversion has expanded dramatically in the last two decades. Once the almost exclusive preserve of psychologists and evangelicals, conversion is now being examined by anthropologists (Harding 1987; Hefner 1993; Jules-Rosette 1975, 1976), historians (Cusack 1998; Kaplan 1996; MacMullen 1984; Muldoon 1997), literary scholars (Viswanathan 1998), sociologists (Montgomery 1991, 1996, 1999, 2001; Richardson 1978; Robertson 1978; Yang 1999), and theologians from many religious traditions. The study of conversion has gained momentum during the last two decades largely due to a global resurgence in the study of religion.

Fundamentalist movements impact virtually all religions—sometimes with striking political implications. Charismatic and Pentecostal Christianity pervades the world (Poewe 1994). Buddhist renewals abound in India and Southeast Asia and have attracted growing numbers of adherents in Europe and North America. Most striking, however, is Islam, which has not only reasserted itself with the conversion of millions of people in Asia, Africa, Europe, and North America, but has also captured the hearts and minds of many who desire to transform the world's economic and political realities—especially those living in places around the globe encumbered by the legacies of Western colonial oppression, military domination, and economic exploitation. In Europe and North America, the most dramatic and unanticipated conversions have been conversions to new religious movements (see Dawson 1998).

Conversion captures the popular imagination and scholarly attention for two basic reasons. At the individual level, we want to know how people change. This issue haunts the minds of many as they contemplate the human predicament. Most of us are keenly aware of the difficulties encompassed in change—even in mundane situations requiring individual initiative and agency like eliminating a bad habit. Changing one's religion is all the more perplexing because religion is believed to be deeply rooted in family connections, cultural traditions, ingrained customs, and ideologies. At the social level, we are impressed by the impact of massive religious change because so much of the world has been and continues to be shaped by world religions such as Buddhism, Christianity, Hinduism, Islam, Judaism, and other religious forces (Hefner 1993; Kaplan 1996; Lamb and Bryant 1999). Therefore, we are at once fascinated and baffled by the transformation of individuals and groups undergoing conversion.

CONTRIBUTIONS OF ANTHROPOLOGY
TO THE STUDY OF CONVERSION

As is evidenced by this collection, anthropologists are making distinct and important contributions to the study of religious conversion. First, anthropologists appreciate and richly describe the context in which religious change takes place. On the one hand, psychologists have tended to focus on individuals—virtually ignoring the rich contextual matrix of conversion except for the role of the family in a person's intrapsychic processes. Anthropologists, on the other hand, pay close attention to the contextual matrix of conversion (see especially Buckser, chapter 6; Norris, chapter 13; and Reidhead and Reidhead, chapter 14).

Second, anthropologists are often in a position to see conversion as it occurs among those who have had little previous exposure to Christianity or Islam; for example, they can examine the intricate and subtle processes that transpire in a convert's first contact with a new religious option (see Farhadian, chapter 5; Lohmann, chapter 9; Mendoza, chapter 15; Menon, chapter 4; Priest, chapter 8). It is hoped that anthropologists will continue this focus. It is also hoped that anthropologists will devote specialized and sustained attention to the processes of conversion. Thus far, ethnographers in the field have not focused exclusively on the conversion phenomenon per se but have combined their studies of conversion with studies touching on a vast array of other topics.

Third, anthropologists contribute to the study of conversion by providing analysis and insight into the long-term consequences of religious change. Psychologists and sociologists often have produced studies of conversion that are synchronic: they offer portraits of conversion at one particular point in time. Because longitudinal studies are more expensive and extremely difficult to conduct, they are generally not attempted within the disciplines of psychology or sociology. Anthropologists, however, tend to establish long-term relationships with particular groups and return to their research sites frequently. For example, Glazier (chapter 12) has conducted research among religious groups on the Caribbean island of Trinidad for over twenty years. Long-term fieldwork often yields rich data on processes of conversion as these processes manifest among particular individuals and groups.

Fourth, anthropologists bring what might be termed theoretical flexibility to the phenomenon of conversion (see Di Bella, chapter 7; Anderson, chapter 10). Anthropologists, it appears, do not rush to impose rigid theoretical interpretations on their data. They seem to accept the complexity of conversion events (see especially Brown, chapter 10; Buckser, chapter 6; Coleman, chapter 2) and avoid hasty or sweeping conclusions. They are willing to restate earlier conclusions in light of new data (see Anderson, chapter 10; Buckser, chapter 6; Coleman, chapter 2; Glazier, chapter 12; Mendoza, chapter 15; Seeman, chapter 3). In my view, this represents a valuable advance in the study of conversion. Unlike the earlier, classic studies (e.g., those of G. Stanley Hall, William James, Edwin Starbuck, and James H. Leuba), which were conducted primarily from the perspective of Christian psychology, anthropological researchers have attempted to fit their theories to the data, not force the data to fit their theories.

PERSISTENT THEMES IN CONVERSION STUDIES

Fundamental issues reflected in this collection are similar to the issues that emerge in the various disciplines addressing topics of religious change and transformation.

Defining Conversion

The definition of conversion remains a vexing problem. The theological legacy of Christian hegemony means that the word "conversion" is generally limited to notions of radical, sudden change (for a critique, see the chapters by Buckser, chapter 6; Coleman, chapter 2; Farhadian, chapter 5; Glazier, chapter 12; Reidhead and Reidhead, chapter 14). Evangelical Christians have tended to "own" the concept for several hundred years, and most conversations about conversion—whether on a popular or scholarly level—are confined to the Pauline paradigm of sudden, dramatic change. The Pauline model of conversion combines notions of an unexpected flash of revelation, a radical reversal of previous beliefs and allegiances, and an underlying assumption that converts are passive respondents to outside forces. Some scholars (Long and Hadden 1983; Richardson 1978) consider the Pauline model too restrictive and have advocated jettisoning the word "conversion" altogether.

Definitions of conversion complicate discussions of conversion. What we are really talking about are a cluster of types of changes that have been observed and discussed. The rhetoric of religion—especially within evangelical Christianity—has often called for radical, sudden, and total change within a person's life (Nock 1933). In fact, most human beings change incrementally over a period of time; even after a long process, often the change is less than a complete 180-degree transformation (see Brown, chapter 11; Glazier, chapter 12; Reidhead and Readhead, chapter 14; Seeman, chapter 3). Asking the question "What is changed?" in conversion certainly initiates a very sobering undertaking—especially for some religious people who have an investment in demonstrating that dramatic changes take place. The search for a workable definition of conversion is perhaps complicated by current postmodern sensibilities in which traditionally accepted verities are held to question.

Paul Hiebert (1978), a Christian missionary who earned a Ph.D. in anthropology, has struggled mightily with definitions of conversion. In the mission field, the nature of conversion for Hiebert was not just an academic question. How much did a person need to know, experience, and do to be considered a "true" convert? What motivations for this process were legitimate and what motivations were seen as illegitimate? Hiebert recognized from the outset that in actual experience, no conversion is total, complete, and perfect. Given the complexities, messiness, and diversity of individual human experience, complete conversion is a goal to work toward, not a "finished" product (see Brown, chapter 11; Buckser, chapter 6; Reidhead and Reidhead, chapter 14).

Insider/Outsider Points of View

Another fundamental issue is the degree to whether "etic" and "emic" considerations should be given priority. As an advocate of the "insider" point of view, I find the emic perspective extremely valuable. At the very least, researchers need to adopt a perspective in which the experience of converts is appreciated phenomenologically. All contributors to this volume seem to have done this. Etic concerns are also crucial. Perhaps scholars of conversion should come to recognize a continuum of concerns that embraces both the "insider's" perspective and the "outsider's" point of view as epistemologically and empirically important (see Jules-Rosette 1975, 1976).

Theology occupies a central place in understanding conversion processes. Whatever one's opinions concerning the validity and value of theology, theology often plays a pivotal role in shaping experience and expectations regarding conversion. Moreover, theology constitutes part of the "DNA" of the conversion process for people existing within a particular religious tradition. Not all conversions are seen in the same way because the theology that informs the psyche and culture of the person going through conversion is deeply embedded in the structures that serve as the foundation, infrastructure, and motivation of the conversion experience itself. The Reidheads' chapter (chapter 14), which skillfully integrates intrapsychic processes, social contexts, and Benedictine theology, provides an excellent example of how theology informs the psyche. Di Bella's chapter (chapter 7) also gives careful attention to the theological ramifications of *Bianchi* and Pentecostal ritual. The theology of converts must be taken more seriously by researchers—whether in the fields of psychology, anthropology, or sociology. This does not mean a simple affirmation of theological beliefs but constitutes a willingness to listen to the theological rationales used by converts to tell their own stories. Again, the various analyses contained in this collection are exemplary.

Religious conversion raises fundamental questions about the human predicament, the meaning and purpose of life, the nature of reality, and the reality of a transcendent realm. It is extremely difficult—if not impossible—to engage the topic of conversion from a disinterested point of view. Assumptions about life, religion, and God necessarily color one's perceptions. Explaining conversion in naturalistic (and/or nonreligious) terms comes "naturally" to an atheist or an agnostic since otherwise an atheist or agnostic would be forced to examine the validity of his or her own assumptions about human nature, reality, and transcendent orders.

Researchers who are both "insiders" and "outsiders" translate the phenomenon of conversion into their own categories and force the experience of conversion into modes of expression that may or may not be recognized by the other. Nevertheless, it should be possible for scholars to write in such a way that their findings are comprehensible to the subjects of their research. Can scholarly works be made useful to insiders, or are the worldviews and approaches to experience so different between insiders and outsiders that their respective understandings cannot be integrated coherently?

Collections as Forums for Conversion Studies

Currently, the most common type of publication in conversion studies is collected works such as this volume (see also Carmody 2001; Collins and Tyson 2001; Conn 1978; Duggan 1984; Eigo 1987; Hefner 1993; Lamb and Bryant 1999; Levtzion 1979; Malony and Southard 1992; McGinnis 1988; Muldoon 1997; van der Veer 1996). Collections of essays are useful as a platform from which to present and examine the innate complexity and diversity of perspectives utilized in the study of religious conversion.

The field of conversion studies is in flux. We may be approaching a state of paradigm exhaustion. No new orthodoxies have been created. A recent book, *Conversion in the Wesleyan Tradition*, edited by Collins and Tyson, illustrates the wide range of topics elicited by serious reflection on the subject of conversion. Collins and Tyson brought together an eminent group of scholars to explore John Wesley's personal experience of conversion, the ways in which that experience was developed and deployed in Methodist circles, and the relationship of conversion to various historical periods of the Wesleyan movement—such as abolition and the women's movement. In addition, contributors were encouraged to employ the latest techniques of biblical scholarship to plumb the depths of the Bible for the meaning and purpose of conversion. Other essays in the Collins and Tyson volume examine practical implications of conversion, the role of rituals such as baptism in conversion, and the foundational question as to whether conversion provides something truly new in theological epistemology. I elaborate on the Collins and Tyson collection to emphasize that even within the Christian tradition, there is growing recognition of the importance of conversion and the complexity, diversity, and elusive qualities of religious change. Anthropologists, psychologists, and sociologists need to recognize that conversion is a source of debate, conflict, and constant reevaluation within the Christian community. The same is true for other religious traditions such as Islam.

SCROGGS AND DOUGLAS:
ISSUES IN THE STUDY OF CONVERSION

After reading these splendid essays on the anthropology of conversion, I was reminded of Scroggs and Douglas's 1967 attempt to discern the thematic contours of the study of conversion within the field of psychology. Scroggs and Douglas focused on seven major issues in the field. At the top of their list were persistent problems of definition. In their survey, they described a number of different types of phenomenon as examples of conversion. Another issue focused on debates as to whether conversion was "normal" or "pathological." If conversion was seen as pathology, this engendered intense debates as to whether conversion results in regressive or even pathological psychological reactions. A related issue, which might be considered quaint today, focused on the so-called convertible type in psychology. In other words, are certain personalities more vulnerable to the sudden, radical dislocations associated with the conversion experience?

Scroggs and Douglas (1967) also explored another typical psychological concern regarding the "ripe age" notion of conversion. Many surveys of conversion in the history of psychology had noted that the most common time for conversion was adolescence. Few psychologists of Scroggs and Douglas's era questioned such a finding as, in part, a logical outcome of the fact that much psychological research was conducted with undergraduate students in psychology classes. Glazier (chapter 12) reports that conversion from the Spiritual Baptist faith to Rastafarianism and vice versa often occurs later in life, but—as he points out—his sample is small.

Scroggs and Douglas's final question is essentially theological: Does conversion result from human or divine agency? Few psychologists would assert that conversion is caused by the interplay of the transcendent in the life of those they study. But psychologists who have carefully observed and/or interviewed converts acknowledge that many converts attribute their transformations to divine intervention. This raises the issue of how to negotiate between scientific explanations of conversion and theological doctrines that mandate the norms against which conversion experiences are measured. How do researchers deal with a theology that asserts God's role in conversion and sees human beings as passive recipients of God's grace? The seventh issue articulated by Scroggs and Douglas attempts to establish the most appropriate theoretical model or paradigm for the study of conversion. Scroggs and Douglas concluded that conceptual schemes strongly influence the methods and models deployed in the study of conversion.

I suggest that anthropologists—as well as historians, psychologists, and sociologists—follow the example of Scroggs and Douglas. Articulating the ways in which conversion has been studied and the major themes that have emerged will provide useful guidance to future researchers.

THE FUTURE OF CONVERSION STUDIES

The future of conversion studies must involve sustained and systematic multidisciplinary research and theoretical exploration. The phenomenon of religious change is so complex that it not only benefits from, but also requires, deploying resources from anthropology, history, psychology, religious studies, sociology, and so on. Each discipline offers insights and methods to examine the full range of issues and dimensions of conversion. Ideally, multidisciplinary studies of conversion will access the full richness of methods and understandings that already exist in each of these disciplines but at the same time will recognize the limitations of each discipline. Multidisciplinary efforts begin with the assumption that each discipline must be self-critical and willing to modify its assumptions, goals, and methods in the face of a phenomenon that cannot be forced into a Procrustean bed.

Some scholars have already undertaken multidisciplinary efforts to gain an expanded understanding of conversion. For example, Donald Gelpi (1998) draws upon the human sciences in his many writings on conversion within the Roman Catholic tradition. Scot McKnight (2002), a Protestant New Testament scholar, uses secular studies of conversion to enhance his understanding of conversion narratives within the Gospels. He examines biblical notions of conversion as these relate to transformations within the inner circle of Christ's disciples. Missiologists, too, borrow from anthropological methods to enrich their understandings and techniques.

With but few exceptions, the human sciences study conversion within the boundaries of a single discipline. Sociological studies focus on recruitment and socialization. Psychologists study conversion in the context of the clinical practice of psychology and psychiatry. Until recently, anthropologists rarely approached conversion as a central focus of study. This collection constitutes an important exception to the above generalization and hopefully represents an emerging trend within the discipline. Missiologists—who form a large and diverse group of scholars working from within the Christian tradition—should also be mentioned. Missiologists use a variety of disciplines (especially anthropology and history) in order to better understand the contours of religious change.

Exemplary studies in the past can also inform future studies of conversion. We have just passed the hundredth anniversary of William James's Gifford Lectures at the University of Edinburgh in 1901 and 1902. The resulting book, *The Varieties of Religious Experience*, has become a classic and is still in print. Few would deny the felicity of style, the embracing quality sensibilities, and the generous, phenomenological approach James deploys. The persistent appeal of this remarkable work lies in James's capacity for appreciating ways in which human beings intersect with the transcendent. A weakness, however, is that James's study is almost exclusively Euro-American and Christian in its philosophical assumptions and methodology. Nonetheless, *The Varieties of Religious Experience* continues to be a major influence in the study of conversion.

It is crucial that scholars of conversion seek out the valuable work of researchers from other disciplines. An excellent example of quality contemporary work in conversion studies is Robert L. Montgomery's *The Lopsided Spread of Christianity: Toward an Understanding of the Diffusion of Religions* (2002). Montgomery is a sociologist who explores various theories explaining the differential rate and extent of religious change before 1500 C.E. A fundamental issue for Montgomery is the question of why Christianity was so successful in spreading to the Roman Empire and Europe but unsuccessful in it attempts to convert Persia, India, and China. Utilizing diffusion theory and social identity theory, Montgomery draws upon historical materials on Christianity in the vast territories west and east of Jerusalem. The scope of Montgomery's study is vast and his theoretical sophistication remarkable. He writes clearly, focusing on his goal of critically applying various theories and their rigorous modifications, and eliminating other theories that do not advance his agenda. His agenda is to develop a theoretical model that elucidates and explains the causes of missionary successes and failures in various religions around the world.

Conversion studies should also include attention to conversion experiences and phenomena in the Roman Catholic, Mormon (Church of Jesus Christ of Latter Day Saints), Assembly of God, and Southern Baptist churches. These faith traditions are among the most effective agents of conversion in many places of the world and yet are rarely the focus of empirical research.

Research on conversion should include more serious studies of Islamic conversion. Especially since September 11, 2001, it is imperative that Islam be better understood and recognized as a force exerting a powerful political, cultural, and religious influence around the world. Second only to the Christian faith in number of adherents, Islam's more than 1 billion followers extend throughout the world. In the study of Islamic conversion, care must be taken to see the phenomenon with new eyes. Christian-based categories must be set aside, at least temporarily, so that the nature and scope of conversion to Islam can be examined without preconception or bias. A special emphasis should be placed on researching and understanding ways in which involvement and commitment to Islam consolidates Islamic communities and — in some cases — propels powerfully politicized movements in various parts of the world. The work of Bulliet (1979), Hefner (1993), Kose (1996), Levtzion (1978), and others can serve as starting points from which to begin a truly new era of the study of conversion.

Few scholars have had the chutzpah, energy, and determination to undertake an authentic, multidisciplinary study of conversion. Sometimes, one gets the impression that anthropology, sociology, psychology, and so on are like parallel railroad tracks. Each discipline has little or no knowledge or interest in disciplines on the next track and even less interest in those disciplines several tracks over. With the exception of acknowledgments to classics like James's *The Varieties of Religious Experience* (1985 [1902]) and A. D. Nock's *Conversion* (1933), scholars either willfully exclude or ignore other disciplines, or they may be unaware of the resources in fields other than their own. Perhaps a modest beginning could be proposed. Brettell and Hollifield's *Migration Theory: Talking across Disciplines* (2000) provides a possible model. Scholars of conversion could begin by organizing a conference and/or a series of articles that focus on the assumptions, methods, and theories of conversion within various disciplines.

Other issues need to be addressed to complete our vision of a multidisciplinary approach to conversion. Among these issues are gender (Brereton 1991; Juster 1989), religious ideology, politics, and the ways in which conversion is not merely a passive or compliant survival strategy but a creative form of resistance and even subversion (Viswanathan 1998). This collection of anthropological essays constitutes an excellent beginning. It contains a number of fascinating case studies, considerable theoretical innovation, and ample evidence of disciplinary sophistication.

REFERENCES

Brereton, Virginia Lieson. *From Sin to Salvation: Stories of Women's Conversions, 1800 to the Present.* Bloomington: Indiana University Press, 1991.

Brettell, Caroline B., and James F. Hollifield, eds. 2000. *Migration Theory: Talking across Disciplines.* New York: Routledge.

Bulliet, Richard W. *Conversion to Islam in the Medieval Period: An Essay in Quantitative History.* Cambridge, Mass.: Harvard University Press, 1979.

Collins, Kenneth J., and John H. Tyson, eds. *Conversion in the Wesleyan Tradition.* Nashville, Tenn.: Abingdon Press, 2001.

Conn, Walter E., ed. *Conversion: Perspectives on Personal and Social Transformation.* New York: Alba House, 1978.

Cusack, Carole M. *Conversion among the Germanic Peoples.* New York: Cassell, 1998.

Dawson, Lorne L. *Comprehending Cults: The Sociology of New Religious Movements.* Toronto: Oxford University Press, 1998.

Duggan, Robert D., ed. *Conversion and the Catechumenate.* New York: Paulist Press, 1984.

Eigo, Francis A., ed. *The Human Experience of Conversion: Persons and Structures in Transformation.* Villanova, Penn.: Villanova University Press, 1987.

Gelpi, Donald L. *The Conversion Experience: A Reflective Process for RCIA Participant and Others.* New York: Paulist Press, 1998.

Harding, Susan. "Convicted by the Holy Spirit: The Rhetoric of Fundamental Baptist Conversion." *American Ethnologist* 14, no. 1 (1987): 167–81.

Hefner, Robert W., ed. *Conversion to Christianity: Historical and Anthropological Perspectives on a Great Transformation.* Berkeley: University of California Press, 1993.

Hiebert, Paul G. "Conversion, Culture, and Cognitive Categories." *Gospel in Culture* 1 (1978): 24–29.

James, William. *The Varieties of Religious Experience.* 1902. Reprint, Cambridge, Mass.: Harvard University Press, 1985.

Jules-Rosette, Bennetta. *African Apostles: Ritual and Conversion in the Church of John Maranke.* Ithaca, N.Y.: Cornell University Press, 1975.

————. "The Conversion Experience: The Apostles of John Maranke." *Journal of Religion in Africa* 7, no. 2 (1976): 132–64.

Juster, Susan. "In a Different Voice": Male and Female Narratives of Religious Conversion in Post-Revolutionary America." *American Quarterly* 41, no. 1 (March 1989): 34–62.

Kahn, Peter J. *Modeling Religious Conversion in Adulthood.* Ph.D. diss., Pacific Graduate School of Psychology, 2000.

Kaplan, Steve, ed. *Indigenous Responses to Western Christianity.* New York: New York University Press, 1996.

Kose, Ali. *Conversion to Islam: A Study of Native British Convert.* London: Kegan Paul International, 1996.

Lamb, Christopher, and M. Darrol Bryant, eds. *Religious Conversion: Contemporary Practices and Controversies.* New York: Cassell, 1999.

Levtzion, Nehemia, ed. *Conversion to Islam.* New York: Holmes & Meier, 1979.

Long, Theodore E., and Jeffrey K. Hadden. "Religious Conversion and the Concept of Socialization." *Journal for the Scientific Study of Religion* 22 (1983): 1–14

MacMullen, Ramsay. *Christianizing the Roman Empire (A.D. 100–400).* New Haven, Conn.: Yale University Press, 1984.

Malony, H. Newton, and Samuel Southard. *Handbook of Religious Conversion.* Birmingham, Ala.: Religious Education Press, 1992.

McGinniss, Michael J., ed. *Conversion: Voices and Views.* Romeoville, Ill.: Christian Brothers Conference, 1988.

McKnight, Scot. *Turning to Jesus: The Sociology of Conversion in the Gospels.* Louisville, Ky.: Westminster John Knox Press, 2002.

Montgomery, Robert L. "The Spread of Religions and Macrosocial Relations." *Sociological Analysis* 52, no. 1 (1991): 37–53.

————. *The Diffusion of Religions.* University Press of America, 1996.

————. *Introduction to the Sociology of Missions.* Westport, Conn.: Praeger Publishers, 1999.

————. *The Lopsided Spread of Christianity: Toward an Understanding of the Diffusion of Religions.* Westport, Conn.: Praeger Publishers, 2001.

Muldoon, James, ed. *Varieties of Religious Conversion in the Middle Ages.* Gainesville: University Press of Florida, 1997.

Nock, Arthur Darby. *Conversion.* Oxford: Oxford University Press, 1933.

Poewe, Karla, ed. *Charismatic Christianity as a Global Culture.* Columbia: University of South Carolina Press, 1994.

Rambo, Lewis R. *Understanding Religious Conversion.* New Haven, Conn.: Yale University Press, 1993.

————. "Theories of Conversion." *Social Compass* 46, no. 3 (September 1999): 259–71.

Richardson, James T., ed. *Conversion Careers: In and Out of the New Religions.* Sage Contemporary Social Science Issues, 47. Beverly Hills, Calif.: Sage, 1978.

Scroggs, J. R., and W. G. T. Douglas. (1967). "Issues in the Psychology of Religious Conversion." *Journal of Religion and Health* 6, no. 3: 204–16.

Van der Veer, Peter, ed. *Conversion to Modernities: The Globalization of Christianity.* New York: Routledge, 1996.

Viswanathan, Gauri. *Outside the Fold: Conversion, Modernity, and Belief.* Princeton, N.J.: Princeton University Press, 1998.

Yang, Fenggang. *Chinese Christians in America: Conversion, Assimilation, and Adhesive Identities.* University Park: Pennsylvania State University Press, 1999.

Index

About the Contributors

Robert T. Anderson, who is a physician as well as an anthropologist, specializes in alternative medicine, which often accesses paranormal and religious beliefs and practices. A professor of anthropology at Mills College, he is also head of the Department of Sociology and Anthropology. His most recent books include *Magic, Science, and Health: The Aims and Achievements of Medical Anthropology* (1996), *Alternative and Conventional Medicine in Iceland* (2000), and *The Ghosts of Iceland* (in press).

Diane Austin-Broos holds the Radcliffe-Brown Chair in Anthropology at the University of Sydney. Based on fieldwork in Jamaica and Australia, she has written extensively on a broad range of topics, including religion, political economy, and cultural change and transformation. Her books include *Jamaica Genesis: Religion and the Politics of Moral Orders* (1997), *Creating Culture: Profiles in the Study of Culture* (1989, editor), and *Urban Life in Kingston, Jamaica* (1984). Her current project examines processes of change among the Western Arrernte of Central Australia. Dr. Austin-Broos is a fellow of the Australian Social Science Academy and a past president of the Australian Anthropological Society.

Thomas Kingsley Brown is a research associate with Zetetic Associates in San Diego, California. His research interests include consciousness, neuroscience, deviance, and intentional communities in North America. He earned a Ph.D. in anthropology from the University of California at San Diego in 2000, and he holds chemistry degrees from the California Institute of Technology and the University of Pittsburgh.

Andrew Buckser is associate professor of anthropology at Purdue University. He is the author of *After the Rescue: Jewish Identity and Community in Contemporary Copenhagen* (2003) and *Communities of Faith: Sectarianism, Identity, and Social Change on a Danish Island* (1996). His research examines religious movements, modernity, and identity in contemporary northern Europe.

Simon Coleman is reader in anthropology and deputy dean for social sciences and health at the University of Durham. His research interests include the study of charismatic Christianity, pilgrimage, religious art, ritual, and globalization. He is the author of many books and articles on the anthropology of religion, including *Pilgrim Voices: Narrative and Authorship in Christian Pilgrimage* (2003, edited with J. Elsner), *The Globalisation of Charismatic Christianity: Spreading the Gospel of Prosperity* (2000), and *Pilgrimage Past and Present: Sacred Travel and Sacred Space in the World Religions* (1995, with J. Elsner). He has conducted fieldwork in Sweden and the United Kingdom.

Maria Pia Di Bella specializes in the relation between religion and law at CNRS-CRAL/EHESS, Paris. She has written widely on Sicily and Italy, on themes relating to speech strategies, the body and pain, and religious and legal practices. Her most recent project studied the popular sanctification of executed criminals in Sicily (1541–1820). She is currently preparing a comparative work on capital punishment in Europe and the United States after World War II. She was a visitor at the Institute for Advanced Study in 1994 and 2002–2003. Her publications include *La Pura verità: Discarichi di coscienza intesi dai Bianchi (Palermo 1541–1820)* (1999), *Vols et Sanctions en Méditerranée* (1998, editor), and *Miracoli e miracolati* (1994).

Charles E. Farhadian is assistant professor of religion at Calvin College. His fieldwork, conducted in Southeast Asia and Oceania, examines the dynamics of world religions and comparative missiology. He received his doctorate in religious studies from Boston University in 2001.

Stephen D. Glazier is professor of anthropology and graduate faculty fellow at the University of Nebraska, Lincoln. He is author of *Marchin' the Pilgrims Home: A Study of the Spiritual Baptists of Trinidad* (1991) and editor of *Caribbean Ethnicity Revisited* (1985), *Anthropology of Religion: A Handbook* (1999), and *The Encyclopedia of African and African American Religions* (2001). Dr. Glazier has served as secretary and vice-president of the Society for the Anthropology of Religion and is currently president of the Society for the Anthropology of Consciousness. He studied anthropology at Princeton and the University of Connecticut where he earned his Ph.D. in 1981.

Roger Ivar Lohmann is assistant professor of anthropology at Trent University. He received his Ph.D. in anthropology from the University of Wisconsin, Madison, in 2000 and has previously taught at the University of Wisconsin, the College of Wooster, Western Oregon University, and the University of Toronto. He is the editor of *Dream Travelers: Sleep Experiences and Culture in the Western Pacific* (2003) and "Perspectives on the Category 'Supernatural,'" a special issue of *Anthropological Forum* (2003). He has conducted ethnographic fieldwork in Papua New Guinea among the Asabano. His major interests include the cognitive and experiential foundations of religion, local forms of evidence behind spiritual beliefs and religious change, and the imagination across all states of consciousness and cultural contexts.

Marcela Mendoza is a senior researcher at the Center for Research on Women at the University of Memphis, where she is also an affiliate faculty member in the Department of Anthropology. She was trained as an anthropologist at the University of Buenos Aires and received her doctorate from the University of Iowa. Dr. Mendoza is the author of *Band Mobility and Leadership among Western Toba Hunter Gatherers of Gran Chaco in Argentina* (2002). She has also published many articles on hunter-gatherer societies of the South American Gran Chaco, analyzing subsistence practices, social organization, and religion. She is the past president of the Mid-South Association of Professional Anthropologists.

Kalyani Devaki Menon is assistant professor of religion at DePaul University. She received her Ph.D. in anthropology from Syracuse University in 2002. Dr. Menon's fieldwork has focused on women in the Hindu nationalist movement in New Delhi. She is currently working on a manuscript that examines the ways in which these women mobilized support for the movement in socially, politically, and economically diverse communities. Her research interests include religious nationalism, gender, cultural memory, postcolonial and feminist theory, and South Asian politics.

Rebecca Sachs Norris is assistant professor of religious studies at Merrimack College. She also teaches a course on Death, Suffering, and Identity at the Boston University School of Medicine. Her primary interests are embodiment and identity in relation to transmission of religious states, and suffering, spirituality, and identity. She organized the Anthropology of Religion Consultation of the American Academy of Religion, for which she now serves as a steering committee member.

Robert J. Priest is associate professor of mission and intercultural studies and director of the Doctor of Philosophy in Intercultural Studies at Trinity

International University. His degrees include both a Master of Divinity from Trinity Evangelical Divinity School and a doctorate in anthropology from the University of California at Berkeley. He has written widely on traditional religion and conversion to Christianity, based on his fieldwork among the Aguaruna of Peru. In addition to his academic appointments, Dr. Priest has served in a variety of church ministries.

Lewis R. Rambo is professor of psychology and religion at San Francisco Theological Seminary and at the Graduate Theological Union, Berkeley. A leading authority on religious conversion, he also studies self theory, psychology of religion, cinema studies, and multicultural systems of care and discipline. Dr. Rambo holds advanced degrees from the University of Chicago and Yale Divinity School, and has conducted fieldwork in Israel, Korea, Japan, and the United States. He is the author of *Understanding Religious Conversion* (1993).

Mary Ann Reidhead is a research associate in anthropology and graduate student in philosophy at the University of Missouri, St. Louis. Her major research includes ongoing ethnography in Benedictine monasteries and among Benedictine Oblates, a lay monastic movement, and includes survey research on spiritual integration. Her publications include both ethnographic articles about nuns and public-policy papers on spiritual integration. Her current work compares the impact of the sex abuse scandal in the Catholic Church on nuns, monks, and diocesan priests.

Van A. Reidhead is associate professor of anthropology and chair of the faculty senate at the University of Missouri, St. Louis. His fieldwork has included extensive studies of monastic orders in the United States as well as archaeological investigations in Ecuador, the Ohio Valley, and Missouri. He is the author of *A Linear Programming Model of Prehistoric Subsistence Optimization: A Southeastern Indiana Example* (1981), as well as numerous articles on the anthropology of religion. In 1995, Dr. Reidhead co-founded the Center for Human Origin and Cultural Diversity; his current projects include the Holy Trinity Abbey Ethnography Project and the Spiritual Integration Measurement Project.

Don Seeman is assistant professor of religion and Jewish studies at Emory University. He was previously lecturer in the Department of Sociology and Anthropology at the Hebrew University of Jerusalem. He has conducted fieldwork in Israel and Ethiopia, and is interested in the cultural phenomenology of religious experience, as well as medical anthropology and Jewish studies.